# Surviving the Krays

# Surviving the Krays

## The Final Explosive Secret about the Krays

### DAVID TEALE

EBURY
PRESS

2

Ebury Press, an imprint of Ebury Publishing
20 Vauxhall Bridge Road
London SW1V 2SA

Ebury Press is part of the Penguin Random House group of companies
whose addresses can be found at global.penguinrandomhouse.com

First published by Ebury Press in 2021

www.penguin.co.uk

A CIP catalogue record for this book is available from the British Library

ISBN 9781529106893
TPB ISBN 9781529108071

Typeset in 11.5/19 pt Sabon Next LT Pro
by Integra Software Services Pvt. Ltd, Pondicherry

Printed and bound in Great Britain by Clays Ltd, Elcograf S.p.A.

The authorised representative in the EEA is Penguin Random House Ireland,
Morrison Chambers, 32 Nassau Street, Dublin D02 YH68.

Penguin Random House is committed to a sustainable future
for our business, our readers and our planet. This book is made
from Forest Stewardship Council® certified paper.

This book is for Debbie ...

... and for my daughters, Diane Teale, Joanne Teale and the youngest, Christine Teale, who arrived when I was away.

# CONTENTS

# A SHORT GLOSSARY

**away** in prison

**bell on** telephone tap

***Bringing Down the Krays*** book by my brother Bobby, written with the help of Alfie and myself, published in 2012

**C.1** Scotland Yard Central Office

**C.8** Flying Squad

**C.11** Scotland Yard Criminal Intelligence Department (sometimes 'branch' or 'bureau')

**carpet** prison sentence

**chemmy** chemin-de-fer gambling card game

**chiv** razor

**CIA** Central Intelligence Agency (US)

**CRO** Criminal Record Office

**D Branch** MI5 counterespionage

**D4** MI5 agent-running section of D Branch

**DCS** Detective Chief Superintendent

**DI** Detective Inspector

**'dilly** gay clubland round Piccadilly Circus, London

**DPP** Director of Public Prosecutions

**DS** Detective Sergeant

**form** criminal record

**GPO** General Post Office (ran UK telephone system)

**pony** £25

**spieler** illegal gambling club

**tool** gun

# INTRODUCTION

Things happen in your life which it might seem better to forget, so why should I want to go back to that terrifying time as a young man in London when I was involved with the Krays?

I was about seventeen years old when I first met Ronnie Kray. I'd meet his twin brother Reggie a little later. My older brother, Alfie, had been introduced to Ronnie by his gay friend, 'Mad' Teddy Smith. He'd been nicknamed that way for his habit of getting off his head and his reputation for being a bit of a tearaway. Some accounts say he was in Broadmoor special hospital for a while when he was just a kid. I never knew that.

Teddy had been topped by Ronnie sometime in 1967. At least that's what the police were putting around through the underworld at the time when I myself was in prison. More about Teddy later ...

For five years of my young life I had been around but never on 'the Firm'. I'd done the driving, run little errands. I wish from the bottom of my heart that it had happened differently. My involvement with the murderous twins would cause years of pain to those I loved. And it still causes me deep pain today.

One way of dealing with bad past experiences is to go back into them. That's what I and my brothers, Alfie and Bobby Teale, did a few years back. Some of what follows has been told in our book, *Bringing Down the Krays*, put together by the three of us when we were reunited in 2010 after a very long time apart. It told the story of how Bobby had been an informer inside the Firm. Alfie and I didn't know. A corrupt policeman exposed him to the twins. Years before, in summer 1966, the three of us had gone to prison in a 'get-the-Teales-off the-streets' operation of which, at the time, I had no comprehension.

Someone high up decided the way to keep we three brothers alive was to put us on trial as blackmailers ('demanding money with menaces', it was called) and find us all guilty. We went to prison. When we were all released, Bobby disappeared.

We assumed he must be dead.

\* \* \*

I'd begun this journey of discovery with a bit of a problem: I could not read or write. Then, a few years into the new century, I started helping people with drugs problems. I had never been into drugs myself, but I knew some who were, including within my own close family. It was while taking someone to a support meeting that I first met a woman called Lally who later helped me learn to read and write.

Lally was an addiction counsellor but was there as much to support the carers as the addicts. So when Lally asked me if I had ever had any help myself, I found myself telling her my whole life story.

During the course of our conversations I told her about my child-hood, my brothers Alfie and Bobby, and our association with the

Krays – the twins from East London who had been so notorious in my young life and who, long after, still seemed to have a terrifying fascination.

Lally was amazed and told me, 'Dave, you have got to write a book.' It was then that I confided in her that I could not read or write. She told me to get a laptop and that she would recommend an adult literacy class. She also asked me where Bobby was. I said we'd been told many years back that he was dead, although I had never really accepted this was true. Lally also told me to start going to the library, where I learned how to use my new laptop – the internet was really getting going by now.

My life wasn't much at the time, it had dwindled to a one-room bedsit in the Caledonian Road in north London. My smart clothes, of which I had always been so proud, now hung on a sad metal clothes rail; expensive suits on plastic hangers with Italian shoes stacked beneath acted as an incentive to try harder.

From the moment I signed up to join the reading class, my life started to change. Although functionally illiterate (how bad does *that* sound?), I had in the past been a very capable man and successful in business. As a result, I had at times in my life been comfortably off.

The kids in the class showed me a new thing called 'Facebook'. Lally suggested I put up a post – 'looking for Bobby' – giving my own name but not much else. So, sitting in my bedsit, I did just that.

No response.

I said to Alfie that we were going to do this, that we were going to find our missing brother and, as Lally said, we must write a book.

So, I went back into my Facebook account:

David Teale. Looking for Bobby.

I tapped the words in carefully with one finger.

He replied.

\* \* \*

That Bobby was alive at all was amazing enough, that we got our story out into the world in the shape of a successful book in 2012 (it was a *Sunday Times* bestseller) was a fabulous bonus. That our book went against a big part of the standard Kray 'legend' (I hate that description) did not seem to matter. There was a wall of accounts out there already – books, websites, TV documentaries – but they seemed to feed off each other, with gaps and time shifts that didn't make sense. Same with films. We brothers, although not named, had been dismissed as cowards and rent-boy blackmailers in one much-filmed book. Well, we're not.

But score-settling is not why I wanted to write this new and very different book. It is not for revenge or retribution. The time for all that has long passed and many who were involved are now dead anyway. But I would like someone just once to say: 'David, we are sorry, sorry that we could not tell you all this at the time, and sorry for what happened to you as a result.' But nobody was going to do that until I myself had made some more discoveries.

Well, I have done.

Lots of discoveries.

If this was a movie franchise, I suppose it would be described as the 'prequel'. It seemed the book we'd written as brothers needed a top-to-bottom shakedown to make sense of what I'd discovered since it first appeared. And I had found out lots in the meantime. Now sort of literate, I could find my way round the internet, access online databases and newspaper libraries and, very important, as it would turn out, get into the UK National Archives in south-west London.

I began to dig. There were tons of boxes of documents, hundreds of witness statements. I found statements by myself and my brothers, our wives and our mother, our neighbours, the telephone man (you can't say they weren't thorough!) taken down in that epic of detective work that brought the twins to justice. I found my name in Ronnie Kray's address book (some interesting names in there), seized as evidence when he was arrested in that famous Yard swoop.

Hundreds of Kray files are closed, thousands of pages. Some of our story remains secret. The file on our trial was closed for a hundred years. I'd been told at the start I must prove that I'm dead and so are my brothers before anyone could see it. Then after a long campaign, a fragment was released to me, giving the name of the judge, the prosecuting counsel and the name of the bank on which the 'cheque' we were alleged to have extracted by 'menaces' was drawn. But more stuff has been coming out. In 2015 a Security Service (MI5) file on a prominent politician of the time was released at the National Archives. It was heavily censored ('redacted') but still fascinating. In fact, other than the spooks, I had known most of the people in it. It took me ages to work out what was going on, but with help, I did.

I had lots of wider questions. Why did so many investigations into the twins fail and fail again? What was really happening on the outside during the two weeks of mayhem in my north London flat, with my wife and young family, when the Krays and half the Firm took it over, straight after the Cornell killing in the Blind Beggar pub?

The siege of Moresby Road, for that's what it was, seemed to have been written out of every published account. It was as if we had never existed. I went looking for answers and, piece by piece, a deeper truth began to surface.

I myself in my young life had seen lots of men behaving badly but I was totally clueless about anything to do with spies or politicians. But so too had been most everybody else. This is what I discovered: the Firm was being informed on from within, but it was not to help bring the most notorious gang in British criminal history to justice (that's what my brother Bobby was trying to do), it was to keep it going. The Krays were being used by MI5 to keep a watch on the sexual adventures of establishment figures.

In one key episode, the UK government's cover-up of a scandal (there'd been a big sigh of relief when that seemed to go away) was about to be exposed by the sexual partner of both Ronnie Kray and a leading politician. A 25-year-old croupier at a gambling club, he lived in the same block of flats as my mum and dad. He was going to 'go to the newspapers'. It was the eve of a general election. The Home Secretary was informed of the danger.

The politician got Ronnie to 'threaten him [the croupier] that it would not be a good thing to do or say anything ...'

I had been on the end of Ronnie's threats: you did as you were told.

The original cover-up had been very clever. Everyone in power knew about it. But in politics, so I'm told, it's the exposure of the cover-up that brings down the House of Cards. Thanks to Ronnie Kray, that didn't happen – he was acting as enforcer in the secret service of the state.

All that came from the file released at the National Archives in 2015. It explained where the information was coming from, an unnamed 'mole' in the Firm. The spooks referred to whoever it was simply as 'Source'.

'We are particularly anxious to protect Source from the threat of savage reprisals if he were blown,' so one inside note said. 'Source' was a 'self-confessed homosexual whose information has proved generally reliable in the past', it was said. And it looks like someone kept a cover story going for years afterwards.

Whoever it was must have been very brave, very stupid or must have done a deal that was beyond anyone's sight. But who was he? Well, I worked it out. In fact, at one very dangerous time for me, he might just have saved my life.

It needed to be someone who was there at almost every meeting, who the Krays would not suspect. During the Hideaway episode, for example, when I was ordered by the twins' older brother Charlie Kray to carry messages from Ronnie in HMP Brixton to put the frighteners on his accuser.

Who smashed up the place? 'Mad' Teddy did. That court case collapsed.

And after the raid on a flat above an east London barber's shop, where the Firm had moved to after leaving my house, guess who was nicked in there with them? 'Mad' Teddy was. He walked free after that. The Cornell murder inquiry just stopped. Then, in early 1967, six months after we'd been lifted from the streets, 'Mad' Teddy disappeared.

And so now I know the answer. I can name the Security Service's informant within the Kray Firm. Join me on the journey and I'll show you why it was Edward 'Mad Teddy' Smith.

# PART I

# 1

## THE EARLY DAYS

I was thirteen years of age and I thought I was big. Nicking stuff was a way of proving it. Mum was skint and needed to go to hospital.

I was stealing from gas meters, breaking into shops, round the back, getting up and down drainpipes. I'd go out about ten o'clock at night when I knew the police on the beat were changing over. I was completely fearless.

The best thing to steal was cigarettes, they were like money, but I got caught selling them. So, I was charged with break-ins, lots of them. The first time I got two years' probation for stealing sixty-one shillings from a gas meter. Then I did it again.

This was Southend in the early fifties, hardly a hotbed of villainy, but I was a teenage crime wave just on my own. Our family was poor, but not so poor as some. Dad had run a greyhound track before the war – he even had a car and chauffeur, so my older brother Alfie told me.

There'd once been a big mock-Tudor house in Chingford, Essex, but that was all long gone when I came along. I'd been a small kid in London, Holborn, in central London, the middle one of seven kids.

We had two floors of an old house in Millman Street, off the Gray's Inn Road. There were big red trolleybuses rolling up and down to Red Lion Square, where they turned around to head back into the East End. We never went there – why would anyone want to? The streets were all grey and brown, peeling paint, broken windows, lots of bombsites.

I'd gone to primary school, St Joseph's RC in Covent Garden. It was run by nuns. School was rubbish – it was just about religion. We often bunked off or were late. We'd bring flowers from Covent Garden market to stop ourselves from getting the cane from the nuns if we were late. Then, when I was about eleven, Dad shuffled off somewhere. Mum brought us to live in Southend, Essex. She did what she could to stay afloat.

Well, Dad had another family living in Chingford, so we'd find out. It was the subject of a lot of arguments between my parents. His other wife's name was Alice. He had other children too although I don't know how many.

We would all help out any way we could. Mum did the odd cleaning job but with seven children to look after and very little money coming in she needed all the help she could get. When she needed to go into hospital for a gynaecological operation, a result of her many years of childbearing, our financial situation became pretty dire. Well, a few stolen fags might help.

My parents didn't care that I wasn't learning to read or write, all Mum was bothered about was getting enough money for food and coal on the fire and making a stew to last three days out of a bacon joint.

There were seven of us kids – our oldest sister Eileen, Alfie, Bobby, then me – David. Then along came George, Paul and Jane.

Because Eileen was that much older, and girls weren't allowed in our gang, Alfie, Bobby and me were always the closest. We all loved one another, but because the youngest three came so much later, we were almost more like two separate families.

I hated school the few times I was there mainly because I just couldn't understand what I was being taught. Since I learned how to read and write, I've discovered I'm dyslexic. There was no concept of that back then when I was a kid, but at the time I just thought, and everybody told me, that I must be stupid.

My brilliant idea was to go out 'screwing' (thieving from shops). Shops in those days were secure at the front, but easy to get into round the back, so I would shin up the drainpipe and get in. First time I did it, I got twenty pounds from a petty cash box. I took it straight to Mum in hospital. The police were not very fit and would usually only blow their whistles if they saw me so I could run fast and get away. It was easy.

Inevitably I was caught by the police selling cigarettes that I'd stolen. I had to appear in the juvenile court in Southend, returning a week later for psychiatric reports. My whole family were there, Mum crying and – he'd turned up – Dad looking stern. It was going quite well for me, I thought. I expected to perhaps get probation or at worst a few months in Borstal.

Next thing I was locked in a room, terrified about what was going to happen to me, while the magistrates, two women and a man, went off and had their lunch. Then they called me back in and said, 'We're giving you three years in an approved school.' They took me to the Redhill Remand Centre in Surrey for assessment. The following morning, I was taken to a room containing a desk with pens, pencils and paper. About ten minutes later, some doctor came to see me in a white coat and gave me tests to do with a pile of bricks and a pencil and paper.

'You alright, Teale?' he asked.

He told me to write my name down and said he would come back and see me a few minutes later. When I told him I couldn't write, he told me to just attempt it. This routine continued with the occasional question about my childhood for the next week before I was finally transferred by car to Red House Farm School, Buxton, Norwich. I was now known only as 'Number 75'.

I'd never been to Norfolk before and couldn't understand the accent at all. Almost the first thing I was told by the other boys was 'We don't like Londoners' – Southend counted as Cockney for them.

We normally slept in a long dormitory but when I came back from running away, and I would do that at every opportunity, I was put in a locked room, like a cell, for a couple of days. I was trying to run away all the time and I always got caught.

The worst thing about being confined like that was what we called 'the night people'. A man coming in and coming up close to me, touching my legs first and then more intimately. I soon realised that joining the boxing club was my only way out, both as a means of taking care of myself and providing me with an opportunity of getting up to London.

In the end I served just over two years. I got to Liverpool Street Station, in summer 1959, with my few possessions in a small bag and made my way to 41 Theberton Street, in Islington, north London, where my family now lived.

No one made much fuss of me even then, apart from Alfie and Mum, looking up with a sort of 'Oh, it's you' when I walked in. To be fair, probably the youngest ones barely even remembered me.

Now sixteen, I had changed from a child to a young man while I'd been away. Mum and Dad had by this time opened a club. We lived upstairs but the shop on the ground floor and the basement had been made into a nice bar. The police passed it and it got a licence off Islington Council. It was called the Theberton Club.

I suppose it had been a natural move for Dad to try and remake the family fortune this way – he was always a showman and Mum loved a bit of glamour. The club was her stage and she was the star in the spotlight up at the bar. Soon, I was working for them as their doorman, cleaner, washer-upper and eventually barman.

You could make good money from clubs in those days. To run one, you just had to find some premises, get a drink licence off the council. You couldn't run a club unless you gave a bung (bribe) to the police or they'd close you down. So that's what my dad did, all the time, in order to stay open. Then there was the little matter of keeping out undesirables. Not just drunks or mugs, but anyone who fancied a slice of the takings. It was called 'protection'. Once upon a time protection had been extorted by the 'race-track gangs' of pre-war infamy. My dad knew all about those and turning over street book-makers for a 'pension'. Now it was clubs. You couldn't get the police to scare them off because more often than not they were on the take too. Anyone who had their own reason not to involve the police – the straight coppers, that is – then their business could be got at.

Clubs were everything in London at the time, the way the laws on prostitution, strip joints and gambling were changing. Everything was changing. The old criminals were in for a kicking – and the Met didn't have a clue what was about to hit them.

One old-time Yard operator realised what was coming. His name was Tommy Butler and, a little later, he would become world-famous as the copper who went after the Great Train Robbers. He would also, as it happens, have a very big impact on the fate of us Teale brothers.

That was all to come.

Meanwhile, I was helping to run the bar at the Theberton, getting tips, being treated as a grown-up. I loved it, knocking around with geezers that bit older, getting a bit of respect even if I was still just a kid. It was hilarious, most of the time.

One of the funniest customers was a friend of Alfie's who he'd met in wicked Soho. His name was Teddy Smith and he was always joking, always doing impressions. Give him a stage and he'd start doing Al Jolson numbers.

As I remember, Teddy looked a bit like Robert Wagner, the actor – smartly dressed, muscular and fit-looking, with a mass of thick curly hair. But it was his self-confidence that you noticed first. He had a kind of swagger about him that marked him out from the rest.

He was seven years older than Alfie, with the usual string of youthful petty theft convictions – stealing bikes, shop breaking, that sort of thing. Aged eighteen, he'd been sent down at the Central Criminal Court for armed robbery with a revolver. That was heavy.

I'd get to know him well. He was the most charming, funniest, most entertaining thug you could ever meet.

# 2

## DOWN THE DOUBLE R

All of a sudden, it's the sixties and, just as music, clothes and every-thing else is going to be shaken all over, so too is crime. In 1960 Detective Superintendent Tommy Butler, aged forty-eight, was high up in C.8 Branch, the famous 'Flying Squad'. That May, he wrote up a long memorandum about 'The Twins', as he called them, the up-and-coming criminal power in the East End of London.

I found it in the National Archives when I was looking for my own story. It explained a lot. The recent changes in the law, and more changes to come, would give the new villains on the block the oppor-tunity of a lifetime. They were, of course, the Krays.

There had been a complaint from a firm of solicitors that their clients, Reginald and Ronald Kray of 178 Vallance Road, Stepney, E2, had been 'followed and observed by members of the police force. Both our clients emphatically deny they are involved in any crim-inal offences whatsoever.' The Commissioner wanted Mr Butler's reaction.

The twins were always moaning like this. They always would. They'd get solicitors, vicars, fashionable writers, lords, whoever, to complain that the police were harassing them. One early rumour that would not go away was that the police were going to 'arrest Mr Ronald Kray for indecency on some homosexual offence so as to humiliate him'.

Mr Butler got very indignant. He had harsh words too for the twins' elder brother, Charles James Kray. He gave the Commissioner (it also went to the Home Office) a long report.

The Krays ran the 'Double R Club', it said, a drinking club that was a 'sink of iniquity, which nurtured both convicted criminals and the many degraded, lower-class newspaper reporters looking for colour and atmosphere for rubbishy news stories' (well, somebody's got to do it). Whatever Mr Butler might have thought, the Double R was in fact becoming a stop-off on trendy safaris to the East End for advertising people, film starlets, and TV directors looking for locations. Soho seemed to be flocking there, if not Mayfair. Perhaps that made Mr Butler especially cross. London was changing and so too was crime.

Reggie first opened the club in May 1957. I never saw it myself, but my older brother Alfie did. Our whole adventure, if that's what it was, began there. More of that later ...

The name of course was a tribute to Reggie's twin, to the two of them. Back then, Ronnie had been away. He'd been sentenced to three years for wounding with intent after a rumble with a rival mob in Stepney the previous year. Reggie got off. The judge said the Krays had 'turned a respectable part of the East End into an abyss of brutality'.

How would they tell the difference?

Halfway through his sentence Ronnie had been transferred on prison doctor's orders to Long Grove mental hospital in Epsom, Surrey, from where, with Reggie's help, he had managed to abscond in early summer 1958. He'd switched with his identical twin who was down there on a visit. It was a big news story. Lots of pictures of them as boxers – I think they got a taste for it. Reggie told the *Daily Herald*: 'He was in the locked ward with no normal people to talk to. Now he's as normal as you and me.'

The reporter's name on that story was Norman Lucas. Mr Lucas (he'd go on to the *Sunday Mirror* as their crime correspondent) pops up more than once in what I have to say. On one occasion, he would try and buy the David Teale story, but I said no.

Ronnie had holed up in a big, four-berth caravan in Suffolk[1] (Reggie had driven it there, two weeks before) discreetly hidden on a farm near Sudbury owned by an insurance fraudster and arsonist called Geoffrey Allen, who my brother Bobby would encounter on his own.

Teddy Smith had been in on the breakout mission and fetched and carried for his big mate Ronnie when he was in hiding,[2] although he didn't exactly boast about it to anyone. More about Teddy in a minute.

Ronnie would make phantom midnight visits from his hidey-hole to the Double R to be greeted with general hilarity, but he was becoming

---

[1] The twins had been evacuated from London to a house in Hadleigh, Suffolk, in 1939 and always liked the county. Mrs Styles, who took them in, remembered that they would never stop fighting.

[2] There is an account of this bizarre episode in John Pearson's original 1972 Kray book, *The Profession of Violence*. Teddy would play elaborate 'hunting' games with Ronnie (he got an airgun pellet in the eye) and once took him to Sudbury's Gainsborough cinema to see the 1958 Hammer Horror classic, *Dracula*.

Teddy was described (it seems to be Reggie telling the author about him in late 1967) as a 'young thief slightly older than the twins who has grown up in Bethnal Green, and been a trusted follower of the Colonel in the days of the billiard hall. He was tough, single and heterosexual [the author would later change his mind about that]. Also, unlike most of the Colonel's admirers, he had a certain vein of humour and common sense.'

increasingly paranoid. His companion-in-hiding, Teddy Smith, sensed danger. On Teddy's urging, Reggie drove Ronnie to Vallance Road, the Kray family stronghold in Bethnal Green, in the boot of a car apparently. In the end, the police were told where to find him.

He went back to Long Grove for a period, responded to medication and was sent back to prison, Wandsworth this time. Then, after a few weeks more, Ronnie had been returned to society in spring 1959 to do what he did best, scare people. As Mr Butler was discovering from his snooping round the East End, Ronald Kray was 'certainly mentally unstable to put it at the very least', so he said in his report of May 1960.

So back to what Mr Butler had to say then. The Krays had perfected the 'protection technique' and the 'keystones of their confederacy are intimidation and violence', he wrote. 'East End billiard hall owners, publicans and café proprietors are already in the twins' thrall and their operation will spread.' He was right about that.

'Nobody will talk about it.'

He was right about that too.

The detective described how the twins had built what he called a 'formidable criminal association' with the Nash firm, the brothers out of Clerkenwell, by intimidating prosecution witnesses during the just concluded murder trial of one of the Nash family, leading to his acquittal.

It was 'a verdict that would enhance their already widespread villainous reputation', he said. That Nash connection would prove important in our story.

Old-time Mr Bigs, like Jack Spot and Billy Hill, still tried to stay on top – while the police tried to stay on top of the old villains any way they could. Back in 1956, Billy Hill had had his phone tapped on Home Office authority. They were looking for corrupt coppers, naturally enough. When that came out in public, there was a big political row. Who was allowed to tap phones and why? There were questions in Parliament and a special inquiry. After that, phone snooping by the 'authorities' went all secret again.

A word about Billy Hill, who my dad knew well. He was the first British celebrity criminal – always in the papers (although he tried his best not to be, unlike the Krays). At the end of his career, he seemed to think what he did was like a public service. He told the *People* newspaper one time:

I have cleaned out the protection racketeers from the West End. Today there is not one club or spieler or cafe under the cosh. And the wicked gang battles, chivvings and beatings that gave Soho its bad name are a thing of the past.

Not for long.

That was the 'King of the Underworld' talking in 1954, the same year that a few threats had been enough for the then 21-year-old Kray twins to win control of their first business venture, the Regal Billiard Hall in Stepney, east London. One day, they had just walked in and taken over. It got a reputation as a place where a newly released prisoner could find a bit of gainful employment. That had been the start of the 'Firm'.

Butler was looking forward, not back, in his 1960 report:

The licensing laws are at present an open invitation to criminals to enrich themselves. They do this by dictating which girls work at which club, who is employed as doorman, and the protection method.

And there was more:

> The Street Offences Act [enacted the summer before, outlawing soliciting in public][3] has greatly increased the importance of clubs as gathering places for prostitutes.

That was obvious across London, across every British city.

And:

> Looking into the not too distant future, it is safe to assume that in addition to these establishments, criminals will batten onto betting shops if the proposed betting bill[4] is made law.

It could have been a business plan for the twins' expanding operations.

> The same comments apply to these private gambling parties and striptease parties which are increasingly becoming a feature of West End and suburban life.

---

[3] The 1957 report of the Wolfenden Committee on Homosexual Offences and Prostitution had recommended the move and also that 'homosexual behaviour between consenting adults in private should no longer be a criminal offence'. That took much longer to enact. After much controversy, it would become so in 1967 with the passing of the Sexual Offences Act.
[4] The Betting and Gaming Act 1960 would legalise betting shops, casinos, bingo halls and one-armed bandits (with a sixpence maximum stake). Three machines were the maximum 'per building'. It was meant to keep organised crime out, but did the opposite. Villainy exploded as a result. The Act also allowed for small-scale gaming in 'members' clubs or for worthy causes. It wasn't quite Vegas, but the old place would never be the same again.

Maybe not so much in genteel Barnes, south-west London, where bachelor Tommy lived quietly with his old mum. Apparently, he liked to read Westerns.

Everything Mr Butler predicted would come true.

Well, I wouldn't see it myself, not yet anyway, because as the sixties dawned, I had decided to go to the other side of the world. It was a big laugh at the club, but I wanted to get away. One day, a friend of Teddy Smith's came up the club with him on Alfie's invitation. This friend had a fantastic tan and when I asked him where he'd got it, he told me he'd been to Australia, working for the P&O shipping line.

I asked my cousin Bertie whether he'd be interested in joining me on a trip to Australia as Alfie wasn't interested. We went to the City and got the application forms. A week later, I had a letter to confirm I was on. We were going on the RMS *Orion* to Australia. Our mission was to deliver British emigrants to various ports along the coast and to return via Bombay.

Thinking I was going on some sort of holiday, I got all my best suits and shirts on hangers and arrived at the ship with Bertie at the appointed time. He was given a job washing up. I was told that someone would come back and sort me out, but as they didn't, I got myself all dressed up and went for a stroll around the deck and to the bar with the other passengers.

Well, that didn't last long so I was put in the dining hall to start – setting tables for lunch. I hadn't the slightest idea how to do this (we'd hardly used knives and forks at home) so instead I paid the head waiter to do it for me.

After that, we travelled all over Australia for the next three months. On the way back, we got logged once or twice for shouting, 'Abandon ship! This is the captain speaking,' and terrifying all the passengers whenever we were bored. I took over the bingo.

I came back with more money than I had when I went out.

When I got home, Mum and Dad's club was doing just fine. And that was with just an all-day alcohol licence. Everyone used to drink there. Small-time crooks, big-time villains, shopkeepers, stallholders from Chapel Market around the corner, coppers from Upper Street nick, the lot. It soon got very crowded, so my parents moved around the corner to a bigger place they called the 'Tudor Club'. I don't know why they chose that name. Above a clothes shop called 'Sandy Scott' in Upper Street, a bit beyond Islington Green, it was three storeys with a big bar on the first floor, half-timbered with oak beams like a country inn and a flat at the top where the family lived.

Alfie had by now moved out of Upper Street and was living back in Millman Street, Holborn. The East End was never his patch. If he had a real home anywhere it was in Soho. Once he'd discovered it, he'd made it his own. He got in with some serious Soho drinkers like the club owner Muriel Belcher (who ran the Colony Room and called everyone 'Cunty', a term of endearment), the painter Francis Bacon and the actor John Hurt.

Sometime in the autumn of 1959 he'd been having a drink in Jack Murray's Club, opposite the Freight Train in Berwick Street. Murray's was quite a place, very fashionable, members only, it was where high society went for a bit of excitement (too exclusive for me, but not so much for Alfie). Christine Keeler and Mandy Rice-Davies worked there. But that night it was completely dead when who should walk in around eight o'clock but his new friend, Teddy Smith. One day he'd tell me all about it.

So that evening Teddy suggested to Alfie going to a club in the East End owned by some friends of his. The East End? Did people really choose to go there?

'What's it called, this club?' Alfie had asked.

'It's the Double R, run by Ronnie and Reggie Kray,' Teddy replied.

Alfie had just about heard of them and he knew they were power-ful. He'd been an old friend of Micky Falco, the son of a big Ital-ian family who lived in Clerkenwell. They'd known one another since childhood, even though Micky had gone to St Peter's Catholic primary in Clerkenwell and Alfie had, like me, gone to St Joseph's in Macklin Street, Covent Garden.

One day, Micky pulled up in a big car as Alfie was walking along the street and told him: 'You'd better be careful. You've got the Firm after you for giving Flash Harry a slap, he's one of theirs.'

The way Alfie remembered it, Flash Harry, one of the local hood-lums, used to hang around the West End – a Mod before there were any. He wasn't a proper villain but he thought he was and styled himself that way, bragging about who he was mates with.

'What's this Firm?' Alfie wanted to know.

'They're called the Kray twins and everyone is frightened of them,' Micky told him.

There'd been stories about the Krays, of course – rumours, bits of gossip. They were quite a bit older than us Teales and had some sort of club in the Mile End Road. Alfie was scared about meeting Ronnie at the Double R because he thought it was about that Flash Harry business and he was going to get hurt. In fact, it wasn't. 'Mad' Teddy Smith was just trying to get Alfie alongside Ronnie because he was young and good-looking.

Could he risk it? The way Alfie had heard it, there was always stuff going on around the Krays, mischief-making, a punch-up or fight – from which the twins would never once come out as the losers, so it was said. They'd been in and out of the nick. Then there was an older brother, too – Charlie Kray. He was married. The twins still lived with their old mum and dad in Bethnal Green.

Alfie was intrigued. He'd go. So, he and Teddy Smith jumped in a black cab and headed for the Mile End Road – and went into what looked like a grimy old tube station. In fact, it had been a disused shop. But when they got inside it was a palace, all red flock wallpaper and chandeliers, exquisitely dressed-up men and women, waiters in bow ties mincing around the tables.

Reggie had said from the start he wanted the Double R to be the 'finest drinking club the East End has ever known'. He wanted smart people; Ronnie's heavier chums were not so welcome. Charlie Kray had expanded the business, it was doing nicely. But now Ronnie, released from Wandsworth on that wounding with intent charge, was back on the outside. And this time Reggie was away. As Tommy Butler said in that report: 'On 10 April 1959 Reginald Kray was sentenced at the Central Criminal Court to eighteen months having been convicted of demanding £100 with menaces from a Finchley shopkeeper' (it's complicated). His accomplice, a fraudster called Daniel Shay, was accused of running a 'Chicago style protection racket' (newspapers were beginning to love that phrase). He got three years; Ronnie was not mentioned at the trial.

The 'menaces' charge was big at the time.[5] Police could bring it with nothing more than verballing, no forensic, no corroborating evidence. Nice and quick. Very popular down the nick, it became a

---

[5] Sections 29 and 30 of the Larceny Act 1916 equated demanding money by threat of violence and by blackmail as the same. Smash up a nightclub or threaten to disclose an illegal activity (such as homosexuality), it was the same crime – 'demanding money with menaces'. The Theft Act 1968 redefined blackmail separately.

class thing – who were you going to believe? There was a whole lot of menacing going on.

But it was Ronnie who was Teddy's special friend. And the Double R was his and his alone that night. As Alfie stood there, taking it all in, Teddy said to him: 'Come on, I'll introduce you to Ronnie.'

Alfie nodded. 'Yeah, I don't mind. Let's go over.' So, they walked into the main room of the club and there, at the centre of it all, sitting at the bar, was Ronnie Kray.

Ronnie was six years older than Alfie. Heavily built, with a fleshy, sensual face, he was dressed in a navy-blue mohair suit. He was sitting half-turned so he could see the people coming.

Ronnie looked ''eavy', so Alfie thought. 'Cor, 'ere we go … he's as big as a house, better be nice to him.' Ronnie was observing everything and everyone in the club. He kept staring hard at Alfie: 'He's either going to kiss me or hit me,' my brother was thinking.

Ronnie announced to the people around him at the club: 'He's a nice boy.'

Then he asked him, 'Would you like a drink?'

Alfie asked for a gin and tonic.

Ron asked Alfie where he lived. He replied that he came from Holborn.

'Ooh, 'Olborn! It's nice round there, isn't it?' he said. The voice was high coming out of such a big body, but not overly effeminate. Alfie told him that our mother had recently opened a club called the Tudor in Islington and he said: 'Got a club, eh? I'd love to go there and meet her. Get him another drink. You're smart, very smart, you must come here again.'

Alfie said he had a brother, Bobby. Ronnie stared even harder at him.

'What's the address of this club?'

'Sixty-six Upper Street.'

'What's the phone number?'

Alfie told him.

'You got a phone at home as well?' He scrawled the numbers on a beermat.

Alfie was flattered. He was smart, despite having left school at fourteen and getting a job as a butcher's boy. Like me, he'd grown up fast and had found quicker ways to make money than cycling round Holborn delivering lamb chops. By now he was making proper money fly-pitching, selling jewellery out of a suitcase on the street. Alfie had been expecting it. Very soon he got a call.

'I thought I'd phone you up because I'd like you to come over to my house in Vallance Road and meet my mum and dad,' said Ron. 'You'll like my mum and dad.'

Alfie said: 'OK, Ron. What time?'

'Come over early,' he replied. 'I've got a bit of running about to do later.'

The next morning, Alfie drove over to Vallance Road, parked his car – a big Humber with a long bonnet – around the corner and knocked on the door. The twins' mum, Violet, answered the door and greeted him warmly.

'Oh, you must be Alfie! Ron is over at the bath-house [in Cheshire Street, there was no bath in Vallance Road] right now but he'll be back in ten minutes,' she said. 'Come in and wait in the kitchen and I'll make you a nice cup of tea.'

Alfie went into the kitchen and saw about ten or fifteen white shirts, all immaculately ironed, hanging up on an old-fashioned indoor drying frame on a pulley. A procession of neatly ironed shirts was Violet Kray's daily tribute to her sons. Alfie sat amongst their folds, drinking his tea, until eventually Ronnie came in.

'Hello, Mum,' he said, handing her the towels and soap he'd been using over at the bath-house. Then he turned to my brother: 'Hello, Alfie!'

Ron sat down with Alfie and started telling him about the caravans the family had, down at a place called Steeple Bay in Essex, where they often used to go at weekends. Alfie told him more about the Tudor, a nice, clean family club which was doing quite well, thank you. Regulars were calling it the '66' – the street number.

There was a big hit American song, (*Get Your Kicks on*) *Route 66*, that had been around for years. Nat King Cole recorded it. So had Bing Crosby. Soon there'd be a TV show called that.

'Ooh, that's good,' said Ronnie. 'I must come up there and meet your mum and dad. Do you mind? We'll take a couple of friends up and have a nice drink with them. That will be nice, won't it?'

Alfie wasn't stupid. He knew what Ron had on his mind. That's what the twins did – they moved in on anyone who was vulnerable. They called it a 'pension' – a slice of every bit of dodgy business, every tickle, every bit of profit from a deal. They had a little army of pension collectors who'd go round taking the money. I was never one of those. Their main interest was clubs. That was no surprise. They wanted 'interests' in more of them. Villains couldn't get a club licence, so they'd get a frontman to do it for them, someone without a criminal record. Nothing was ever in the Kray name.

Soon, Ronnie was phoning Alfie up all the time. He would tell him: 'Come on, we're going to The Pigalle,' or Churchill's, or the Astor Club in Berkeley Square, the Celebrity, the Society in Jermyn Street, Danny La Rue's in Hanover Square once that had opened.

Going out to a club with Ronnie was something else. If a place was full, an empty table, freshly laid, would magically appear. Service was instant. When that first happened to Alfie, he'd tell me, 'I thought I was a big boy, one of the chaps.'

'We'll pay for it later,' Ron would say at the end.

But no money ever changed hands.

And it went on from there. First, it was 'protection', a club owner having to pay out to make sure there was no trouble. Then the Firm would become 'staff'. Then all of a sudden, the place would be theirs. Well, we, the Teale family, were now in the club business. That's how Mum and Dad made their living. Although we didn't quite know it yet, we would be on the twins' takeover list and soon I'd be having my own encounter with Ronald Kray.

# 3

## THE COLONEL

Back from my seaborne adventures with a glowing tan and a wodge of money, I'd found a new talent. Alfie and I were natural money-getters – we'd get gear off wholesalers and go out fly-pitching. My older brother had been out street trading since he was nine years old, starting with rain hats for sixpence and working his way up, selling stuff out of suitcases in the street: jewellery, perfume, wind-up toys, anything. We'd work Oxford Street, Berwick Street, Petticoat Lane on a Sunday. Alfie did the banter and the selling while I would watch out for the police.

They could only do you for obstructing the pavement and move you on, but you had to be constantly on the move or you'd get done. The fine at the magistrates' court was half a crown, sometimes seven and six.

I'd shout, 'Alfie, slow up!' which meant he could serve the customers but that there was a policeman further up the street. If I said, 'Up for your life!' the coppers were getting very close. Meanwhile, when not dodging coppers while street trading with Alfie, I was helping out best I could at the 66. One night, there was some loud banging on the door at the bottom of the stairs. Mum called out to me: 'Tell them we're closed.'

I opened the door to the street and said to the two men standing there, 'No, you can't come in,' and shut the door in their faces.

*Bang, bang, ring, ring!*

They kept banging and ringing until eventually I had to open the door on its metal chain. Peering through the gap, one of them said to me: 'D'you know who I've got here with me? It's the Colonel.'

'I don't care who it is,' I said. 'My mum said you can't come in, so that's it. We're finished, we're closed.' And I shut the door again in their faces.

Alfie was around the place. He came clattering downstairs to find out just what was going on, then said very quietly to me: 'Oh God! You'd better open the door, it's Ronnie Kray.'

'Go up to the kitchen and stay there,' he told me. 'Stay very quiet.' He opened the door. I didn't know who Ronnie Kray was, but my big brother certainly did.

The man who'd done the talking was Dickie Morgan, a friend of Ronnie's since his less-than-glorious National Service days in the army. I'd never heard of him either.

I got over my embarrassment and went back into the main room of the club, where I saw a man in a flash suit sitting up at the bar, laughing and joking. I started collecting glasses and he said: 'Come over here and sit with me. I do like it here, it's lovely and private.' So I did what I was told, got a stool and sat next to him.

'Well done, son, you're a good boy,' he said in a squeaky voice. 'You look after your mother, and if your mother says don't let anyone in, you don't. I need someone like you in our clubs.'

I thought this geezer was taking the piss.

That was it. Ronnie (for that was who it was) stayed until about four in the morning, drinking brown ales, one after another. After that, he started coming up the 66 Club night after night. He practically lived there.

Sometimes Teddy Smith would turn up with him. They'd get drunk, then even drunker, and Teddy's routines would be all a bit camp. Ronnie would say, 'Look at 'im, he's like a girl! He's a big poof!' They'd end up fighting. I'd go and hide in the kitchen when it went too over the top. Anyway, as I remember, Ronnie liked to call Teddy 'Smithy' so that's what I'm going to do from now on.

A little bit later, I was in the 66 when Scotch Pat Connolly – a member of the Firm who was effectively next in command after Ronnie and Reggie – came in and said I was wanted at the Green Dragon in Whitechapel. I didn't know much then, but it was an old Jack Spot place, which Reggie and Ronnie had simply barged into and taken over years before. It had a spieler (an illegal gambling club) upstairs.

'I can't leave Mum, I've got to work the door,' I said.

Pat said: 'I can't go back to Ronnie without you.'

You didn't argue with Pat, eighteen stone of Glasgow hardman.

I had a girlfriend at the time. A hairdresser, she had her own shop in Islington Green. She was about ten years older than me and seemed really sophisticated. I was really flattered that she was interested in me. Well, she had turned up. Pat went down to some car in the street and got Billy Exley, an old boxer who hung around the Firm, up the stairs telling him to look after the door.

'Can I bring my girlfriend?' I asked. Pat looked at me as if I was crazy, then said: 'It won't be long. Come and see Ronnie and I'll bring you straight back.' I agreed. Then we went to the Green Dragon in Whitechapel.

It was a private drinking club, which meant you had to sign members in to keep your alcohol licence and stay legal. When I got there, Ronnie was sitting at a table: 'Come in, boy, sit down and have a drink,' he said. Then his older brother, Charlie Kray, and some of the Firm showed up. I didn't really know much about it, but Reggie was away again, in prison. They all sat down and had a drink. Ronnie asked me: 'What do you think, David? Lovely club, isn't it?'

'Yes, Ronnie, it's lovely.'

What else could I say?

With that, three drunks came stumbling in, signing their names at the door. Whatever they'd written, the girl at the desk wasn't having it. She came over to Ronnie and read him what they'd put in the visitors' book. The three of them had written 'Dickie Bird' as their names and their addresses as 'Up a tree'.

Ron said, 'Oh, right.' He went up to them and had a word.

'You're not Dickie Birds, are you?'

'What do you mean, mate? Who are you?' one answered back.

'And you don't live up a tree, do you?' said Ron. 'Sign your names in properly next time.' And with that – wallop! Ronnie took a swing, and like a cartoon, the three drunks fell over, one by one, into a heap on the floor.

Ronnie just sighed and walked up to the bar while dusting his hands down: 'Giss a drink, will you?' he said.

Nobody moved to stop him, nobody said it was wrong. He behaved like it was nothing to knock three men out stone cold.

'Can I go home now?' I asked.

'We'll all come back to the 66,' he said. And they did. It was nearly midnight by now.

That was the beginning of it all. The club regulars soon fell away. It was all villains now – or police. Ronnie and Reggie (when he got out of prison in 1961 after that demanding money with menaces conviction) often had meets with the police at my mum's club, where they would give up other names to them – what they called 'bodies' (they always wanted those) so they could clear their books of 'unsolved' crimes, get little tip-offs on what was going down or about to. Half the coppers in London at that time were bent.

I'd be cleaning up the 66 Club and I'd see Ronnie giving them money in brown envelopes all the time. The Krays had police officers in their pockets on every manor. This was the Flying Squad, coppers on the beat, every level. Billy Hill would bring top coppers up to the club to meet the Krays.

Ron would say when we could open and close, who we could let in. It was becoming a right den of thieves. There were guns in the kitchen, guns in the oven, guns in the fridge … Often, Ronnie would hand me and Alfie a handgun and we'd have to hide it anywhere we could think of.

It wasn't just the club that Ronnie was taking over, it was our mum too. He came to really love her, I think, and she, at least at first, could only think of him as a 'lovely boy'. Often, we'd come home from a night out to find Ron having tea and sandwiches in the kitchen with Mum and his gun left in the fridge.

Neither Ronnie or Reggie could read or write properly (then again neither could I). They used to get Smithy to do all their Christmas cards for them, about five hundred a year. A lot were to other villains, say in faraway Scotland, or in prison. But Ronnie also used to send cards to the families of those he'd just cut up. 'Send her a card' was a code I learned to recognise. Sometimes it was a bunch of flowers or a bowl of fruit to someone's sister or mother. We'd put the stamps on the cards and post them. I used to sit for hours in Vallance Road, sticking stamps on envelopes.

And Ronnie always knew how to play the clown. We'd be driving along somewhere and he would suddenly shout out to a complete stranger: 'Oi, bollock-chops, what's the time?' Or 'Soppy-bollocks, come here!' 'Bonzo' was another common nickname and 'Basil'. One of his favourite catchphrases was: 'Smashing, innit?' It was all very funny, when he wasn't smashing somebody in the face.

Like this. We were at the 66 one night, having a good time, everyone relaxed and enjoying their evening, when all of a sudden Ronnie went to sit at a table by himself and began staring menacingly across the room at Smithy. Really staring.

We all started to get nervous as when Ron went like that you never knew what might happen next. With that, he jumps up and runs at Smithy, smashing him in the jaw and knocking him out cold.

We ran over to Smithy to get him to his feet and make sure he was OK. Once he started to come to his senses, he asked: 'What was all that about, Ronnie?'

Ronnie said: 'Do you remember when you came to get me out of jail? I was in the car [after absconding from Long Grove mental hospital by switching places with Reggie in summer 1958] and you were driving and you said: "What's that over there, Ron?" and I answered, "A bus stop." "What's that?" you asked. "A black taxi," I said. You thought I was nuts, didn't you? You were checking me out. Well, I'm not nuts. That was what that punch was for.'

Smithy just shrugged. And they called him 'Mad'.

\* \* \*

Mum didn't know about the violence. Dad did. He used to sit down with Ronnie and tell him stories about all the old gangsters he had known. Ron loved the old-time yarns, saying: 'I knew a few of them.' And he really had done. When he was a teenager, not long after the war, he used to work for Jack Spot and Billy Hill: it was his apprenticeship. Jack taught him the golden rule: 'Only nick from thieves, that way you'll never get nicked.'

Both my parents knew the Krays were criminals but didn't mind – we were all criminals in our own way. After they met, Violet Kray and our mother Ellen, known as Nell, bloody loved each other. Every weekend there'd be a party with our parents and the Krays' parents until two or three in the morning. It was known as 'ATs' or 'After Times'. They would go to musicals together – *Fings Ain't What They Used to Be*, *Oliver!*, *West Side Story*, the big shows of the day. Ronnie would get them tickets off Sammy Lederman, who was a showbiz agent. They'd meet the stars, it was all very glamorous.

Ronnie brought good spenders to the club. We'd make loads of money on a good night but it soon went out the door again. Over time the twins 'borrowed' lots of money off Dad … and never paid any of it back. When he said he wanted to sell the club, they said they'd buy it off him. They made lots of promises about the money they'd pay him back and, despite the debts they already had with him, he still went for it, saying, 'Don't let me down, Ron.' He wasn't physically frightened of them, I suppose he knew there was no way out.

One night, Mum asked Ron to bar the both of us, me and Alfie, from his clubs so we wouldn't 'go with dirty women'. Ronnie told us this the following day with great amusement, pretending to bar us when we turned up at the club. It was like he wanted to control us completely.

As much as Ronnie would come to the 66, so Alfie and I would be required to attend wherever he and Charlie were. If we didn't come immediately, he'd send a car round for us. Sometimes it was to go to another club, sometimes to Vallance Road.

Whatever it was the Colonel wanted, you couldn't refuse. It seemed Violet Kray liked the idea of us being there because it made Ron happy. Smiling, she would greet the two of us with: 'Oh, Ronnie will be pleased to see the pair of you! Come in the kitchen and I'll make you a lovely cup of tea. Do you want a sandwich?'

'Yes, please, Mrs Kray. Thank you so much, Mrs Kray.'

When Ron got the hump, the rest of the family would all be tiptoeing round him, trying not to upset him. But we'd walk in there and say, 'Look at the face on him! Isn't he ugly?' and that would start Ron laughing and blow away the brooding tension. It was as if we had a licence to insult him. Nobody else did.

Except maybe his own father. Old Charlie Kray used to go around town being dead rude about him: 'I've got a poof of a son.'

Ronnie would tell his mum: 'Say goodbye to him, kiss him. I'm gonna kill him, I'm gonna bury him in Epping Forest – I'll put a tree there so you can pay your respects.'

I didn't realise Ron was gay. Alfie and Bobby and I knew loads of homosexuals and always respected them, but I certainly didn't know Ronnie was one when he first came up the club. But it was pretty obvious. I thought all gangsters were gangsters, not gay – as far as I knew then, the two just didn't go together.

# 4

## ALL THINGS KNEES-UP

Now it was my turn to meet the other Kray twin – the still mysterious Reggie. On 10 September 1959, Reggie had appealed against that demanding money with menaces off that Finchley shopkeeper charge and been released on bail. 'For reasons not known, this appeal is still outstanding, and Kray is at liberty', DS Butler had noted in his long memo on the 'The Twins'. He'd be out for quite a time.

Ten months later, Reggie had had his appeal turned down, his bail revoked and was away again. But not for long. When he was let out of Wandsworth Prison in September 1960, the twins came to the 66 Club that night to celebrate.

This was the first time I'd ever met Reggie. He was a lot like Ronnie, obviously. He looked at you like he was trying to weigh you up, much more serious than Ronnie. Ron was beaming. It was like he was showing off to Reggie that he had got my mum and dad's club as a trophy: *You got the Double R when I was away, now I've got this!*

You had to watch everything you said, even the way you looked at Reggie. He had a horrible habit of walking up to people he didn't like the look of and offering to light their cigarette. Then, as their chin went out to accept the light, he'd hit them so hard on the jaw they'd be knocked unconscious.

There was one night I was with him when he pulled a bird and suggested the three of us went back to Vallance Road. The girl was up for having both of us and I thought Reggie wanted it too. So, we all went into Reggie's bedroom at the back of the house and got into bed. But after I'd had sex with the girl, Reggie said he'd changed his mind and let it go. I never considered Reggie being involved sexually with a girl before he met Frances Shea. He'd end up marrying her.

After Tommy Butler had taken a special interest, the Double R was raided by the police late one night in June 1960. No one was arrested but the drinking licence was revoked soon afterwards. But it didn't take them too long to be back in the club business. In September 1961, the twins set up all over again. Called the 'Kentucky', it was in Stepney, just across from the ABC Empire cinema in the Mile End Road, and was supposed to be a posher version of the Double R. It had once been a shop, more like a warehouse at the back really, but the bar had been done up with crimson velvet and mirrors.

It was managed for a while by a disbarred barrister called Stanley Crowther. He'd tell the police one day: 'It had been run by a coloured man and many of his customers were coloured, he chose the name and the Krays evidently decided to retain it.' There was a little house band, a trio. Crowther would end up running Long Firms, fraudulent companies trading on dodgy credit lines, for the twins.

The East End was getting all a bit trendy. The Double R had begun it really. Dockland pubs were tourist attractions. Joan Littlewood's Theatre Royal, Stratford, was doing *Oh! What a Lovely War* and face-off-the-telly Dan Farson (a pal of Smithy's) made a TV show about pub singers like Queenie Watts. All things knees-up were fashionable for a while and while it lasted, the twins were the big stars of Cockneyland. The Kentucky might just get to be the smartest place in London. So they might dream. But to make it so, you had to get proper faces in. They wanted pop singers, people their mum had seen off the telly or in films, so they employed their old army chum, Dickie Morgan, to cruise the West End to persuade celebrity customers to head east, getting the faces in.

He was dreadful at it. Alfie and I were meant to do the same, so was Smithy. I managed to get Colin Hicks (entertainer Tommy Steele's brother) and two black tap dancers from America called the Clark Brothers, Steve and Jimmy. The Clark Brothers were amazing, very stylish smartly dressed tap dancers, thin as whippets the pair of them. They'd been on TV several times and were friends of the singer, Kenny Lynch. They went down very well at the club but as Ronnie never paid anyone and they couldn't even afford the cab fare home, eventually they came to me and I had to ask Ronnie to at least give them a few quid for their trouble. Which thankfully on this occasion he did.

I was summoned to the Kentucky one night. It was really dead that evening because it was too far out and no one would go there. Ronnie was arguing with Reggie and Charlie, screaming and shouting up at the bar. Then suddenly he grabbed hold of a lemon slicer from the counter and ran it across the back of his hand in a single movement. Waving his bloodied hand in the air, he shouted: 'If you say you're going to do something, fucking do it!' After that they had to take him down the London Hospital to fix him up. He was permanently scarred as a result, but he didn't seem to care.

So, if the West End was a bit too slow in coming east, the twins had a new plan – they were going up west. This was the time of the infamous landlord Peter Rachman with his slum property empire, letting rooms to prozzers at high rents and enforcing payment by thuggery. It was the badlands of Bayswater, Paddington and Notting Hill, a lot of villainy round there.

The twins wanted a slice so they put the frighteners on Rachman's frighteners. And they'd always be sending people out spying to find out who was spending money and where. Right then, a lot of money was crossing the tables of a certain gambling club in Wilton Place, Knightsbridge. To keep the Krays off his back, Rachman introduced them to the owner (in fact, he had a big share of it through a hotel firm): a man called Stefan de Faye.

The club was Esmeralda's Barn. Once a smart society place, it had then secured one of the very first of the new gaming licences. It had come the twins' way in typical fashion. A posh bird called Esme Noel-Smith owned it. When she died, it was bought by this man de Faye, who soon lost interest. In fact, he advertised it for sale in the *Evening Standard*, where a face called Leslie Payne saw it. I found a note of all that happening in the National Archives.

Payne had been a sergeant in Italy in the war. He'd sold hoovers and used cars before graduating to fraud. He was the twins' money-man adviser. Tall with pale blue eyes, he wore spotty bow ties like a politician. One writer has called him 'stylishly dishonest'. He went on to write a very readable book called *The Brotherhood* – very instructive, a kind of *Long Firm Frauds for Dummies*. It tells you how to do it.

There'd be a big falling-out with the twins, but that was all in the future. Payne did the deal with de Faye and it was Rachman who brought the twins to the party. It was his way of paying them to leave his slum landlord operation alone. The Krays just took over a slice of the ownership (they never actually paid for it), with its staff and upper-crust membership not much the wiser. Reggie and Ronnie were company directors for the first time in their lives. That was early January 1962.

I got to see it myself soon afterwards. We were all up the Green Dragon in Whitechapel one night when Ronnie suddenly said: 'Come on, let me take you up my posh club, Esmeralda's Barn.' So, we went there and I was really impressed. It had a lovely restaurant and a bar. The men were in evening dress, black tie, and the women wore pearls. All very smart. I could see how pleased Ron was by my reaction. The casino was on the top of three floors with a restaurant below and the Cellar Club below that in the basement. The old boxer Billy Exley was the doorman there for a while. The Cellar Club was popular with lesbians but there were also gay men and straight couples there too. In those days no one knew who was who so it was difficult to tell sometimes! But let's say the club had a bit of a reputation and began to build up quite a following. It was a members only club and you had to sign the register when you went in same as you would at the Savoy.

So it went on. What Ronnie really liked about it was seeing what he'd call the 'flash cunts' losing money. 'Don't they make you fucking sick?' he'd say. (That's a quote from Les Payne's book, *The Brotherhood*, by the way.) Guards officers and their dopey girlfriends. But if Ronnie didn't like a punter, he'd be thrown down the stairs. It was all part of the entertainment. As Les Payne would write: 'They all thought it was amusing at first, that the place was run by gangsters. Later they changed their minds.'

Years after it closed, DI Leonard 'Nipper' Read went around collecting stories from the Barn as part of his investigation. I found some of them in a box in the National Archives called 'Kray: Wounding and Assaults' – there's a lot of boxes like that.

Billy Exley told this tale. He was rung at home at four in the morning and told to get over to Knightsbridge quick: Les Payne was there, Ronnie, Teddy Smith and the croupier, Bobby Buckley. In the kitchen, the gas ring was on, a sharpening steel glowing red-hot on it. A face called Lennie Hamilton 'arrived and was taken into the kitchen,' said Exley. 'Ronnie pushed the hot steel into his face. Ronnie said, "It's over now but if you tell anyone about this, I'll put it across your eyes."'

Here's another yarn from the Barn I found in the National Archives. One night in March 1962, a wealthy club member called Hyman Diamond stood guarantor up to £30 for a lady chemmy player called Eva Blackburn. She'd rather play all night than go home to her flat in Curzon Street, Mayfair. Mr (he styled himself 'Commander' apparently) Diamond did go home and left her to it. The next day, Les Payne rang up, demanding £600. Diamond refused to pay. The following morning, he found his Roller smashed up with a sledgehammer round the back of Harrods. He didn't tell the police at the time (he 'didn't make the connection with the Krays', he said. Of course, he did, he was too scared to say so), but he did seven years later. In fact, he would tell DI Nipper Read all about it.

The *People* newspaper did a peek round clubland soon after the Krays moved in and discovered a young man called Bobby Buckley, aged nineteen, working as the croupier for a very 'high-rolling chemmy game'.

It was Esmeralda's Barn of course. Bobby was reportedly making £200 in tips a week. He had a younger brother, Jimmy. On that kind of money, no wonder the Buckley brothers liked the trendier-by-the-minute King's Road scene of which the Barn was now such a feature. So what if some of the upper-crust clientele had had enough of Ronnie's antics, there was a new Chelsea set of rich kids moving in.

There was one punter called David Litvinoff, a fast-talking homosexual who'd got out of the East End on his wits. He's in several Kray accounts. I must have met him, but I don't remember. This Litvinoff couldn't stop telling his fashionable friends about the party-loving criminals he'd discovered. He'd been losing big at the tables. He traded his gambling debt for a lease on his flat in Kensington. It was in Ashburn Gardens, off the Cromwell Road. Ronnie moved in, not just the flat, but on Litvinoff's boyfriend: bisexual croupier Bobby Buckley. Ronnie was enraptured.

Bobby Buckley was Irish-born. He'd been a stable lad in Kildare. He came from Exmouth Market, Finsbury, round that manor. His younger brother James was the Barn's cloakroom attendant for a while. Bobby would get married one day. His wife, Monica, and a 'close relative' called Moira, would, unusually for women, become good friends of Ronnie's. He called Monica 'Angelface' and used to send her flowers by Interflora.

Bobby Buckley would be a Kray loyalist to the end. I found a police notice from 1969 of him as a Firm associate in the National Archives. He's described as 'a dangerous man of effeminate appearance'. According to the writer John Pearson, Buckley was a big source for his first Kray book, *The Profession of Violence*, and both Bobby and Monica 'died in the early seventies from overdosing drugs'. Some say Monica put that about as a disappearing act.

There was another east London face who 'crouped' the tables at Wilton Place. His name was Leslie Holt and his parents had a flat in Cedra Court. He was fair-haired, blue-eyed and had briefly been a boxer when he was billed as 'Johnny Kidd'. Ronnie would take a big fancy. But it wasn't that long before Ron left the flat of ill repute in Ashburn Gardens with Buckley and Litvinoff and moved back to his mum's house. Maybe he needed his ironing done. Then the twins just started arguing again. Their mum couldn't stop them. Ronnie put a caravan at the back of Vallance Road on some bombsite – it was somewhere to go and sulk when they'd had a row.

Moneyman Leslie Payne's role had been to run the gambling club. Now it was to get the Krays' latest venture up and fraudulently running in an old scam called a 'Long Firm'. It was outright crim-inality: you set up a company, bought goods on credit from legit-imate suppliers but based on phoney references. You found some short-lease premises and sold the stuff at bargain prices, took the cash and disappeared overnight. It needed fast footwork. The suppliers and the banks would be left holding the loss. The money could be really big. It was too tempting for the twins to stay out. That's how the Firm got some important new recruits to join the old-time cons from Regal Billiard Hall days, old fraudsters like Sammy Lederman and Nobby Clark.

One day, Ronnie asked Alfie over to meet Leslie Payne. He said: 'I'm going to give you some money and you've got to do what this man tells you.' Ronnie, Reggie, Charlie and Alfie all had a meet-ing with Payne in the front room in Vallance Road. There were two front rooms at the Krays – the one downstairs was for more social ordinary meets but if it was more important, you went upstairs. This was one of those.

Alfie was told he was to be the frontman in a Long Firm. He'd open a bank account, set up a business and trading accounts, order the goods in and start getting credit. But my brother didn't want anything to do with it – he had more sense than to get mixed up in it. He said to me: 'This ain't my game. I'm a trader, not a crook.'

In February 1961 Ronnie and older brother Charlie were charged with 'loitering with intent to steal' – trying the door handles of parked cars in Queensbridge Road, Hackney. As if they'd do that. They got off, claiming police harassment. They had a big party – there was always a party.

Then in April Reggie found himself arrested again, for 'housebreaking' this time. But the woman who filed the charges failed to identify him in the magistrates' court and so the case was dismissed.

There was another big party that night, 8 May 1961. Not at our mum's club this time, but at Esmeralda's Barn. Ronnie proposed a toast to 'British Justice' and all the journalists and photographers were given champagne. The Krays for the first time really were national news. Several newspapers the next day carried big articles about 'the celebrated boxing twins' and their claims of a police vendetta against them. The twins loved the company of celebrities. Might they not be celebrities themselves? What was to stop them? They would end up famous alright.

The articles proclaimed their declaration to 'go straight'. And this time it seemed Reggie at least really wanted to do just that. He spent much of that summer at the Steeple Bay caravan. I myself would one day get to know the place well. There was a girl called Frances Shea from Hackney who had started coming down for weekends. Reggie proposed to her there when she was eighteen. She herself said she was too young.

Alfie knew her brother, Frankie Shea. He ran a used-car business on Pentonville Road in Islington, where Reggie used to get his cars.

Frankie was also a getaway driver. Frances was a beautiful girl, stunning. Alfie thought she looked like the young Brigitte Bardot.

The Kentucky Club wasn't entirely forgotten. And it came really good one time. The premiere of the film *Sparrows Can't Sing* was held at the Empire Cinema in Bow Road, on 26 February 1963. It was a Cockney love story. Joan Littlewood directed. There was a souvenir programme with ads from local businesses, the proceeds all going to charity of course. The whole Firm was told to attend, including their wives. Princess Margaret was meant to be graciously attending, but Lord Snowdon turned up without her. People were told she had flu, but Special Branch had warned her off.

There were jellied eels and mash at Queen Mary College over the road, then it was all back to the Kentucky Club, so everyone could have their photos taken with the twins. Not Lord Snowdon, sadly. He left the Empire straight after the credits rolled. All the women, including the film's star, Barbara Windsor, were done up in furs and diamonds. She wasn't that famous then, but soon would be.

Frances Shea was there with Reggie, along with James Booth and George Sewell out of the film. Alfie was there with his Soho drinking pal, the Welsh actor Victor Spinetti. The journalist and MP Tom Driberg was also there and Donald Bridgehouse, a homosexual barrister.

My job that night had been to go and get the blind singer Lennie Peters and bring him to the club. He lived in the flats up Seven Sisters. When I got there his wife Sylvia opened the door and said: 'He doesn't feel too well.' He had three or four kids there with him. Lennie said: 'Can you tell him I can't come?'

So, I went back and told Ronnie and Ronnie said: 'Just go back there and tell him he has to.' I went back to Lennie and said: 'Ronnie says you've got to come.' I felt bad bullying a blind man, but Ronnie would insist.

So, Alfie and I had done our best roping in faces for the big night. But Ronnie went mad. It was a big night, it just wasn't big enough. The celebrities weren't big enough. I don't know who he was expecting. Did he really think Princess Margaret was on her way to join him and Reggie for a brown ale? The real diehards went back to Esmeralda's Barn for even more drinking. I did some of the driving that night, two return trips: I took Bobby Buckley and the Colonel.

In any case, the Kentucky didn't last long after its turn in the spotlight. Just as had happened to Double R, the police at Arbour Square objected to the renewal of the club's licence. It closed its doors for the last time on Sunday, 7 April 1963.

The twins had another big moan about police victimisation – I saw a long report on it in the National Archives. One night, Leslie Payne and Reggie were pulled in Payne's Mercedes in the Mile End Road and made to go to Commercial Street nick to prove it wasn't stolen. Payne complained in person at New Scotland Yard.

Members of the Kentucky Club committee raising money for Mile End Hospital were scrutinised. It featured Dr Morris Blasker (the twins' resident stitch-you-up doctor) and Daniel Farson, 'a television commentator who has several recent convictions for drunkenness and has all the appearances of a homosexual personality', so the report said. Plus, a vicar. All the money seemed to be going into the twins' pockets. The do-gooders were either complicit or fools. 'Their charitable ventures are a thin mask,' the report said.

Anyone could have told them that.

# 5

## SMASHIN'

By now I was a little bit older, not very much wiser and doing all sorts of little errands for Ronnie. Ron was always sending one of us out for salt beef sandwiches from his favourite shop in Windmill Street, Soho. The twins wanted all the trimmings, gherkins and schmaltz, or they wouldn't eat them.

Ronnie was a terrible driver. Reggie wasn't much better. And although they had cars, flash cars – Ronnie had a big, Yank Ford for a while – they were useless behind the wheel themselves. They needed to be driven everywhere and anywhere. That's what I did a lot of the time. I'd go over in my little Ford Pop and be told to pick up a bigger motor from such and such a place.

Every so often I used to have to go round Vallance Road at 7pm to get our orders if we were going out on 'meets'. And I carried guns for Ronnie. If we were going to a pub, he'd give me a gun and say, 'When you get inside, stand by the toilet.' He'd know I'd be there so that if he had a meet with someone, he could then go to the toilet and collect a gun from me on the way. He wasn't stupid enough to carry a gun himself because he knew he was being watched the whole time.

Then one time I was called upon to run a more unusual errand. One morning, I was asleep with a girl on the couch – her name was Lucy – when there was a bang on the door. Scotch Pat Connolly and Charlie Kray walked in and told me I had to take some money to 'Ronnie in Jersey'. It was early spring 1963, about eight in the morning.

'Are you joking!' I said, but they insisted I go. They told me to go to Vallance Road. So I did as I was told and waited for about five hours before Charlie Kray eventually came in and said, 'I've got a packet here with some money in it and an air ticket.'

'Keep this on you whatever you do,' he added. 'Get a case and put some clean shirts in and get a cab to Heathrow. When you get to Jersey, someone will be there.'

I felt quite excited, to be honest. I don't know exactly how much money there was, but it looked like a lot. Arriving around eight in the evening, just as it was getting dark, there was no one to meet me. I didn't know what to do. I waited for an hour. Then I remembered Charlie saying to Teddy Smith at Vallance Road that the hotel was 'near a castle'.

I jumped in a cab, keeping a close hold of the packet, and asked if there was a hotel that was near a castle. The cab driver said there was and took me there. Running up the steps into the reception, I asked: 'Have you got a Mr Kray staying here?'

'Try the bar,' she said.

I walked in and saw Ronnie sitting down on the sofa with another man and a girl – I didn't know who they were. I was very relieved. Ron looked over at me and said to the others: 'Get David a drink.'

He then asked me: 'Have you got that packet for me?' as if I'd come from just across the road. I looked at him to see if he was joking or not, but I couldn't tell. Ron left the bar for a moment. The girl then said: 'Thank God for you, Dave!'

Ron came back, took out a wad of notes and gave the man some money. Afterwards, when we started drinking and talking, he said he worked at Scotland Yard. This was some kind of fancy pay-off, but why come all the way to Jersey to pass money – to whoever it was?

Almost as soon as we arrived Ronnie noticed a man and woman, a supposed honeymoon couple, watching us. Following us around the hotel wherever we went, they were clearly, as he said, coppers.

Later we went back to Ronnie's room. By this time the policeman (if that was what he was) was well lagged and had passed out in the chair, drunk as a sack.

When I said to Ronnie, 'Where do I sleep?' he answered, 'We'll sort it out later.' Then he looked at the policeman, who had by now slid onto the floor, stared at him as if he'd like to kill him then and there, then stepped over him, rolling him over with his foot contemptuously as he did so, leaving him in a collapsed heap on the floor.

Turning to me now he pointed to the girl, the grafter they'd brought over for the policeman, and said: 'Just get in there and give her one.' The girl was happy enough to oblige. But it would turn out later that watching, as Ronnie did on this occasion, was one of his *little things*.

On the plane coming back we noticed the undercover couple again, the 'honeymooners', and Ronnie advised us to split up so that we didn't look so obvious.

Three months later, I was sent out to Jersey again to take more money to Ronnie. Smithy was there with us this time and the man 'from the Yard' was there again too. That night the five of us, me,

Ronnie, Dickie Morgan, Teddy Smith and the policeman, all had a lot to drink in the bar. It was another pay-off. The police officer was again very drunk but this time went to bed, leaving early the next morning before we were up.

Along the way of our little adventures, Alfie had told Ronnie (Alfie always gave far too much away) that our brother Bobby 'had got a beautiful place on the Isle of Wight'. With a business partner, a South African-born naval veteran called Phillip Filmer, he ran self-drive speedboats for hire and a launch called *The African Queen*. We'd work down there for the summer season.

One day, the twins suddenly arrived. Bobby had never met the Krays before, but we'd often described them, telling him they were villains but also how smart and glamorous they were, and how we were taking all the people we knew to their clubs. As soon as Ronnie saw the speedboat, he wanted to go out in it, so I took him round the bay for a spin.

A big thing came out of that trip. I saw a young girl walking along the boardwalk in Shanklin and that was it. She was called Christine French and she wasn't quite twenty – I was ten months older.

Meanwhile, Alfie had also met his future wife, Wendy. Our mother predicted it wouldn't last for either of us, so I said to Alfie: 'We'll prove them all wrong and have a double wedding,' and we did. We both married on 26 September 1963, in Russell Square Registry Office, one after the other. After the wedding, the girls went to Oxford Street, me and Alfie went to the pub.

That night, we all went to the Talk of the Town in Leicester Square for a big party. It was lovely, a stage that came up out of the floor and swirled round. I often met the Welsh singing star Shirley

Bassey and her husband and manager, Kenneth Hume, there. He was both ways – bisexual, I mean – but he thought the world of her after picking her up in Tiger Bay.

At the time the guest stars got paid by the number of people who turned up, so Kenneth asked my Christine and me to come down as often as we could. We used to arrive there about ten. People liked us because we were young and smart, and because the Krays seemed to be our best mates. And not a soul had a bad thing to say about the Krays. Of course, they didn't.

Everything, as Ronnie might say, was smashin' …

# 6

## ONE BIG HAPPY FAMILY

Ronnie was still treating the 66 club as his own. Same with the family flat upstairs. He'd turn up and say he was going to have a kip for an hour. Or we'd get a phone call out of the blue, saying, 'Come over, we're going out.' On one occasion it wasn't for some meet in a club this time, it was to go for a drive in Epping Forest. We had no idea what for – Ron kept going on about getting fresh air and telling us to take big, deep breaths. Smithy came along for the ride.

The car got stuck in the mud so everyone had to get out and push it. I got the giggles because Ron got mud all over his clothes. Ronnie didn't like me laughing at him so drove off with Smithy, leaving me and Alfie in the forest. We had to get four buses home, we felt like mugs. And when we got in, Ron was tucking into Sunday roast at our house.

A little later, Alfie was called to a pub for an 'urgent' meeting. He was told to 'bring Wendy' as well (which was very surprising because Ron didn't like to have the women around). When they arrived, loads of the Firm were there – all sat at a big table with two empty spaces next to Ronnie. Father Richard Evans was also there, he was a

Catholic priest from the Krays' local church in the East End. He liked a drink, and he liked the money, and I am pretty sure he was also gay. But he was useful to Ronnie so that meant he was kept around just in case he needed to be brought out as a supposedly trustworthy witness.

Ronnie explained what it was all about: 'I'm buying an island and we're all going to live there. Father Evans is coming too. I'm going to build him a church. We're going to kidnap your favourite tailor and take him. We've all got to learn to grow our own vegetables. We're going to have armed guards to keep people off the island ...'

Alfie says he couldn't stop laughing and nor could his wife. Ronnie was obviously completely cracked. Wendy was saying, 'He's gone!'

It was all absolute bollock-chops hilarious, of course. We were part of the entertainment. Alfie and I would do close harmony duets. My brother could make up poems on the spot, like one he wrote about a villain being up in front of a judge. When Ronnie was in a good mood, we could take the mickey as much as we liked. Judging that would become a matter of life and death.

Each time after some new outrage, I'd say to Ronnie, 'You're mental.' And he might say, 'Do as you're told ... your mother told me to look after you.' Or he might sulk and walk away. I never thought he'd go for Alfie or me in a violent way, although I did get a couple of slaps off Ronnie: 'Don't be saucy,' he'd say.

So now Alfie and I were married with kids either toddling around or on the way. Of course, our wives didn't like the association with the twins because it meant we were hardly ever at home, what with all the calls to come out with them. 'Come on, child,' Ronnie would say down the phone, 'it's going to be smashin'. We'll have a nice meet tonight, alright?'

You weren't allowed to say no.

But when we were at home it was even worse. Ronnie, or both the twins, would suddenly arrive with a crate of drink and settle in for the night. My wife Christine hated that especially. There were lots of rows. I'd say to her it was 'only for a while' to try and fob her off, but that just wasn't true. Ronnie in particular seemed to like Christine and was always polite to her. Christine would smile back but kept away from the twins as much as she could. She would sit in the kitchen or busy herself with housework if they came round. She would be whispering to me, 'Can't you get them out? When are they going?' She was always glad to see the back of them.

And there was simple jealousy of other women in the clubs: the cigarette girls, hostesses, coat check girls, showgirls, all that kind of thing. None of it was good for our marriage and it wasn't fair on Christine, not fair at all.

Charlie Kray was the worst for the women – he loved them, he really did. He was always bringing birds up the 66: Barbara Windsor, the model Christine Keeler once. The rumours that it was Reggie who was going out with Barbara were just put round by the twins to keep Charlie's wife Dolly quiet. Dolly had a problem with him from the beginning. And whether it was stolen out of a bank or took off a church collection, Charlie was always the first in the queue for his money. He didn't care where it came from. Then he'd say: 'I've got to go, Dolly wants to go to the hairdresser's.'

Dolly must have lived in the hairdresser's, the number of times I heard Charlie say that.

My wife Christine didn't like me driving Frances Shea, Reggie's by now established girlfriend, around the whole time. She'd ask why couldn't someone else do it. I still don't know why it always had to be me.

I'd first met Frances in the Regency Club in Stoke Newington some time in 1962. Reggie was there, Ronnie and Teddy Smith too.

Smithy felt sorry for Frances. He knew that she was trapped by Reggie in the way that we all were by the twins but she couldn't get away even if she tried. Smithy was funny when he was drunk. He'd get all camp, which Ronnie hated but used to make Frances laugh a lot. It was good to see her with a smile on her face for once. But that first night I met her, she was doing anything but smiling, even at Smithy's jokes. Reggie came over, he knew that I'd just got a car: 'Dave boy, take Frances home for me.'

I could hardly say no.

He came out with her and showed her into the back. 'Drop her home and make sure you see her go through the front door, then come straight back, Dave boy,' he said. Frances lived with her mum and dad and brother in Bethnal Green – I knew where to go.

I could see her in the rear-view mirror. She seemed very upset. I tried to talk but she just blanked me, staring out the window. I got her home and went back to the Regency.

'Did Frances say anything on the way back?' Reggie wanted to know.

'Not a word,' I said.

He seemed relieved.

So now I was Frances's full-time driver. I'd pick her up, take her to a pub or a club or Vallance Road. Sometimes Reggie would say, 'Take Frances shopping. Take Christine with you, if you like.'

'OK, Reg,' I'd say.

I used to take Frances shopping, sometimes with Christine as well. Occasionally Frances would buy Christine a lipstick if she was getting one for herself but it was always a bit as if Christine was her lady-in-waiting rather than two female friends going on a shopping spree together. I resented that a bit and I am sure Christine did too.

To be honest, I hated driving Frances. She wouldn't talk to me and she was very quiet; 'bookish' is how I'd describe her. She very rarely smiled, always had a long face and it was as if she was weighing you up when she looked at you. She was moody, like Reggie, and would stare at me the whole time. I suspect she was on pills. But once she was with Reggie, she seemed petrified the whole time, staying quiet for fear of saying something out of order. For good reason.

The boozing, and there was a lot of that, didn't help the rows at home. Already a big drinker, now Alfie was caning it. One day he went out for a pint of milk and came back two weeks later. He'd been on some massive bender, ending up in Cannes in the South of France, where he claims to have met Pablo Picasso: 'You know my mate Francis Bacon!' he'd told old Pablo one day, strolling along the Promenade de la Croisette. At least that's what he would tell me anyway. But for now, it was a big happy family: the Kray brothers and the Teale brothers, Violet and Nell. Sometimes, after some particular piece of Ronnie madness, Alfie and I would look at each other and sigh: 'It can't go on like this.' But it did.

Going out with Ronnie meant you'd never be got at. Anyone in a club, unless they were very pissed or stupid, would back away or be very polite as soon as he showed up, with or without Reggie. You were in a magic circle of calm. Any trouble was only caused by the Krays. But not everyone knew the rules. One night, I was having a drink with Ron in the 66 when a rich 'fence' (a stolen-goods middle-man) we both knew had a few too many and started laughing to himself about how he had kept a lock-up garage around the corner for years, which the police believed belonged to Ronnie.

Big mistake.

Ronnie turned round to the man and, still smiling at him, said: 'Ten years you've had it and the police thought it was mine? I reckon that's £10,000 you owe me.'

He didn't know what to say. Ronnie just stared at him, waiting, still smiling. Then, right in front of me, Ron went into the kitchen, took out a gun from some hiding place and shot the man straight in the foot. He stood over him, laughing, as if it was nothing.

'Sit him down on that chair over there,' he told Smithy. 'Give him a light ale and a whisky and then take him in the car and drop him outside the hospital to get fixed up.'

Smithy looked shocked – he hated physical violence. This time, he seemed visibly disgusted by what Ronnie had done.

And episodes like this kept on coming. I was in Esmeralda's Barn one night. Everything's lovely. Everyone's smart and the evening is looking exciting when all of a sudden Ronnie says to me: 'You got your car, David?' I say: 'Yeah,' but dread what's coming next. 'I should probably go home,' I add. Ronnie announces: 'I'm coming with you.'

My stomach lurched. I couldn't argue with him. If Ronnie told you to do something, you had to do it, but I did try. 'Ronnie,' I protested, 'where are you going to sleep? I've only got one room.' If I thought that would put him off, I was wrong. I had a couch at the end of the bed and he said, 'I'll sleep there.' Then finally, I got what the plan was: Ronnie was trying to come off Largactil (an anti-psychotic drug) as well as some of the numerous other pills he was on, so he'd decided being with me was the safest way to do that.

Anyway, he got on the couch, I got into bed with my wife Christine, our baby daughters' cots alongside (we'd had two little girls by then). So, we got up the next morning, Christine made us some tea and we started chatting. Ron was smoking a lot, un-tipped Player's Navy Cut.

At first, I thought he was OK, but then he started to shake. It got so bad he was lying on the floor, trembling from head to toe. He told me, 'You'd better take me back,' so I did, but as soon as we got to Vallance Road, Reggie went for me as if he would kill me. He only stopped because Ronnie finally managed to convince him that he had told me to take him back to my place. Reggie had been going mental, wondering where his brother was all night, and had blamed me. I kept away for about a week and after that everyone had forgotten about it. Shortly afterwards, I was sent for again. Ronnie had got over his crisis, whatever it was, and soon it was business as usual.

Another time, I was in Esmeralda's Barn at closing time when Ronnie asked me to drop him and Smithy off at the Regency, a Kray drinking club in Stoke Newington. Smithy got in the back, Ron in the front. Coming along Shaftesbury Avenue I noticed a police car was following us and pointed it out to Ron.

Smithy said, 'I've got a tool on me, Ron.'

Ronnie answered, 'So have I.'

I couldn't believe what I was hearing.

'Just drive careful, don't look round,' Ronnie told me, his voice calm.

I started to panic. 'Look, Ron, I can see them in the mirror, the Old Bill. They're going to pull us.'

'If they stop us, I'm going to kill them,' Ronnie said. He wasn't so calm now.

'Please, please don't do that!' I was shouting.

Ron just kept repeating, 'No, I am … I really mean it.'

And he did. In that moment I saw myself being caught up in the middle of a police killing – they hanged you for that.

I turned sharply off the main road to try and lose them: it worked and we got to the Regency.

'You know, I would have shot the fucking lot of them,' said Ron.

'Ron, you know you're not all the ticket! I'm off,' I said.

'Be round the house in the morning,' he told me as if nothing had happened.

And of course, I was. That's how Ron worked – you did do what you were told or were put away yourself.

\* \* \*

One day, Ronnie asked me to take him to a pub in Stoke Newington for a meeting so I drove him there in the back as he liked. I waited in the car for half an hour, then Ronnie got back in and they went back to Vallance Road, where Ronnie gave me his coat and told me to very, very carefully put it at the back of the yard – 'Don't drop it, don't knock anything on the way.' There was a bomb in it, he said. He had thought that the people in the pub were 'Home Office spies', whatever that meant, and his plan was 'to blow them all up if things had turned nasty.'

Was this paranoia? Not really. There were always watchers outside Vallance Road. Unmarked cars, vans. Men in macs and large black boots. Or the rubber-heel mob. Sometimes they were deliberately obvious. Other times not at all.

DCS Nipper Read would say in his memoirs:

We quite brazenly set observation outside their house as it was my intention to let them know we were going heavy-footed into certain areas ...

There was a running gag about Ronnie taking cups of tea out to watching coppers: 'Milk and sugar? You must be freezing out here. Take your time ... I'll send someone out for the tray after.' Sometimes it would be me who'd go out and collect the empties.

Then there were phone taps. Ron knew about those. Maybe Billy Hill had warned him. Wire taps were dodgy as evidence in court but could be a part of an investigation. In his memoirs Nipper Read describes using a Home Office-authorised tap to get a tip-off at the start of his second run-in with the twins.

The twins' cousin Ronnie Hart told Norman Lucas in 1969 about the twins' obsession with being snooped on. It's in Norman's book, *Britain's Gangland*. For the Firm's little talks on the dog and bone, there were code words for people, places, pubs and more. 'If you went to do anyone, you had to report by phone that dog lost [failure] or that dog won [success],' Hart explained to Lucas.

'The twins never trusted the phone because they were convinced that it was being tapped by the police. Sometimes Ronnie would pick up the phone and just swear into it for the benefit of any listeners.'

The twins were taught how to do it themselves by their tame private investigator, George Devlin, with the spy gear he got from shops in the Tottenham Court Road. Hart told Lucas about a micro tape recorder hidden in 'a packet of American cigarettes' and buttonhole cameras to photograph 'men watching their home who were suspected of being detectives'.

Some of it would later come out in the DS Townsend 'corrupt copper' episode, with Teddy Smith fitting up a tie-pin microphone to a tape recorder in a shoulder holster, playing Q to Ronnie's James Bond.

There were always old-fashioned letters. Ronnie had got Harry Granshaw, manager of the Cheshire Street Baths, to be his discreet mailbox round the corner from Fort Vallance. No steaming open allowed there, big-shot airmail letters from America would come that way.

That's why Ron liked the 66 so much, because it was out of the way, a frontier post halfway between east and west. By now he was using it like it was his front room. All the rules were Ronnie's rules: 'This is perfect for us,' he would smile. 'A nice straight, clean little club, the ideal place to make a meet.'

It was tragic really. The 66 was now a Kray fiefdom with all the attendant villainy. Dad was too old to make much of a fight of it. Mum was heartbroken. She loved the business. It was the family's living and there were still loads of young ones to support. Alfie and I couldn't help – we were not on the Firm, but we didn't dare cross it.

How was I to fend off the wolves when I was running with the pack myself? I knew how easy it was to lean on club owners, I'd done it myself and so had Alfie. Ronnie would say to us: 'Go down to [wherever] and cause havoc. Smash it up, start a fight, get drunk.' Ronnie and Reggie would then come in and say, 'We hear you had a bit of trouble yesterday. We can deal with all that. You give us a little pension, we'll sort all that out.' It would usually be about £25 a week, sometimes more. And there were loads of clubs – they were raking it in.

Alfie and I never hurt anyone, we'd just get drunk and act like idiots. I only did it two or three times, but I feel terrible about it now. This was people's livelihoods and I deeply regret treating anyone like that.

Meanwhile, Alfie had got into the club scene himself as a partner with a man called George Hardy, who was in the music business. They set up a place called the Two Decks in Rupert Court, on the south side of Shaftesbury Avenue in Soho. Pubs used to close at 3pm back then so afternoon drinking was really what it was all about. Members-only, it was licensed by Westminster Council; you had to sign in the book as you went up the stairs and guests were allowed. He fitted out the place like a ship, with portholes, brass lamps, that sort of thing. It got a reputation as a quiet place where stars like Cliff Richard could go for a drink without being pestered.

Alfie got some big showbiz names in there: drag performer Danny La Rue, comedians Ronnie Corbett and Frankie Howerd, Victor Spinetti, Shirley Bassey (that's where I first met her) and Beatles manager Brian Epstein. He did well with it when he wasn't drinking away the profits. I'd come over and help out a bit. Back then, I thought I was it, I really did – I thought I was the business. I used to get my suits handmade by Sam Arkus, a trendy tailor in Berwick Street.

When he wasn't at the Two Decks, Alfie would take me down the 2is in Old Compton Street, where Tommy Steele and all that lot used to go. We'd go there or the Freight Train or the Ad Lib, where Alfie knew the doorman.

So, one afternoon about four o'clock there's a ring on the bell at the Two Decks. I looked out and saw Brian Epstein – I knew what he looked like because he was a friend of George Hardy. There's four fellas with long hair waiting to come in with him. I told Brian they couldn't come in, they were too scruffy. He just shrugged, he thought it was funny. 'C'mon guys, they're too posh for us,' something like that. Guess what!

Alfie told me he'd never let Ronnie near the Two Decks. If he had found out about it, he would have moved in, just as he and Reggie always did. After about five years it folded – just as well maybe – before the twins got the chance.

# 7

## THE CEDRA CIRCUS

In summer 1962 Ronnie changed his domestic arrangements. He departed Vallance Road (but not altogether, he could never do that) for a block of mansion flats in Stamford Hill, a north London suburb with a long-established Orthodox Jewish community. It looked like an ocean liner. He moved into Flat 8, Cedra Court, Cazenove Road, N16. The tenancy, rates, HP agreements, phone, all of that was in Leslie Payne's name. He'd always be getting menacing letters demanding payment, so he would write later. The twins never paid for anything.

My mum and dad were already living there. Dad had got a flat through the Freemasons, mainly Jewish people. It was actually our dad who got Ronnie his gaff. Ron decked it out like some sultan's palace. There was an ebony elephant, stuffed birds, scimitar swords on the wall, a pink-tiled bathroom with a black bath, mirrors everywhere, joss sticks. He installed a four-poster bed with muslin curtains for Bobby Buckley (I found a note of that in the National Archives). According to the crime reporter Norman Lucas, who'd taken an interest in the twins from the start, there was a mynah bird which would squawk, presumably in Ronnie's voice: 'Go and Get Some Money!'

There was a Labour MP new on the scene, Tom Driberg. He was a homosexual and didn't care too much who knew it. That was quite brave for a politician as physical acts at any age were criminal and moral disapproval (in public at least) was near universal – even if all that was changing fast.

He'd first met Reggie at the Kentucky Club when the theatre producer Joan Littlewood took him there. And it was Smithy who introduced Ronnie to Driberg because he was sleeping with him.

Both of the Krays met Lord Boothby, the famous 'TV-peer', soon after that through Driberg, who brought his political chum to Esmeralda's Barn one night in 1962. Boothby had gone mad for it. The two of them were very different. Boothby was fleshy and blustering, a natural television personality on shows like *This Is Your Life* and *What's My Line?*, big hits of the time. Driberg was small and sickly-looking, like you wouldn't want to get too close to him. Both got a real kick out of being friends with the Colonel.

The link between them all was Teddy Smith. Smithy was everywhere and into everything. He was like a scout for the Krays, searching out people who might be useful. One time, he went with Ronnie to have lunch with Driberg in the House of Commons. Just like Boothby, Driberg loved the set-up around Ron.

Then there was Soho. It was quite dangerous but that's why those MPs did it of course. Teddy was always hanging out with that crowd – he used to go around like he was the Mayor of Old Compton Street.

Now that Ronnie was away from Mum, up in Stamford Hill, he could party any way he liked. He had boys there, lots of boys, 'willing East End lads' who were passed around Cedra Court parties. That bit has been quoted over and over in Kray accounts.

But there were a lot of girls around too. Reggie used to say to Alfie: 'Go and get some women.' My brother was a real ladies' man, he was the one bringing the birds back. But Ronnie would be saying: 'No, go and get some boys.'

The pubs around the East End at that time were just full of girls waiting to be pulled. They'd sit around waiting for some punter to come in so that they could make a few quid. One night we'd been having a drink up at Cedra Court when Ronnie had sent Alfie and me out to get people to make up a party. About four or five girls came back for drinks with us. One had short hair and slim hips and looked more like a boy than a girl. I could see Ronnie was taken with her and after going over to talk to her he took her into the bedroom. A short time later I heard her scream, not from pleasure but more as if she needed help.

I was worried and went and knocked on the door and called, 'Ron, Ron, what's going on?' Ronnie shouted 'Fuck off!' but the girl came running out, shouting that Ronnie was 'mental'. Then she went and found her friend and they left. Ronnie gave them some money but I doubt that made up for what she'd been through that night.

Ronnie did what he liked. What he liked a lot was seeing a boy-girl couple having sex.

He also loved blue films. I was at a party one night at his flat. Everyone was watching them and getting very drunk. The film kept breaking and everyone started booing. It was funny really. There's been plenty of accounts in print (and a scene in a major film) of live sex shows in Ron's exotically decked-out parlour at Cedra Court. I myself never saw one.

Like Esmeralda's Barn, it became quite the thing for the smart set, faces off the telly and politicians to mingle with villains. Plenty of people thought a night at the Cedra Circus was worth the risk.

And it *was* a risk. Like Fort Vallance, it was being watched. And it wasn't just local police. As I remember, you could tell because if it was local coppers, Ronnie would go out and talk to them. So, who was doing the watching? It's still a bit of a mystery, but more of this later ...

You might ask why Ronnie wanted all those fashionable people trooping through his flat. Well, it was flattering and a bit of fame was nice. His mother Violet liked it too. And that's what all that charity stuff was about, all those photographs of Reggie and Ronnie with boxers, singers and film stars, all that trouble to make sure the press were tipped off whenever there was some gift to a kiddies' hospital.

Reggie wanted to manage pop groups. Since the Kentucky Club days and me and Alfie's efforts to pull in smart young faces we knew, the twins were all too aware that some old boxer wasn't going to do the business. But as Leslie Payne would put it in his book, *The Brotherhood*: 'It didn't occur to them that there was more to managing than going out for an evening with the stars.'

Some of the old Kentucky Club crowd had stayed loyal – the actor Ronald Fraser, Barbara Windsor, a few others. But not enough. So, to keep the celebrities flowing, Charlie just took over old Sammy Lederman's business. He set up in Esmeralda's Barn before that shut, then in Cork Street, Mayfair, as the 'Charles Kray Theatrical Agency'. He didn't have a clue. And Sammy would become another hanger-on for the twins – as a barman.

What the Kray brothers really wanted was to rub shoulders with top American stars – and they did. For a while it worked like this: Sammy was an old Soho face. He could still pull a few contacts in big sports, in Hollywood, on Broadway. Whoever it was, if they were coming to the Palladium or the Talk of the Town, Sammy and now Charlie would try and fix it that big acts coming on a UK tour would take in the sights of Old London Town. This of course included a meet with the lovable Kray twins, Cockneyland's very own royalty, so Ronnie, Reggie and Charlie could have their picture taken with them. It might be in the contract. It was all 'for charity' – *their* charity. In fact, the money went straight into their pockets (and into Charlie's pockets) most of all.

One day, in late summer 1963, Ronnie told me: 'Come over this evening, you're going to meet Sonny Liston.' The heavyweight champion of the world, he was here in London on a month-long nationwide exhibition tour. Charlie had fixed it with Sammy Lederman.

Liston was staying at Brown's Hotel in Mayfair. He didn't have a clue who the Krays were. Like everyone else, he was just told he was doing an appearance 'for charity'. I picked him up in a limo from his hotel and drove him and Ronnie to the Grave Maurice in Whitechapel Road. God knows what he made of that. There were crowds of people in the street and loads of photographers too.

A local paper took a photo of me and Ron with Sonny Liston in the pub. There we are with Liston between us and reporters asking whether Sonny had ever deliberately thrown a fight. Bit cheeky. Sonny took the mike from one of them and said: 'What would you do? I am one of eleven. The gangsters picked me out of the gutter and put me on a pedestal. Who do you think I am going to look after, the gangsters or the mugs at the ringside?'

A few days later, that September 1963, I drove Sonny to the Cambridge Rooms, a roadhouse pub on the Kingston Bypass in New

Malden that the twins had set up as a sort of smart supper club with a cabaret. They'd taken it over the same way as usual, just agreed a majority shareholding without actually paying for it. Les Payne had done the paperwork. In fact, this was the opening night. Smithy was supposed to be the manager, but he was pissed most of the time. It was a big, big party. Liston really didn't have a clue what it was all about. A very drunk Reggie drove him back to his Mayfair hotel. I know that.

After that, the Krays just helped themselves to all the drink, to the cash in the till. It was all 'a loan' or for charity. There was a house-band and a resident singer called Dave Nelson who Smithy was supposed to 'manage'. When he tried to get out of his contract the twins got heavy. After a year or so they walked away from the place leaving £2,500 in unpaid bills. Suburbia and the Krays was not a marriage made in heaven.

One night, Alfie and I went to a party down in Brighton. It was a big house, full of MPs, including Tom Driberg, as well as Ronnie and Reggie. Lord Boothby was there. There were more men than women there certainly. But there were couples too – well dressed, fashionable. Everyone was terribly drunk. Teddy Smith was also there, with Driberg, who had a gold cigarette holder and was walking around like Princess Margaret, his drink balanced in one hand.

Now Smithy had a reputation as a 'creeper' – a cat-burglar, that is. We all thought we knew where he got his money from and that shinning up drainpipes was his thing. Smithy seemed very good at it. He was never without plenty of readies. People used to ask him where he got his money from and he'd answer: 'Well, let's just say I know a lot of rich people.'

Night-stalking burglars in black polo necks robbing filmstars and millionaires were all the rage at the time. It was glamorous, it was in the movies, in TV adverts. There was a famous real-life one called 'The Human Fly' who was supposed to have lifted Sophia Loren's diamonds when she was filming at Elstree Studios in 1960. Well, I was told it was Ronnie's big mate Charlie Clark, who turned over Miss Loren with an apprentice, Teddy Smith. It was all set up by Charlie Kray.

That night at the Brighton party, I was told that Driberg used to tell Smithy about the houses of rich friends and political rivals he could burgle. He and Boothby would send Smithy out on house-breaking missions to turn over anyone who had crossed them. It was their idea of fun apparently. I have a different theory, but more of this later ...

Round about this time, the Krays got involved in a scheme to fund the building of a new town in Enugu, Nigeria, which was newly independent and wide open to all sorts of chancers. Ronnie had been introduced to the project through the moneyman Leslie Payne.

I was driving Ronnie round for meets and heard little bits about it. Payne had set up an investment vehicle for this Enugu plan, what-ever it was. It was called the 'Elukokwa Development Company'. The Minister of Health, a Mr Okwu Oko, was on the board of directors. Charlie Kray was in charge of the 'introductory fees' – big bundles of cash. What could go wrong?

Anyway, it was the start of the next big Ronnie rumble.

# 8

## 'SOURCE'

I didn't know much about politics. Why should I? I knew who the Prime Minister was. I knew the hard way about some of how the police worked, with the local coppers and big men at Scotland Yard, the Flying Squad, the Murder Squad. I'd never heard of the Criminal Intelligence Bureau, the Special Branch or MI5 – although I knew there was some kind of secret Security Service. I kept a sort of eye on the newspapers too. Although I couldn't read (I only could do so many years later), I knew what people were talking about.

There was a big spy scandal, something about a homosexual at the Admiralty (this was before there was a Ministry of Defence), an official blackmailed by the Russians into passing secrets. That was in autumn 1962. A minister who was alleged to have been protecting him resigned. There'd been all sorts of stories of a secret 'ring of queers' in government. The newspapers got very excited – that's how it was back then.

The British civil servant's name was John Vassall and the story centred on goings-on at his 'luxurious' London flat, 807 Hood House, Dolphin Square. It was one of the apartment blocks on the

Thames, much-favoured by politicians, establishment figures and, it would turn out, spies. I would see inside one of those flats myself before too long.

Then a year later, there was the Profumo affair: Secretary of State for War John Profumo and his affair with the model Christine Keeler, who was having sex meanwhile with Captain Yevgeny Ivanov, a Soviet intelligence agent in London. Now that had got people very excited. Mandy Rice-Davies, the Denning Report ... The stories kept coming. Then one day, the story came to me.

In 2015 the National Archives opened the MI5 'personal file' on a top politician of the time. It was full of crossings-outs and blanks ('redactions') but clear enough. It's about Lord 'Bob' Boothby, the Conservative peer – he was famous off the telly. At the time, I knew Boothby a little for all sorts of odd reasons. With some help, I read the file. Turned out I knew quite a few more people named in it. That's why I'm pleased to get this part of the story out there. It's the bit of the Kray legend you won't have heard before.

This file also explained, if you looked hard enough, where much of the information on its subject was coming from. It was from a mole apparently close to the twins, referred to simply as 'Source'. He would be working undercover for almost two years. If his identity was blown, he would be subject to 'terrible reprisals', it was said in the file. Why would MI5 have a spy in the firm? To help the police bring down the Krays? It wasn't quite like that. So, it's worth going into a bit of detail to understand why MI5 should take such an interest in 'twin brothers named Kray', as they are first described. Were the Krays spies? No. But the twins, especially Ronnie, were involved with powerful men behaving badly who might be blackmailed. And that could blow up into a new political storm.

It very nearly did.

It all went back to the homosexual spy business that had happened a few months before 'Source' sent in his first message. And that's why the Security Service and their political bosses were so keen to have a listening post in the gay (the word wasn't used then – it was 'queer' or 'homo') underworld.

The file had lots more mysteries within – scribbles in the margins, people identified only by numbers and initials – so I'm grateful to the journalist Clare Campbell for helping decode them and explaining the political ding-dongs of the time. When 'Source' started work, being 'queer' was a crime. In 1967, the law would change. That change was relevant to a lot of what was about to take place.

It began like this. In 1962, a senior KGB officer had defected in Geneva and offered his services to the CIA. The Americans told MI5 about what he could reveal. There was 'a spy in London', a homosexual who had provided Moscow with 'all NATO' secrets from a 'Lord of the Navy'. The defector had seen copy documents in Moscow which he recognised as having been photographed with a special camera. The spy hunt pointed to an Admiralty clerk dealing with 'high security technical matters'.

John Vassall fitted. He had been a clerk in the office of the British naval attaché in Moscow. Might he have been got at? 'An eavesdropping operation [whether bug or phone tap was not revealed] against his flat got nothing about espionage,' according to MI5's official history, but 'it was soon established that Vassall was a practising homosexual who was living way beyond his means'.

That last bit is in the words of Peter Wright, the self-styled 'Spycatcher', the retired MI5 electronic specialist who would so enrage Prime Minister Margaret Thatcher with the unofficial publication of his memoirs in 1985. 'Armed with this knowledge, we arranged to burgle Vassall's flat when he was safely at work,' he continued.

They found a hidden copying camera and piles of letters, plus rails of expensive suits. Vassall was arrested by Special Branch officers that night. The flat was further turned over. Holiday postcards marked 'Dear Vassall' were found, sent by the junior navy minister, Thomas 'Tam' Galbraith, a posh Tory politician and friend of the Prime Minister. The lead MI5 investigator was Ronald Charles Symonds of D (counter-espionage) Branch.

The letters were later purchased from the imprisoned spy by the *Sunday Pictorial* (soon to be *Mirror*) for an enormous sum. Norman Lucas did the deal through Vassall's solicitor. In the flat he found perfume bottles and 'a teddy bear'.

Clearly a deviant.

'We have arrested a spy who is a bugger, and a minister is involved,' the Director of Public Prosecutions told the Attorney General that evening of 12 September. Vassall quickly confessed to having been compromised in Moscow in 1955 in a sex photo sting. He'd been passing secrets to Moscow ever since. The Prime Minister was told directly: 'It was unfortunately true he had earned large sums of money as a male prostitute.'

The arrest (the work of 'spy-hunters at the Yard,' said the papers) and the first day of the committal at Bow Street on 9 October were made public. The Old Bailey trial that followed was in secret. On 22 October, Vassall was sentenced to eighteen years in prison.

Was he the only one? Not so far as Fleet Street was concerned. 'Spy Catchers Name Sex Risk Men' was the heading of a Norman Lucas exclusive in the *Sunday Pictorial*. He could reveal the existence of 'a secret list prepared by detectives [which] names homosexuals who hold top government posts'. Who was on it was not revealed.

The *News of the World* led the same day with 'Spies Vice Probe ... Frankest details of the private lives of all government workers, men and women, who handle secrets are to be probed in a sweeping new security drive ordered by the Cabinet'.

Well, they would have a lot of probing to do.

'Every aspect of the private lives of government workers is being investigated,' said the story. 'Sexual activities and the clubs these people frequent will come in for special scrutiny.' The paper editorialised a week later:

Is it possible, MPs are asking, that somewhere amongst senior officials lurks a 'Mr Big', who is able to protect homosexuals from stringent inquiry?

Everyone was getting very excited.

To calm things down, the government announced a big inquiry conducted by the lawyer Lord Radcliffe. It would take evidence from officials in secret then hear from journalists in open session about what they knew or thought they knew. That would get very lively. A couple of hacks would go to prison for not revealing their sources.

In those days, being 'queer' officially counted as a 'character defect'. You could not be trusted, you were open to blackmail – the Vassall case proved it.

Newspapers loved public men getting caught like this. There'd been the Ian Harvey case, a junior foreign office minister who had resigned in 1958 after being up in Bow Street for indecency with a guardsman. A rising politician called John Profumo took his place.

A Labour MP, William Field, had been fined back in 1953 for importuning in Leicester Square toilets. Then the former Conservative MP Sir Ian Horobin was jailed for four years in 1962 on ten counts of indecency.

There were stories of gangs doing it to order. As the 'teenage leader of a blackmail gang' told the *People* newspaper: 'It's easier than breaking and entering. We pretend we're queer, let them take us back home, and rob them of everything they've got. They're too afraid of the police to say anything.'

All this sold newspapers and the press fanned more rumours. The convicted spy had had a homosexual relationship with the navy minister, Tam Galbraith, it was whispered. They had been planning to flee the country together. Prime Minister Harold Macmillan agonised. The Chief Whip, Martin Redmayne, went to Galbraith's flat with a letter of resignation and ordered him to sign it. The MI5 Deputy Director, Graham Mitchell, told the Prime Minister, 'There are four or five [similar cases] coming up from other departments. Whether the conduct of ministers could lead to allegations it was difficult to say.'

That note is in the National Archives – no wonder there was panic.

Vassall had been exposed as part of a 'secret ring of homosexuals in public life, where loyalty to their kind overrode all other obligations', wrote Peter Wright in his very unofficial memoirs published over two decades later.

Well, Mr Spycatcher certainly had no doubts about that.

Wright also famously said of his own clandestine career: 'For five years we bugged and burgled our way across London at the state's behest while pompous bowler-hatted civil servants in Whitehall pretended to look the other way.' The official history of MI5, *Defence of the Realm*, portrays Wright as a fraudulent conspiracy theorist but judges this statement to be 'broadly true'.

Wright also recorded that he had interrogated the Labour MP Tom Driberg over links with Czech intelligence officers in London.

As well as the Vassall operation, Wright's book tells of a long campaign of covert break-ins and bugging of London embassies. He describes having to get through rooftops and party walls to plant the then new electronic bugs.[6] They were called 'SFs' (Special Facilities). To do that you needed climbing skills. You could say 'cat-burglars' might come in handy.

One of the fellow snoopers Wright mentions in his memoir is Freddie George Beith, who is described as 'an energetic agent runner working for D Branch'. He was clearly 'FGB', the agent runner to whom the mysterious source in the Firm would soon be reporting.

So why was 'Source' being employed in the first place? The Boothby file explained it. It really gets going in early 1963. By now the convicted spy John Vassall was in Wormwood Scrubs. He was on exercise periods with a man called Colin Jordan, a bachelor schoolmaster and self-styled 'Leader' of the 'National Socialist Movement', imprisoned for nine months in August 1962 for public order offences. That spring of 1963, he started writing what Vassall was telling him down on bits of prison-issue lavatory paper – he had quite a story to tell.

Open-session testimony to the Radcliffe Tribunal had been in the papers for weeks meanwhile. It had come from fact-hunting

---

[6] Unlike phone tapping and letter opening (done at the telephone exchange or sorting office) which required a 'Home Office Warrant', bug-planting in defence of the realm could be done under 'Crown prerogative'. But it needed clandestine entry to the target premises.

journalists waving chequebooks, not intelligence sources. Some of it really was sensational. For example, there had been two 'copy-cat' murders in London in February 1962. The naked body of an Admiralty clerk, Norman Rickard, was found asphyxiated by a ligature in a Paddington cupboard, his hands tied behind his back. The room was otherwise undisturbed. The next day, a TV-studio wardrobe assistant called Alan Vigar was found the same way in Pimlico. The murders, as the coroner judged them to be, baffled police. They remain unsolved and the files on them are sealed for eighty years.

Reports of both victims' backgrounds implied that they were homosexuals who frequented 'the many West End clubs that had sprung up recently'. Which were now full of 'Iron curtain agents', apparently. What the press of the time liked to call 'Queer Soho' had been around for decades but was becoming increasingly open in its goings-on. A Sunday newspaper could always nip down the 'dilly to pick up a yarn. And there were ever more twists.

Like this. At the height of Vassall hysteria, Roy East of the *People* newspaper sensationally reported that unsolved murder victim Norman Rickard had been working for 'admiralty security as an informant on homosexuals in Government departments':

According to a high police authority, it is possible that, finding Rickard on Vassall's trail, the Russians sent an assassin to kill him and make it look like a sex murder.

What a scoop! This was something for the Radcliffe Commission. On 22 January 1963, Mr East was duly called to give evidence. On his investigative tour of Soho, he could testify, one club owner had told him he'd seen Vassall and Rickard drinking together with two 'senior naval officers' in the Music Box Club in Panton Street, a well-known pick-up spot.

Two days later, a 'grey-suited' man, announced only as 'Mr X', gave testimony. He could say openly, however, that he was the 'Director General of the Security Service' (which, to add to the confusion, officially did not exist). 'Do you know of any security operation [to expose homosexuals in government] of that kind in which Rickard was used?' Lord Radcliffe asked.

'I am quite sure there was no such operation and that Rickard was not used or employed by the service at any time,' so Mr X replied.

Definitely not.

Back to that MI5 file opened (some of it) after fifty years. The Vassall affair explained why it existed in the first place.

Lord Boothby had been on the Security Service's watch list for a long time because of 'dubious business interests', so it says right at the front of the file. No sex scandals, not yet. All very dull, in fact. Then, according to the file, 'a new Source thought to be reliable' first went live on 6 February 1963 with a short report. 'Action copy to D1/HDD'[7] it is marked, who forwarded it in turn to 'D1/RCS'.[8] This would get much more interesting.

---

[7] HDD is identifiable as Harold ('Hal') Doyne-Ditmas, one of ten case officers in D1, the counter-espionage section, and a collaborator of Peter Wright's – who says in his book *Spycatcher* that in 1964 the section had already been working for four years on 'Movement Analysis', using data from A Branch surveillance agents known as 'the Watchers' to track movements of individuals and suspects.

[8] RCS is identifiable as Ronald Charles Symonds, who had been the lead case officer in the exposure of the 'Admiralty spy' John Vassall in 1962.

He was known throughout simply as 'Source'. There is no open indication of how the informant was recruited, when or why. Only that he seemed to have been known to the service for a little while already. He would later be described as a 'self-confessed homosexual'. That first report said:

Lord Boothby's current homosexual fancy [is] a Shoreditch ex-boxer called Johnny. Johnny [to be identified later in the file as 'Leslie Holt'] has been invited to be Lord Boothby's chauffeur from April '63 next.

It was written up and put on file at MI5 by someone known as 'D4/ FGB'.

Boothby had been gambling heavily, 'Source' could also reveal. It did not say where, but it was at Esmeralda's Barn. The peer was also set on some personal mission to Moscow 'to see [the Soviet leader] Mr Khrushchev', so 'Johnny' had told 'Source'.

MI5 got quite excited. But this wasn't about Russians, it was about homosexuals.

As the Vassall story began to fade, sharp-eared journalists and opposition MPs picked up on whispers that a 'freelance model' called Christine Keeler had had a sexual liaison with a junior government minister eighteen months before. A Soviet intelligence agent was involved. She had a flat in Dolphin Square (bugged by the Russians, it would later be claimed). Press innuendos reached screaming point. On 22 March 1963, the minister in question, John Profumo, told the House of Commons: 'There was no impropriety whatsoever in my acquaintanceship with Miss Keeler.'

There was a short, unrelated story in the *Daily Mirror* three days later: 'Youth on forged cheque charge'. A certain 17-year-old James Buckley of King's Road, Chelsea, had presented a cheque for £1,800 to a west London bank three days earlier, saying 'he was from Lord Boothby', so Marlborough Street magistrates had been told. 'The bank made inquiries and found that Lord Boothby had not sent the youth.' He was arrested and remanded in custody for a week.

The case would go for trial at the Old Bailey on 2 May 1963. How did he get the cheque? In court, Buckley said he found the book in the King's Road and 'someone' gave him a signature which he practised forging. He took out one cheque, signed it and put the book down a drain. But the chequebook, it turned out, was safely in Boothby's flat all the time. Buckley had to admit he lied about that, but 'the rest was true'.

On 6 May, he was sentenced to a period of Borstal training. Several papers reported the sentence, but the *Daily Express* gave more details, describing Buckley as 'a cloakroom attendant at Esmeralda's Barn, Belgravia'.

It was around this time too, late March 1963, just as 'Source' had predicted, that a 'nice fair-haired chauffeur' would be engaged by the TV-peer. He came with the blessing of his current employers, the Kray twins, so that was alright: his name was Leslie Holt.

Colin Jordan was released from the Scrubs on 31 May 1963. There was a miniature Nazi rally held at the prison gates. Folded up in his inside pocket was a list of names.

That early summer of 1963, the ever-deepening Profumo sex and security scandal meant the British government's survival hung by a thread. On 4 June, John Profumo at last told Harold Macmillan that he had lied about Miss Keeler. His resignation was made public the following day.

From out of nowhere, a letter to the Prime Minister arrived addressed to the House of Commons. The letter dated 13 June 1963 was typed on 'National Socialist Movement' headed paper: 'For Race and Nation'. It was from Colin Jordan and contained some shock allegations. It's in a file in the National Archives which was supposed to be closed until 2043, but the substance of it was released 'early' a few years back.

The substance of the letter, published in the *Daily Telegraph* that day, was that its author could reveal 'a shocking picture of a still-operative homosexual network of corruption involving Members of Parliament, high civil servants and even intelligence officers themselves which manifestly jeopardises our national security'. No names were given.

The Labour opposition was baying, the press slavering. A big parliamentary debate on the War Minister's shock resignation was due for eleven days' time. Would something even more damaging than Profumo explode?

One man might know. The 'Leader' was urgently brought in a government car from his home in Coventry on Saturday, 15 June 1963, to be 'interviewed on behalf of the Prime Minister' at the offices of Special Branch in New Scotland Yard. It turned out Colin Jordan had scribbled names that Vassall had disclosed in their exercise-period chats on bits of toilet paper, which he had kept, then typed up into a list on his release from prison a few weeks before. Both versions were solemnly retrieved for the attention of Sir Roger Hollis, MI5's Director General, the 'Mr X' of the Rickard murder tribunal appearance, eight months before.

And there, in the middle of the interview, was this: Jordan had revealed another Scrubs inmate called 'Ward' had told Vassall that Lord Robert Boothby, the prominent Tory peer and TV personality, frequented a west London address – 31 Airlie Gardens, W8 – where the mysterious Ward (no connection to Stephen Ward of the Profumo affair) 'ran a homosexual brothel'.

Ward had told Vassall (who told Jordan) directly that the peer visited there on more than one occasion, looking for 'chickens' – 'homosexual parlance for young boys'. That part of the interview transcript was extracted by MI5, typed up and put on Boothby's Personal File.

So, the British government knew in the summer of 1963 that Lord Robert Boothby was (allegedly) a predatory homosexual with an interest in young boys. There is nothing in the file to say that he wasn't. What else might his lordship be up to?

It was implied that Vassall might divulge more names. The list (two pages, to be kept secret until 2063) was said in another note to contain those of 'present and former ministers and certain civil servants'.[9] It was passed to the Prime Minister and to the Chief Whip, Martin Redmayne, who also noted that he had the names of two colleagues alleged to 'have used Vassall's flat' (for sex, presumably). Mr Redmayne seemed unshockable by now.

---

[9] In a later interrogation, Vassall would tell MI5 that Jordan's list was 'all true apart from one individual referred to'. The 2015 book *Closet Queens* by Michael Bloch names a number of 'promising' junior ministers (and one senior minister) in the Conservative governments of the period, none it would seem with Kray connections. After minor scrapes with the law they were quietly removed from office.

Sir Roger Hollis, the MI5 chief, clearly thought the whole thing deeply disagreeable. Political or sexual scandal involving public figures was the service's business only if it threatened national security. That had been his stance throughout the Profumo affair.

Lord Robert Graham Boothby, the bisexual Tory who had been MP for East Aberdeenshire for over thirty years before being given a life peerage in 1958, was a very public figure. He'd been a wartime junior minister. Churchill was a fan. But now he had no access to real secrets. That was openly admitted in the file.

But others on the 'list' might well be security risks. The Boothby file, barely ticked over for years, was suddenly hot. That was why 'Source' was such an asset. He was MI5's mole in the 'queer' underworld. You never knew what might pop up.

Someone was pumping up a right moral panic meanwhile. The existence of Jordan's 'list' was reported in *The Times* on the day of the Profumo debate, 17 June 1963. But the big show in the top people's paper that same summer morning was a full-page advertisement addressed: 'To All Who Love Britain':

The issues to be debated in Parliament [today] are not questions only of sex and security but of survival. When perversion infiltrates, subversion follows, the ring of men who for so long have protected each other and [operated] at the heart of our affairs in politics, society, and civil service must be exposed ...

So there it was in *The Times*, not some neo-Nazi news-sheet. A self-protecting ring of perverts was corrupting the nation and endangering national security.

Profumo might have written himself out of the scandalous picture by resigning, but the British government's woes just seemed to be deepening. Boothby might not be a 'security' issue, but as for 'deviant' sex, this was a new frontier full of potential disasters.[10]

A salacious Fleet Street could hardly wait for more. There was a rising power in the East, which might engender even more dangerous liaisons. But it wasn't pesky Russians, it was much closer to home.

Rumours were still spreading after the press reports of Jordan's letter. A parliamentary question had been put down for 9 July. Mr Macmillan thought it might all turn out to be 'malicious gossip', but felt 'the Government should be protected against any charge that they had ignored or made light of this information ...'

That was political reality. The government had to be seen to have been doing something. A note inviting the Home Secretary to take charge of the matter expressing the PM's view was drafted on 5 July 1963.

On 9 July, an MP asked a question: 'Can the Prime Minister give the House an assurance that the interview which one of the security services undertook with this man Jordan did not disclose anything prejudicial to the interests of the State?'

'The Radcliffe tribunal has gone into all these questions,' Macmillan replied.

---

[10] Two days later, the US CIA London Station drew up a secret report on possible successors to Macmillan, whose resignation was seen as inevitable after the Profumo debate. It's on the internet. Five possible candidates were named (but not the eventual winner, Alec Douglas-Home). Of one contender, 47-year-old Edward Heath, it said: '[He is] considered by many as Macmillan's personal choice but recent revelations about homosexuality in government have made Conservatives quite gun-shy about bachelors.'

Perhaps not deeply enough. Thank goodness for the secret watch on Lord Boothby and his deviant pals. What might they get up to next?

An old friend of MI5 came back online the very next day. It was not a coincidence. A note (heavily redacted in the file, the first of two pages is blanked out entirely) was typed on 10 July 1963.

Who it was forwarded to is not clear, but it is marked 'the following information has been given to me by a source known to you who has given reliable information over the years'. It gave its mystery addressee a summary of what 'Source', who'd been quiet since February, had to report right now.

The report's author, D4/FGB, talked of 'a certain Chelsea cafe or restaurant owned by two genuine East End gangsters, twin brothers named Kray who operate a protection racket ranging from brothels to bookies':

> The Chelsea cafe frequented by [redacted, but has to be homo-sexuals] is also clearly a place frequented by criminals as one of the cheques lost or stolen from Boothby a short time ago was passed at this establishment.

It was Esmeralda's Barn.

The stolen cheque reference looks like an elaborated version of the press reports on 27 March and 7 May of the arrest and sentencing of James Buckley, the Barn's cloakroom boy, for the £1,800 Boothby cheque sting. That looked a bit tricky for a 17-year-old to have dreamt up all on his own. And James Buckley would not admit to anyone how he got the cheque.

He never would.

Boothby had subsequently told 'Source' in conversation, according to the summary, that 'shortly after the foregoing incident, two smooth-looking young men who announced themselves as the Kray brothers', had turned up at the peer's flat to apologise. 'They explained that one of their chaps had been responsible, but he was no longer employed by them.'

The visitors then asked Boothby 'if he would like them to provide him with a nice young [he was 25 years old] chauffeur', whom they described as 'pleasant and fair-haired'. That was Leslie Holt. In fact, 'Source' had been reporting the twins' attempt to get their boy alongside Boothby full-time since soon after the start of the year. And it had worked a treat: Holt had been driving Lord Bob around town since April.

But Holt was already very much known to Boothby. They'd met at Esmeralda's Barn in its earliest Kray days. There's a scrappy note from early August 1964 in the MI5 file in which it is reported

Source says Boothby himself denied about four years ago when Source called on him to complain that Holt might have stolen his (Source's) watch and keys, that he never knew or had ever heard of Holt, yet Source had even then heard an account of this odd relationship from Holt himself. Anyway, the association of Holt with Boothby was a fact and had lasted for years.

The Security Service seemed keen for whatever reason to fix the exact length of the peer and the young boxer's relationship. 'Source', who had provided the information for FGB to summarise, clearly knew Boothby himself quite intimately, referring in this report, 10 July 1963, to his habit of carrying private letters around with him which might be prey to pickpockets.

On 13 August 1963, Colin Jordan published his Top Ten Queers allegation in his newspaper, the *National Socialist*. It described but did not name 'a stream of high-placed men' who had passed through Vassall's Dolphin Square flat. Jordan mentioned 'an address in London W8 catering for sexual perversions', which numbered amongst its distinguished clients 'one of our most televised peers' and his 'preference for chickens, which is homosexual parlance for young boys'.

It was obvious who the TV-peer was. But nobody was in the mood to sue the news-sheet's Hitler-worshipping publisher. The wider press ignored the claims completely.

On 18 October 1963, Harold Macmillan resigned due to 'ill health' and was replaced by Sir Alec Douglas-Home. It was to be hoped his new administration would be less troubled by sex scandals and open to mockery by TV 'satirists'. The Profumo affair had at least swept the Vassall homosexual vice probe off the front pages. A bit of calm would seem to be in order, but it would not be for long.

Meanwhile, it seemed the twins had also quit the pages of the sensation-hungry press to pursue new careers as 'respectable businessmen' – even if their ways of going about it were proving distinctly dodgy.

Of the clubs, Esmeralda's Barn was going down the pan in a shower of unpaid tax bills and bounced cheques. The Cambridge Rooms out in New Malden had sought to attract the suburban stockbroker set, but they'd all fled in horror. Now it was just the Firm drinking their way through what was left of the booze. Even so, there was all that Nigeria business to look forward to. Les Payne and his accountant partner, a face called Freddie Gore, were leading the twins straight.

The sun was shining in Enugu.

# 9

## PEER AND A GANGSTER

It was a new year, 1964 – the year London would be thought by some to actually start swinging. The 31-year-old twins seemed to be growing up, they seemed to want respectability even. Their 'charitable' ventures were all over the papers.

Nigeria, here we come.

But what about Ronnie's goings-on at Cedra Court? The partying, the celebrities, the 'orgies'? 'Source' had gone quiet for a while on the line to MI5. What were the police up to?

It's hard to know. It's long been said that the Metropolitan Police were snooping round Ronnie's set-up from 'the beginning of 1964'. And from that time onwards 'Detective Inspector Leonard Read' had been leading a probe into a growing empire of 'protection rackets, blackmail and vice'.

Veteran Kray historian John Pearson said that in his 'official' (that's his own semi-ironic description) biography, *The Profession of Violence*, first published in 1972.

Well, that was wrong and would lead to much continuing confusion.

Later accounts by Pearson and other Kray writers accredited the elusive six-month investigation to the Yard's Criminal Intelligence Bureau (C.11)[11] led by Superintendent John Cummings. He was building up a 'considerable dossier' not only on protection rackets but also 'the sexual shenanigans at Cedra Court', it would be said.

'C.11 had turned up sensitive information about a number of public figures and politicians involved with one of the twins in a homosexual vice ring,' so John Pearson would later write of the goings-on in the first half of 1964. Superintendent Cummings told the author that in person apparently. Once kinky Lord Bob was safely dead, his alleged scatalogical party tricks could be revealed. The 'Pervert Peer' has been in published accounts, TV documentaries and films ever since.

The other major political name to be publicly outed in all of this was Tom Driberg. He had died in 1976.

But it seems that the 'considerable dossier' disappeared somewhere along the way or in fact never existed at all. There's nothing like that in the National Archives. Nothing open, that is.[12] But there was something (see Chapter 10).

---

[11] C.11 was an intelligence clearing operation set up experimentally in the early sixties, an index of villains and villainy with a staff of fifty. It was described (in 1976) as having '8,000 files on suspected and proven big-time criminals, each of whom has a personal file including extensive information on personal lives. This information is regularly updated by informers and personal surveillance by C.11 staff'. Nipper Read later said it didn't work because 'police officers were naturally jealous and hated sharing their information.' Well he should know.

[12] There are hundreds of Kray files at the National Archives closed until the 2080s, most of them post-conviction prison reports. Substantial extracts from Inspector Read's long 'Kray Inquiry' of 1968 into 'wounding and assaults' and the 'Cornell killing' are closed until the 2050s, as are some files on the Hideaway affair of 1965. Most contentious seemingly was a file titled

While Scotland Yard was reportedly looking that spring for a homosexual vice ring around Ronnie and his new political chums, in the deeper secret world older liaisons were being shaken out. In April 1964, former wartime MI5 officer, Sir Anthony Blunt, was given immunity in exchange for his confession to having been a spy for Soviet Russia. It was all kept very secret. Blunt's admitted homosexuality was coincidental to his exposure, but his revelations gave the 'queer-hunting' faction in the service its best day yet.

MI5's official history (without quoting sources) says:

> Telephone taps were authorised in 1964–5 on four suspected homosexuals in the public service, one of which generated an immense amount of material of a revolting nature involving over 250 men.

And investigative journalist Duncan Campbell would write much later:

> According to former MI5 staff, one particularly valuable source of information about MPs and peers was a large archive of telephone intercepts which were operated against the Kray family. I was given the example of one prominent peer, now deceased, who became vulnerable in this way. The Kray intercepts had disclosed his interest in sadomasochistic sex, and the twins' role in helping supply his lordship with partners.

---

'Office of the Commissioner, Parliamentary Questions: Police investigation into the blackmail and protection racket 1963–1966'. It was closed until 2042 for 'reasons unknown', but partially opened at my freedom of information request, heavily redacted in July 2020. It explained a lot of what had really been going on.

That's Boothby of course, but it could be that MI5 'staff' were keen to distract attention from the existence of a human source (still alive when the article was written in 1988) and claim information was all obtained by phone-tapping.

Whatever, from snippets like these, it's clear that the 'queer-hunting' faction within the Security Service was keeping busy. And so, it seemed, were the Metropolitan Police. In 2019 as part of the Independent Inquiry (IICSA) into reports of historic child sexual abuse at Westminster, the Metropolitan Police published details of 'Operation Banway', its investigation of allegations going back to the mid-sixties.

It had a line about a Whitehall meeting in late 1965: The Home Office minister [who had been present] recalled the Home Secretary asking the Commissioner [Sir Joseph Simpson] why it was his men were spending so much time hanging round public lavatories in order to arrest homosexual men for importuning. He claimed the Commissioner replied to this effect: 'We don't do that in all toilets' – implying that certain toilets were avoided in case they found Cabinet Ministers in them.

It makes you wonder.

It was judged irrelevant to the wider inquiry as it involved only adults. It was almost comic. There were sniggers at the Home Office in 1964–5 when it was revealed that Sir Joseph Simpson and his deputy visited public conveniences around Westminster to see for themselves what MPs were up to – no mention of peers.

But Tom Driberg, Labour MP for Barking, was a different matter. His taste for living dangerously was notorious, as was his ability to escape clod-hopping coppers hanging round public toilets. He wrote about it himself. His autobiography, *Ruling Passions*, is pretty up-front about his sexual misadventures. It came out not long after he collapsed in the back of a London taxi in 1976 and died in hospital aged 71. But just what he actually got up to with the Security Service will remain mysterious until his MI5 Personal File is transferred to the National Archives for opening at some far-off future date. A few snippets have come out. In 2015 it was alleged by a retired copper that the Metropolitan Police had been warned off investigating him in 1968 by the Director of Public Prosecutions (it was 'not in the public interest'). Then in February 2019, an MI5 lawyer (name redacted) gave a witness statement to the independent child abuse inquiry. It was promptly posted to the internet where it was reported:

In 1981 MI5 received information that suggested that Tom Driberg had engaged in sexual activities with young boys.

Well, that was no surprise. What was interesting was that MI5 should still be adding to its Driberg file, five years after his death.

Back then of course when it was all illegal, it was the threat of blackmail that made homosexual politicians a 'security risk'. So why not remove that risk by decriminalising it? Some people had long been saying that. Going after men who complained to police about blackmail for being homosexual themselves seemed increasingly ridiculous. There was no consistency in police forces deciding to bring prosecutions or not.

Thus it was on 10 June 1964, the new Director of Public Prosecutions, Sir Norman Skelhorn, instructed a meeting of chief constables not to bring charges against homosexuals without consulting him first. It was done 'verbally'. Nothing was to be recorded of the meeting, it was so sensitive. He did not tell ministers. Nor was the move publicly announced, but of course it would all come out.

A big new sex and politics row was about to explode.

\* \* \*

It happened like this. On 12 July 1964, a front-page headline appeared in the *Sunday Mirror*: 'Peer and a Gangster: Yard Inquiry.' It would become famous. There'd been no build-up, no press campaign. No one was pictured. And no one, other than senior policemen and the Home Secretary, Henry Brooke, were named. The reporter was Norman Lucas. What was it all about?

I saw that headline fifty years later at the National Archives when I was researching what had happened to me. Pasted into the MI5 Boothby file was an original cutting of that famous front page. The story went that a senior Scotland Yard detective, named as Detective Chief Superintendent Frederick Gerrard, was investigating 'an alleged homosexual relationship' between a 'leading thug in the London underworld' and a 'well-known member of the House of Lords'.

Police had been 'watching [their] meetings for several months', the report said.

The probe had been ordered by the Metropolitan Police Commissioner, Sir Joseph Simpson. It was said to have looked into 'a West End protection racket', 'clergymen', 'Mayfair parties', 'allegations of blackmail' and 'the private week-end activities of a number of prominent public men and the peer during visits to Brighton'. The Commissioner was set to meet the Home Secretary within the next 48 hours and give him 'details of the reports', said the front page exclusive.

And that was it. It seemed to be the Vassall 'ring of queers' scare all over again, with protection racketeers and blackmailers pulling the strings instead of Russians.

The 'facts', if that is what they were, seemed to have come from inside the police. No sources were given. It would become clear later that the writer had not checked his yarn, formally that is, with anyone at the Yard. Mr Lucas meanwhile had been conducting his own investigation into the 'thug milking thousands of pounds from London's clubland'.

So where had the story come from, and why publish it now?

# 10

## THE BIG THREE

Soon after midnight on Sunday, 12 July 1964, the 'Peer and a Gangster' story started coming off the *Mirror*'s printing presses in Holborn.

When the headline appeared, certain faces across London became very agitated. Leslie Holt rang 'Source' that morning to say: 'Have you seen the front page of the *Sunday Mirror*? What's all that about?' 'Source' himself had yet to see it.

The story seemed to be saying that the ageing peer (it was obvious who that was) and 31-year-old Ronald Kray were homosexual lovers. Well, that was a load of rubbish. Everyone who knew them knew they were both into boys.

Holt told 'Source' that Ronnie had phoned him already and asked, 'in a pained sort of way, what's all this in aid of?'

Exactly.

'Source' told Leslie: 'I think it's a mistake, they're mixing you up with Ronnie [they had]. Have the police been to see you?'

'No,' he replied, 'but Ronnie's upset with this stuff in the papers.'

'Source' told him to keep his mouth shut.

'Source' was right: it was all a colossal cock-up. They had mixed up Leslie aka Johnny (his boxing name) with Ronnie. What the fuck was going on?

We know all this because a few days after the headline triggered that round of frantic Sunday morning telephoning, 'Source' contacted his MI5 agent runner to offer a full 'inside account' of what he knew. And he would have lots more to reveal in a full debriefing, but more of this later ...

There was general bafflement at other London addresses on that sleepy Sunday. The duty press officer at New Scotland Yard was given an indication of what was coming late on Saturday night by the *Mirror* newsroom and 'after making proper inquiries, telephoned the newspaper to deny the veracity of the article'. No one at the *Mirror* seemed to care evidently. But DCS Fred Gerrard, head of 3 Division CID (East London), named in the story as the officer in charge of the mystery probe, was by now on red alert.

There was more excitement on Monday the 13th. The Sunday writer, Norman Lucas, had more to say in the *Daily Mirror* – and dropped a big clue as to where the story came from.[13]

Yard men started probing the affairs of the gang after receiving information about them from three underworld informants.

---

[13] For whatever reason, it would be said for years afterwards that the story had been sold to the *Sunday Mirror* by a corrupt policeman. Lucas never revealed directly where the story had come from although he made it pretty obvious in print from Day Two.

The informants, who have alleged that a leading mobster has a homosexual relationship with a peer, have also told Yard officers that the gangsters have slit the tongue of a man who has told reporters about their activities.

The peer and the gangster were frequently seen together in Mayfair, where the gangster has a luxurious flat.

That same day, two Labour MPs, Arthur Lewis and Marcus Lipton, put down parliamentary questions to the Home Secretary about DCS Gerrard's supposed 'report' and whether he would publish it. They were due to be answered on Thursday 16 July.

The baffled Metropolitan Police Commissioner, Sir Joseph Simpson, sought an urgent meeting with Fred Gerrard, who assured him the Lucas article was a 'pack of lies'. The rest of Fleet Street was in uproar, the press office overwhelmed. So, Simpson, on his own admission without consulting the Home Office, put out his own press release at 6.05pm that Monday evening. '*None* of these statements is true,' he said. He had *not* ordered officers to investigate alleged homosexual relations between a peer and a man with a criminal record. It was *not* his intention to make a report to the Home Secretary.

There were ongoing investigations into 'various aspects of underworld life', but then there always were. Sir Joseph was not going to disclose them.

The story was basically bollocks.

But on Tuesday the 14th there was more: 'A secret CID squad' was on the trail of the 'crime big three whose every movement has been shadowed by undercover detectives from Scotland Yard in the past three months', so the *Mirror* reporter (not Lucas this time, he was having a day off) could reveal:

> One of them, detectives have discovered, has been consorting with a well-known peer and visiting him at his London flat [they'd clearly seen a picture]. Club owners have made full statements naming the Big Three.

Everyone on the inside knew the peer was Boothby – and had some clue about who the 'Big Three' were: Ronnie, Reggie and Charlie.

Fred Gerrard meanwhile had drafted a long memo covering his version of events. He asked that it should go straight to the Home Secretary as well as the Commissioner. Dated 15 July, it's hard to follow through the redactions (there's no open mention of the Peer and a Gangster affair) but he did indicate there were 'special arrangements' to watch the Krays in spring 1964. It was in connection with a criminal plot (by others) to rob cash 'in transit to a bank'. 'The Krays were said to be associated with this gang. The robbery did not take place,' so Gerrard noted. But he did say this:

> Concurrently efforts were made to secure evidence linking Reginald and Ronald Kray with the alleged protection rackets. Every CID officer in the District [east London] was supplied with copies of their photographs and a sheet giving their descriptions, relatives, legal advisers, places frequented, vehicles used [some flash motors in there] and their criminal associates.
>
> The younger officers were additionally briefed about these notorious characters by representatives of C.11 (Criminal

Intelligence) department. Divisional Officers were further assisted by members of C.11 and the Home Office (Room 115).

There was no assistance from the Krays' alleged victims, Gerrard said wearily, 'but the situation might develop favourably and lead to prompt and appropriate action'. Meanwhile there was no 'report' to forward to the Home Secretary or anyone else, whatever the MPs might have supposed. All this was secret until March 2020.

So, there *had* been a probe into protection in the East End. C. 11 had provided background intelligence. But on the allegations of investigations into illegal sexual relationships, clergymen and seaside parties, made in the two articles, DCS Gerrard was 'not able to recognise a single vestige of truth'.

Fred Gerrard was ordered meanwhile by Assistant Commissioner Ranulph (inevitably known as 'Rasher') Bacon to actually do some proper investigating. Not so much the protection rackets, but the potential for a government-toppling sex scandal. That is what this was now clearly all about, not the supposed woes of menaced East End bookies or Soho club-owners.

The same day the 'big three' story appeared, Gerrard went in person to the Mirror Group's Holborn HQ to see *Sunday Mirror* editor Reginald Payne and crime reporter Norman Lucas. It was, so it would be said, an 'uncomfortable interview'.

The names Reginald and Ronald Kray were mentioned but the pressmen offered little more. Why should they? Because it was their duty to produce what evidence they had about protection rackets, Gerrard pointed out. If not allegations about deviant sexual behaviour.

Anyway, the *Mirror* had more to come, and although they didn't tell Gerrard that morning, this time they had a picture – even if it was now the subject of an injunction against publishing it by the person who provided it in the first place.

There was deep bafflement at the top of government. What was the Labour-supporting newspaper trying to achieve? Goad the police, or generally attempting to 'denigrate the Establishment'? There was a lot of that going on at the time. 'Does this mean another scandal involving the private lives of people in high places?' asked the *Daily Mirror* that Tuesday. It might mean exactly that.

The *Mirror* kept it up with a front-page editorial on the 15th demanding action 'against a gang so rich and powerful, that the police are unable to crack down on it'.

That day, 'Source' contacted his agent runner to offer a full 'inside account' of what he knew. It was typed up that Wednesday night. All this had been 'offered up freely by Source in a debriefing called at his request', noted FGB. From the government's point of view, his timing could not have been better.

'Source's account revealed the animated phone calls between certain interested parties (including 'Source' himself) on the Sunday morning the story broke. And he had had lots more to say. The day before, Tuesday 14th, 'Source's 'flatmate' had got the 'lowdown' on how the *Mirror* got its story in the first place, so he told his agent runner.

He'd heard it from a journalist in Fleet Street and from a 'Bayswater crew'.[14] 'One of the Nashes' (brothers Jimmy, Johnny and Roy out

---

[14] The Nashes had been fingered by Tommy Butler back in 1960 as being especially dangerous confederates of the Krays. There'd been a big falling-out since then. There was a Nash operation running vice and protection around Bayswater Road and Paddington Station. DI Leonard 'Nipper' Read tangled with them while working out of Paddington nick in the early sixties.

of Clerkenwell, and there were more Nashes than that) had got upset at always being accused by the pop Sundays of running protection rackets and 'peddling pep pills to teenagers'.

According to 'Source': 'One of the Nashes is supposed to have told some journalist, "I'll give you a real story if you leave me alone."' The journalist bought it. Then Nash told him some yarn about Boothby and Kray having 'a long-term [homosexual] affair'.

It was a load of cobblers. 'Source' certainly thought so because Ronnie was 'ugly' and would not appeal to Boothby, who was 'a hunter of young men'. Ronnie Kray had rung Leslie Holt again later that same Tuesday. It was clearly a difficult conversation. Holt rang 'Source' again, this time in some desperation, to ask: 'What can I tell Ronnie?' 'Source' said, 'He had heard from his flatmate that it's all a big try-on by the Nashes, who hate your friends' [the twins] guts.'

'Source' told Holt: 'Not to worry, just sit tight.'

Ministers might not be aware of it yet, but a political lid could be kept on the scandal. 'Source' had revealed why: it was in that line about the 'Nashes'.

Then on Thursday 16 July came the anticipated parliamentary questions, including the one from Arthur Lewis MP to the Home Secretary about 'what report he has received from the Commissioner of Police [about] East End gangsters connected with the protection racket, blackmail, and *other* illegal activities?'

'It would not be in the public interest to disclose the progress of particular inquiries,' Brooke replied. If he thought that was the end of it, he was mistaken.

That same day, the Director of Public Prosecutions' new line on prosecuting homosexuals was leaked to newspapers. The Home Office didn't know what to say. The move had been put into effect 'informally'. In press and Parliament, protection rackets, homosexuals and blackmail were blurring into a generalised panic.[15]

* * *

The 15 July debrief of 'Source' had provided plenty more information. D4/FGB forwarded it as raw intelligence to the head of D4 (the agent-running section), as he said, 'almost verbatim'. It said:

> The peer is of course Lord Boothby, the so-called racketeer is Ronnie Kray, and there is a young man called Leslie Holt, alias Johnny Kidd, who intervenes in the affair.
>
> Leslie lives in Kingstown St. NW1 in the dirty part of Regent's Park with a girl. She has been with him for about a year. He has a telephone number on the JUN[iper] exchange. Boothby has been using him for a long time. He has given him expensive cars, wads of cash, and they have been to the opera a couple of times which is rather bold. They are genuinely attached, this no fly by night affair.

'Source's 'flat mate' had seen them at the opera a couple of months ago, with Leslie sitting between Boothby and the fashionable journalist Bernard Levin.

---

[15] Popular culture fans will note how 'protection' by mobsters menacing clubs and coffee bars had become a major plot-line for newspaper crime reporters and fictional cops on film and TV. Sean Connery played the lead in the 1961 movie, *The Frightened City*, as a petty thief who is 'lured into a West End protection racket by an oily mobster'. The Shadows had a top three hit with the twangingly menacing main theme.

'Now Boothby is a kinky fellow and likes to meet odd people and Ronnie obviously wants to meet people of good social standing,' 'Source' said in the debriefing. 'Both are queers.

'Leslie Holt never suggested there was any villainous connection between the two and they were not likely to be linked by a queer attraction to each other for both are hunters of young men.'

There's a big paragraph blanked out in the document but it picks up like this in the voice of FGB:

> It was either at this party or around this time that Leslie told 'Source' he had introduced Boothby to Ronnie Kray. They attended several homosexual parties together, at one of which they were photographed (in a normal social pose) together.

They had been to each other's flats [Leslie lived at Cedra Court] for 'parties' and 'on the Continent' together.

There was no known link to Brighton, as the *Mirror* story claimed, although they might have links to 'Peter Churchill'[16] and his 'queer set' by the sea, it was noted. FGB's report continued:

> There had been [a] mention of an MP, too, in the *Mirror* items and 'Source' wondered if some of the Labour people mightn't be going to burn their fingers if they tried to make much of it all for their own purposes because [name redacted] had said

---

[16] Wartime intelligence officer and party-loving resident of Brighton suburb of Ovingdean. Tom Driberg was a pal.

his information was that the MP was Driberg although source could not confirm this.

[Name redacted] said the story was all over Fleet Street. It was just a question of who will bring the whole thing out.

In fact, other than the Home Secretary and the notice on the 14th of Labour member Marcus Lipton's parliamentary question, no other MP was named in the *Mirror*'s four-day sequence of stories to the moment the agent runner put in his report.

Why bring Driberg into it?[17]

\* \* \*

'Source' thought the *Mirror* story had been in preparation for some time. He recalled 'about a month ago Leslie Holt had told him again? [question mark is in the original] that Boothby and Kray had been photographed together' and that 'some men from the BBC' had asked him whether he could be filmed driving his E-Type Jag. Which he had thought strange. 'Source' had advised against it – he wasn't a racing driver or film star, who would want to film Leslie Holt driving his flash, Boothby-provided sports car round London?

Making a big deal of protection rackets was another mistake by the paper, said 'Source'. The twins had run the now-closed Kentucky in the East End, which was 'frequented by queers', he added, but they got Esmeralda's Barn more or less legitimately.

---

[17] The conspiracy theorist Peter Wright noted it was MI5 practice to disguise source reports by 'bowdlerising' them, by inserting contrary information. It's tempting to think that Smithy's well-connected flatmate was Driberg himself and blurting out his name like this was a way of hiding him in plain sight.

'Ronnie and his brother were now living respectably in the West End although they kept up the house in Vallance Road. They'd installed their mother in it. It looked like it always did from the outside,' said 'Source', but the inside is 'very smart and looks beautiful'.

He had clearly been there.

Violet Kray was the GPO telephone subscriber at 178 Vallance Road. The number was 'XD' (ex-directory), it was noted on the MI5 file.

Was someone in the Security Service taking an interest in that particular phone number?

The report went up the chain at MI5. Director D, Malcolm Cummings, sent it to the newly appointed Deputy Director-General, Anthony Simkins, with a note: 'this has come from an unpaid source of ours'.

So, the mysterious 'Source', who, as it was acknowledged, was at risk of 'terrible reprisal' if he was blown, wasn't doing it for money. So, what was he doing it for?

The next day, according to the file, someone identified as 'D4HDW'[18] discovered from a 'Fleet Street Source' that the *Mirror* has a photograph of Lord Boothby with two crooks called Cray (sic) who are involved in protection rackets'. A writ had been served for it not to be published. Just who had done that was not yet known.

The veteran MI5 agent and former Reuters journalist Courtenay Young, head of D4 Section, told his director the same day that he

---

[18] Identifiable as Harry Wharton, MI5's agent-running contact with Fleet Street. Just to complicate things, according to Peter Wright, Cecil Harmsworth King, the Mirror Group's chairman, was an asset of MI5.

himself had been informed by 'a Fleet Street Source' that the snap depicted 'Boothby, Kray and another, and this might blow up into a minor Profumo affair'.

So, who was 'another'?

There were some senior figures in MI5 who knew exactly who it was. His identity had been announced in the very first message from 'Source', back in February 1963. It was 'Johnny Kidd' – better known as Leslie Holt.

It turned out a freelance photographer based in Hoxton called Bernard Black, favoured by Ronnie for celebrity snaps, had gone round to the *Mirror* the morning after that first story appeared. He had offered them certain pictures 'free of charge' (said the rival *Observer* newspaper in a big analysis published soon afterwards). For whatever reason, he'd gone back later in the day and asked for the roll of negatives back.

The newspaper would rather hang on to them, thank you very much. Mr Black sought and got a legal injunction later in the afternoon from a judge in chambers against their publication or copying. A note of that, a cutting from the *Evening Standard*, is in the MI5 file. The injunction was obtained by the celebrity criminal barrister of the day, Victor Durand, engaged by the solicitors Sampson and Co. – always a favourite of the Krays. It looks like Ronnie wanted to be in charge of where and when and which picture appeared.

Mr Durand would successfully defend the twins themselves in their next big rumble with the law.

# 11

## THE PICTURE WE MUST NOT PRINT

The government had done nothing since the first 'Peer and a Gangster' story broke that fateful Sunday morning, other than leave Commissioner Sir Joseph Simpson to make his home-made 'what's-all-this-about-then?' statement on the Monday night. 'Sinister rumours' were multiplying. I've seen the notes in the National Archives from the politicians and top civil servants of the day. They seemed terrified that the 'opposition was going to detonate a scandal' and that 'rumours would mushroom' just as they had done with the Profumo affair the year before. Right then, the Krays seemed more dangerous than nuclear attack.

The Opposition were trying their best. 'The police are investigating the existence of a blackmail, extortion and protection racket, which I am told is connected with homosexuality,' so Labour MP Arthur Lewis told the *Mirror* on 18 July 1964. They put that on the front page. 'What I want to know is this. Is there any link between the various investigations and the allegations that prominent people are involved, and the government change in the administration of homosexuality laws?' thundered the MP. 'If there is, it would mean there was a plot, *a cover-up.*'

The government was deliberately hiding a sex scandal.

On Sunday, 19 July, there was another front-page shocker. The *Sunday Mirror* ran a story headlined: 'The Picture We Must Not Print'. It was ingenious journalism, considering. There was a photograph in the paper's possession, it could be revealed, of the still-unnamed peer and the equally anonymous 'gangster' sitting on a sofa (later described as 'lemon-coloured') with 'drink poured out on a nearby table'. The picture was of 'the highest significance and public concern'.

But it was now the subject of a legal dispute, so the story had to admit without giving further details, so they must not print it. The very lack of a picture made it a press sensation. What could it show?

An inside piece to go with the story mentioned the disclosure the week before of the new Director of Public Prosecutions guidelines on 'consulting him before prosecuting homosexuals'. That was the biggest 'sinister rumour' of all, that a devious 'Whitehall' plan was in hand to cover up the deviant peer and the gangster's goings-on and plenty more like them besides.

Some gay-bashing newspaper columnists were getting cross about the hypocrisy of trendy liberals and 'TV-pundits' attacking ministers for seemingly protecting perverts – while these were the very same people who otherwise loudly supported 'Soho queers'.

Confusion was general. The *Mirror* was a supporter of decriminalising homosexuality. Why had it reverted to smutty innuendos about clergymen and seaside parties in its front-page scoop?

Published alongside 'The Picture We Must Not Print' yarn was some actual reporting with a story about 'the terror behind the bright lights of the West End'. Two 'mobsters in sixty-guinea suits' were imposing 'a reign of fear over clubland', apparently.

A 'former underworld boss who knew them' declared:

> their contacts are everywhere, not only thieves and blackmail-ers, but film stars too. They have been mixing with actors and actresses and even organise charity shows as a demonstration of public spiritedness. [In fact] they are the most ruthless and certainly the cleverest gangsters ever to rule London.

Some chats with some supposedly menaced beat-club owners went with the tale. This was hardly a sensation.

However thin the story, ministers and officials gathered at Chequers, the Prime Minister's country home in Buckinghamshire, that Sunday with a sense of dread. The PM, Sir Alec Douglas-Home, Henry Brooke, Home Secretary since summer 1962, and Lord Dilhorne, the Lord Chancellor, were wreathed in gloom.

The Home Secretary could report that Cecil Harmsworth King, Chairman of the Mirror Group, had declared since the first story appeared a week before that this was 'the beginning of a scandal that would wreck the Tory Party'.

It would also sell newspapers.

There could be big trouble ahead. It was agreed that they 'should move the handling of the situation as quickly and as far as possible away from members of the government acting as politicians to law officers acting in their non-political capacity'.[19]

---

[19] There's a big 'OHMS' manila envelope loose in the prime ministerial file. Scribbled on it in a mystery handwriting are the words: 'Keep Govt. out of it especially H. Brooke' and 'Blackmail 24 10 1963'.

It was obvious who the peer was. It was Boothby, already identified by MI5 in the Colin Jordan allegations of the year before as
a visitor to an address in west London where young boys might be
procured for sex.

The Home Secretary knew that, even if his colleagues might not.
But what would this 'picture', now in the hands of a national newspaper (even with an injunction against publishing it), possibly show?
Some backbench Tory MPs had already made their minds up that it
was 'disreputable' and were saying so. The government was staring
down the barrel of a vice probe shock that would rock the nation.

So why didn't Boothby sue? Because he had not been named,
so why invite trouble? Boothby wrote to Brooke the same day the
unprintable picture story appeared. His handwritten letter on House
of Lords notepaper is in a file in the National Archives released
twenty years before the MI5 documents. It had caused quite a stir
on public release, back in 1995. Put the two together and you get a
ringside seat at the scandal that had to be hidden.

In this letter, Boothby confessed that he knew Mr Kray. He had
been rung up by him six months earlier and the 'name was familiar'.
You bet it was. There had been two meetings to discuss 'a construc-
tion project in Nigeria'. At the first meeting, Mr Kray had left the
prospectus and then at the second meet a week later, Boothby had to
say sorry, he was turning it down. But this time Mr Kray had brought
a photographer and asked if he could take a snap of them together
as he was a big fan of his on radio and television. It would have been
'churlish to refuse', Boothby said. 'I suppose that somehow or other
they [the *Sunday Mirror*] got a copy of the photograph.'

Pretty soon he would know exactly how they had procured it –
and it wasn't 'somehow or other'.

Mr Kray seemed 'an agreeable chap', continued Boothby in his letter. 'I have met Mr. Kray twice in this flat at his request and nowhere else,' he said. Now that was an outright lie. 'If I was a homosexual, which I am not, I should not choose either gangsters or clergymen.'

The allegations were gutter-press lies. 'Every other paper has held off it,' he pointed out. Perhaps it 'was a hang-over from the Vassall and Profumo affairs'.

No one in government needed reminding of that vale of tears.

The Boothby letter was circulated. Sir Peter Rawlinson, the Solicitor-General, thought it highly implausible. Who brings their photographer to a business lunch? But he thought he might know why the picture was taken. 'The Krays were trying to become respectable,' he suggested to Sir Charles Cunningham, the Home Office Permanent Under-Secretary. 'We learned from *a secret source* they were attempting to engineer the same sort of thing with Sir Winston Churchill, specifically a photograph of them together.'

He knew all about Bernard Black (from the legal moves in play in the Law Courts) and the attempt by the hapless snapper to get the photograph back.

Things were looking even dodgier for the government. On 21 July, a 'note for the record' by Sir Alec's private secretary, Sir Timothy Bligh, said that two Tory MPs had told the party's Chief Whip 'that Lord Boothby and Mr [Tom] Driberg had been importuning males at a dog track and were involved in gangs of thugs who come to dog tracks to dispose of their money':

Apparently a Chief Constable knows about this but is taking no official action. It is understood, however, that he is prepared to sell his knowledge to Conservative MPs.

According to the MI5 file, they had turned up outside Boothby's flat at one in the morning to confront him.[20]

This was getting out of control.

Brooke put together a crisis committee. It first met on Tuesday, 21 July, at 2.45pm in the House of Commons. Top of the agenda was the apparent softening in policy on prosecuting homosexuals. If 'pressed in parliament, the Home Secretary and Attorney General could say this was not of their doing', so the meeting agreed.

Next up were 'the rumours which were spreading involving members of the Government'. There was a hint that the Mirror Group (which included the *People* newspaper) had an even more sensational story. 'The government must be seen to have taken immediate steps. Any allegations of homosexual relationships, no matter who they involved, should be followed up,' so the meeting agreed.

Same with the importuning at a dog track. The Commissioner of the Metropolitan Police should investigate that one. And the Home Secretary should secure Boothby's agreement to being interviewed by the police 'to give them any information he possesses about the Kray brothers'.

Boothby phoned the Home Secretary late on the same Tuesday afternoon of 21 July. Yes, he would talk to a police officer, but he doubted he could add anything to his letter. But somehow, he now had information the *Mirror* was 'frightened to death and were anxious to withdraw'.

What did he know?

---

[20] The two MPs were called Burnaby Drayson and Brigadier Terence Clarke and were linked to Boothby in an east-west trading company. From the MI5 file, they seemed to be bitter enemies of the peer.

The Home Secretary was having a busy day. That Tuesday evening, Sir Roger Hollis, Director General of MI5, was summoned. At last the Security Service, whose job was chasing Russian spies, not saving the government from sex scandals, had been formally brought back into the matter of Lord Robert Boothby's little walks on the wild side.

The last time that had happened, in July 1963, it was because of the allegations on Colin Jordan's lavatory paper list. The Krays were already in the secret picture back then because 'Source' had told his MI5 runner about Boothby's cheque being 'passed at Esmeralda's Barn' – and how two 'smooth young men' had turned up in person thereafter to apologise.

Might that be significant?

As soon as he got back to his office, Hollis wrote up a note of the meeting for the file:

The Home Secretary asked if I had heard anything of the matter. [I told him] we had heard a story that associated Lord Boothby with the Krays and allegations that he was a homosexual. I said that no security position was involved as Lord Boothby held no official position which gave him access to government secrets.

Hollis had reminded Brooke of the Colin Jordan tie-up with the Vassall allegations of the year before, that a 'prominent TV-peer' was a homosexual. Everyone knew who that was. Brooke had been Home Secretary at the time. In return, he told Hollis about the unsavoury-sounding dog-track allegations about Boothby and Driberg. The Home Secretary doubted 'there was any substance in it'.

Boothby had phoned the Home Secretary that morning to say he would give a statement to the police. Thus it was, early in the evening of 21 July, Inspector Frederick Gerrard headed for 1 Eaton Square, notebook in hand, to have a chat with the flamboyant TV-peer in his gracious Belgravia home.

So, how had the Peer met the, er, 'Gangster'?

Mr Kray had 'rung him to complain about being harried by the Yard' some time ago, Boothby told Gerrard. 'If he went into business and played it straight, the harrying would stop,' the peer advised. He himself had rung 'someone at Scotland Yard' – just who, he could not remember. But that is why he was in Mr Kray's sights about the West Africa project.

And thus it was Mr Kray had rung the peer about six months ago and made proposals about a development scheme in Enugu, Nigeria. He had met Mr Kray several times since then to discuss investing in it, so he told Gerrard. Boothby had mentioned it to his old friend, Mr Driberg, who thought it better if he stayed out, as he thought that Mr Kray had 'at one time been connected with the underworld but had given up these activities', indeed, 'now having enough financial resources to play it straight'.

'I asked [Mr Kray] to call on me a week later,' said Boothby, 'which he did accompanied by a friend who had a camera. He asked if he could take a photograph of us sitting together. I accepted without giving it another thought.'

So how had the picture ended up in the hands of a national newspaper? Boothby explained three days before, early on the afternoon of Sunday, 19 July (the day 'The Picture We Must Not Print' appeared), a 'greatly alarmed' Mr Kray had rung. He needed to come around urgently in person to Eaton Square. Mr Kray told him that 'a man called Nash' had persuaded the photographer to sell the snap to the *Mirror*.

Boothby was 'sure Mr Kray had not done so himself', so he told the detective. It was just as 'Source' had told his MI5 agent runner the week before: the story had come from the Nashes.

The name Nash would ring a big bell with Gerrard. The rival Firm fronted by brothers Jimmy, Johnny and Roy, originally out of Clerkenwell, was as notorious as the Kray twins. They'd been at it since the fifties with protection rackets in Soho and Paddington.

Boothby's explanation continued: 'I have never been to any party with Mr Kray nor visited any club which he controls or has controlled in the past,' he insisted (MI5 knew differently as the 'Chelsea cafe' report of 10 July 1963 would confirm).

Gerrard went back to the Yard to type up his notes.

The next day there was another parliamentary question:

It has been alleged that a protection racket is being run by criminals among club owners in London, and that there is evidence of an unlawful relationship between a leading criminal concerned in the racket and a Member of another place [Boothby].

'[The police] have no evidence to support the allegations published in this newspaper,' the Home Secretary replied. On any supposed unlawful relationship with a homosexual gangster, the Home Secretary made no comment.

The crisis committee went back into session later that afternoon. Ministers and officials were informed of 'the contents of Boothby's latest statement to Inspector Gerrard', which had been sent by Ranulph Bacon to Sir Geoffrey Otton at the Home Office that morning, so it was minuted. Whether they were given the line about Ronnie Kray's urgent personal visit to Belgravia and 'a man called Nash' who had caused the picture to be passed to the pesky *Sunday Mirror* was not recorded.

The meeting also discussed a rumour that the *People* newspaper had more information. The police should follow this up, it was urged.

They would.

Sir Roger Hollis added a new note to the file that day to put the service's position on record after his meeting with Brooke the evening before. 'It would be right to give the Yard the information we have alleging Boothby is a homosexual and the report we have of Boothby and the Krays,' he wrote. 'We shall have to be careful about the source of this report which we cannot reveal to the Yard.'

Meanwhile, the Commissioner's urgings about 'public duty' had seemed to work. Ernie 'Hooter' Millen and Frederick Gerrard visited the Mirror Building in person on the 22nd to be 'handed a dossier' and inspect certain pictures. There were twelve images on the roll, none of them compromising.

'Except in one there is an ill-dressed beatnik youth on the sofa with Boothby and Kray. This boy we have yet to identify.' That's what Millen's boss, Assistant Commissioner Ranulph 'Rasher' Bacon, told Sir Geoffrey Otton, Henry Brooke's private secretary at the Home Office, the next day.

MI5 could have told them exactly who it was: Leslie Holt.

Boothby was not being wholly truthful, said Bacon. Same with not going to Brighton, they had information that he had been there. *Mirror* reporters had given Inspector Millen 'a short history of what they knew about the Krays. One or two passages might be useful,' Bacon said.[21]

Gerrard meanwhile could confirm by seeing for himself in the picture sequence that the third person on the sofa, the 'beatnik youth', was not Gordon Goodfellow, the manservant, who he had seen in the flat.

On the morning of the 24th, the MI5 Deputy Director, Anthony Simkins, sent Commander Evan Jones of Special Branch a summary of the information supplied to date by 'Source' and a note of what Hollis had told the Home Secretary at their meeting three days earlier. High up was a paragraph about a cheque being 'passed at Esmeralda's Barn' and 'the arrival of two smooth characters who announced themselves as the Kray brothers', who had come to see his lordship in person to apologise.

That had been in May 1963.

The information had been acquired 'as a by-product of our normal security inquiries', Simkins stressed.

Inquiring into what, he did not say.

Simkins told Commander Jones he must not 'disseminate this information and not take any overt action on the basis of it, for reason of libel and Source protection. We are particularly anxious to protect Source from the risk of savage reprisals if he were blown.'

---

[21] Veteran *Mirror*-man Brian McConnell, while not commenting in any other way on the Peer and a Gangster affair (because he was legally bound not to), said in his 1969 book, *The Evil Firm*, that two senior detectives took away 'a gargantuan file marked Kray'. Rival *Sunday Times* journalist John Pearson said in 1972: 'There was no dossier, although a phalanx of reporters had been working hard since dawn trying to make one.'

Jones told the MI5 man by return, 'most of what your Source said is already known to the Assistant Commissioner Crime'.

That was Ranulph Bacon, the senior policeman who'd been running Gerrard. But clearly some of 'Source's intelligence was 'acted upon' by being briefed to Gerrard in preparation for his next little chat with Lord Bob – but not where it came from.

Later that day, Gerrard went to Eaton Square to interview Boothby for the second time. He had by now seen the *Mirror* 'dossier' on protection rackets and the picture of the mysterious beatnik youth. But for whatever reason the 'cheque from Esmeralda's Barn' would be almost the sole topic of conversation. That, and when his lordship had *really* first met Mr Ronald Kray.

The peer's memory was magically refreshed. He could now recollect exactly when and why he had 'originally met Mr Kray'. It had been on 17 July the previous year, 1963, he said. And he had good reason for being so certain of the date.

It had happened like this. A mystery 'woman' had phoned the Brompton Road branch of the National Commercial Bank of Scotland and said a 'Mr Masterson' would be round with a signed cheque to collect cash from Lord Boothby's account, which was needed urgently. Specific quantities of five- and one-pound notes were requested – it was a very large amount.

The bank manager's secretary 'did not recognise the voice as being that of my secretary Miss Taylor', said Boothby. He himself had dialled 999 to warn of the apparent impending fraud and the police promised to respond. A 'well-dressed young man' duly turned up at the bank. The manager, Mr Strachan, chatted about the weather until the police arrived.

'You seem very well dressed,' the police had said.

'You would be if you were Lord Boothby's secretary,' the youth replied.

'You'd better come along with us,' said the police.

'I've been expecting this,' said the youth.

He was duly arrested. Mr Strachan had rung Lord Boothby from the bank to say what had just happened.

Boothby had clearly been relaying a detailed account he had kept of the conversation he'd had with his bank manager on 25 March 1963 for whatever reason. Boothby's account continued: 'The following day a story appeared in the *Daily Express* saying Mr Buckley had been caught in an attempted forgery and was in the employment of Esmeralda's Barn.' In fact, that report was of the guilty verdict and sentencing, which was on 7 May 1963.

'That day [implying 8 May] Mr Kray rang up and said he wished to see me urgently in connection with the forgery and came round,' said Boothby. Mr Kray had explained that Buckley had had 'a rough past but was now going straight. In fact, he had had no connection with Esmeralda's Barn now or since. Nine months later [Mr Kray] rang me about the Nigerian project.'

He had remembered the date of that first meeting because: 'I was lunching with Lady Diana Cooper [the 1920s society figure] when the bank manger rang to tell me about the attempted forgery that day and had it in my diary.'

Yes, it was 17 July 1963, no doubt about it.

Boothby signed the statement. DCS Frederick W. Gerrard countersigned it: 'Dictated and signed in my presence'.

But James Buckley's arrest had been almost fifteen weeks earlier. Scotland Yard had a record: it was on 25 March. Never mind any confusion over the newspaper cutting, whether about the arrest or the sentence, Boothby had pushed the date of his first meeting with Ronnie Kray (and indeed Reggie) back by many weeks. Why would he want to do that?

Boothby wanted it all to go away as it linked him with Esmeralda's Barn and put his first meet with Ronnie much closer to the truth. Or it might have been a blackmail payout.

Leslie Payne offers an alternative. 'All real transaction were cash,' he wrote, but if 'Inland Revenue inquired, there was a sheaf of dud cheques which absorbed all the profits. I could account for £16,000, some of which had bounced from very high places. Business was great.'

Lord Bob's carelessness with his chequebook could come in handy.

Bacon sent a copy of the latest statement to Henry Brooke's private secretary. It was clearly tosh. Commenting on the time slip, 'Rasher' Bacon told Sir Geoffrey Otton: 'I can only suppose that Boothby had two lunches with Lady Diana Cooper and his bank manager rang him up each time.'

How very amusing. They knew he was lying his head off – everyone did.

Gerrard had told Bacon some more stuff that he picked up in his visit. He'd spotted Gordon Goodfellow in the flat, who was not one of the other two people in the photograph (he'd seen it on his visit with Millen to the Mirror building). 'According to Boothby himself, of the two other people in the snap, one was the photographer Black and the other was the chauffeur used to bring Kray and Black to Boothby's residence,' however many weeks before.

That would turn out to be another lie.

Boothby said he had met Kray on three subsequent occasions, always in his flat and he brought 'at least two other people'. His own manservant Gordon Goodfellow was present each time.

And there was more Gerrard could report. Boothby had 'shown signs of preparing for a civil [libel] action, apparently in the hope of settling out of court. He was going after their meeting to see his solicitor for the purpose of taking statements from Kray and Black.'

Friday 24 July was a busy day all round. 'Hooter' Millen went to see the editor of the *People*, who, although his staff had been working on stories about protection rackets for months, denied they had anything more than the *Mirror* had already published.

In fact, it would turn out they *did* have something.

# 12

## A LEMON-COLOURED SOFA

That morning of 24 July 1964, the satirical magazine *Private Eye*, which had baited Harold Macmillan mercilessly throughout the Profumo affair, came out with this line: 'The papers should name names or stop scaring people with this horror show.' It was obvious who the gangsters were: 'The Krays. Why have they suddenly become a matter of such grave anxiety?'

So now everyone knew. Boothby embroiled the Tory Party in potential scandal, Driberg did the same for the Labour opposition. Everyone stood to lose politically.

Then, untroubled by British libel laws, on the morning of the 28th, the German magazine *Stern* revealed their journalists had actually seen at least one of the pictures. It depicted Lord Boothby, 'once Mr Churchill's parliamentary private secretary'. And his neighbour on the settee was 'one of the homosexual twins, Ronald and Reginald Kray ... rulers of London's underworld'.

There was a big meeting chaired by the Home Secretary at 4.15pm that day. In fact, things were looking brighter. Henry Brooke could report that the dog-track importuning investigation by police had revealed nothing. The police had approached the *People* newspaper, which had been rumoured to be holding something compromising, but it was an apparent dead end.

Boothby had been in discussion with William 'Bill' Deedes, Minister Without Portfolio, about 'getting a libel action on its feet', so the meeting heard. But after speaking to the Attorney General, Sir John Hobson (who had led the prosecution of John Vassall), it was clear 'there was no advice the government could offer in the matter'.

A messy action in the High Court was the last thing the government wanted.

Rumours of even more damaging allegations persisted. Deedes told the meeting he would ask around 'with his contacts on the *News of the World*'. On the supposed 'cover-up', there was a question in Parliament that day: 'Is it not high time that this House was kept informed so that suspicions and rumours which are running through the country could be shown not to be the case?'

Then, very suddenly, it all went away.

\* \* \*

It happened like this. On or around the morning of 28 July, Boothby had engaged the powerful solicitor Arnold Goodman (who had Labour Party connections, so MI5 would later note). Bill Deedes says in his memoirs that he made the introduction via his chums at the *News of the World* and their legal department. There are other explanations. However it came to be, Goodman offered his services and very quickly brought in the heavyweight barrister Lord Gerald Gardiner, QC to assist. Goodman heard Boothby's story but 'because of the facts doubted an action for damages would succeed,' according to Bill Deedes. He was right about that: he suggested an operation to 'flush' the Mirror Group out. There need be no sordid allegations in public. It clearly worked; Boothby had dropped the idea of a libel action 'on advice from Lord Gardiner' so the Home Secretary's crisis committee was told late on the 28th. Relief all round. But how would the promised 'flushing' be done?

On the morning of 31 July, Goodman and Boothby visited Gardiner's West End office to discuss just how. Leslie Holt drove them in Boothby's car. The TV-peer was asked 'point-blank' by Gardiner: 'Are you a homosexual?'

'Certainly not,' he replied.

'Have you engaged in homosexual practices in the past ten years?' Gardiner persisted.

'Certainly not!' came the reply.

We can know this because MI5 had a ringside seat at the meeting. Although Leslie Holt had waited in the car outside the plush Albemarle Street offices, he told 'Source' what had happened as Boothby had told him on the drive home. 'Source' in turn told his agent runner at MI5.

It was noted on the heavily censored MI5 minute of the 'are-you-now or have-you-ever-been a homosexual?' exchange that Holt had been saying [to 'Source' presumably] not long ago that Boothby, 'if not a "true" homosexual, practised perversions and had used Holt himself to perform them'.

At their meeting, Lord Gardiner had urged the peer to write a letter to *The Times* admitting that it was him in the (still unseen by the public) picture with Mr Kray but denying all of the *Mirror*'s allegations. He was outing himself. It was duly published the next day, 1 August. Boothby said:

> I have never been to all-male parties in Mayfair. I have met the man alleged to be King of the Underworld (Ronald Kray) only three times, on business matters, and then by appointment at my flat, at his request, and in the presence of other people.
>
> I was photographed, with my full consent, in my flat (which is also my office) with a gentleman who came to see me, accompanied by two friends in order to ask me to take part in a business venture. Lastly, I am not, and never have been, homosexual … the whole affair is a tissue of atrocious lies.

The next day, Sunday, 2 August, the *People* newspaper had this to say:

> There need be no further mystery. Together with a Mr Ted Smith and another man, Ronald Kray visited Lord Boothby to place a business proposition before him.

And they didn't say much more than that. But they were right about who had been in the flat. The *People*, of which ministers had seemed so frightened in the tempestuous two weeks before, were doing a little flushing out of their own. They'd smuggled a bit of the truth out there. Ronnie had attended the infamous meeting with two companions, the photographer Bernard Black and Ron's driver, who it would seem, unlike Boothby, Ron would rather not leave waiting in the street outside. They were all old friends after all – *very* old friends.

Ron's driver was Smithy – Teddy Smith. Leslie Holt was already in the flat on that morning in May 1964.

It was quite a little party. Mr Bernard Black snapped away. Nothing inappropriate, nothing compromising. Whisky and soda and cigarettes on the sofa while discussing Enugu.

* * *

According to the MI5 file, 'Harry Wharton's Source on the *Mirror*' made contact two days later, 4 August, to say 'they were dropping the Boothby story'. But the peer would not 'dare to sue as he had so much to hide'.

Boothby didn't need to sue. Behind the scenes, Arnold Goodman was in the process of negotiating a record out-of-court settlement, £40,000, from the owners of the *Sunday Mirror*. There was a confidentiality clause binding anyone involved from discussing it. How it was fixed was, and would remain, secret. But fixed it was.[22]

On 6 August an abject apology signed by Cecil Harmsworth King appeared on the front page of the *Daily Mirror*. Unconditional surrender. That same morning, the *Daily Express* had something a little more engaging, a picture of Ronnie and Boothby (and nobody else) on the lemon-coloured sofa.[23] A cutting is in the MI5 file. The morning before, Boothby had given an interview to the paper's reporters expressing his 'happiness to see it published at last'.

---

[22] Otherwise fact-filled books by Mirror Group journalists published at the end of the big Kray trial in 1969 make no references to the Peer and a Gangster affair.

[23] According to Bill Deedes' memoirs, Ronnie's 'girlfriend' (?) had sold it to them for £100.

Halfway through this little chat, the phone rang. It was Ronnie to remind the noble lord the copyright was his – as he had paid the photographer.

Very Ronnie that.

From Belgravia, the *Express* reporters headed north to interview the twins themselves at home in Cazenove Road. 'We are ordinary business people,' said Reggie as Ronnie 'paced the carpet'. And Boothby? 'He was everything I expected of an English gentleman,' said Ronnie. Was he being ironic? They were photographed a little later that day in a much-reproduced sequence in the grounds of Cedra Court.

Ronnie (in public at least) got no money – but he'd get a front-page apology a few weeks later.

So why did the *Mirror* give up? The newspaper had messed up the Ronnie-Boothby lovers' yarn completely. It was suggested at the time and many times long afterwards that the *Mirror* chairman, Cecil Harmsworth King, had been seized with an anti-government rage and gone more than a little crazy rushing it into print.

His boardroom rival, editorial director Hugh Cudlipp, would never have been so stupid, it has always been suggested. But he'd been bobbing about on his yacht in the tempestuous eight days the string of stories ran. He'd come back to find the biggest cock-up in Fleet Street history. He 'called for the dossier and having studied it, made his views forcibly known', so it was reported at the time by a rival newspaper. You can guess what he said.

The clubland terror yarn had the thinnest evidence. 'Source' himself thought that it was all wrong in the first place. Nothing would be forthcoming from the police rackets probe (there hadn't really been one) to back the paper's claims.

Most damaging of all, it would all come out that the 'homosexual relationship' shocker had been the gift of Johnny Nash. That's what Ronnie Kray had told Boothby in person on 21 July (the Home Secretary knew the next day) and as 'Source' had reported to MI5 almost at the very start. What had 'Source' said? He had heard that 'it's all a big try-on by the Nashes who hate your friends' guts'.

No wonder Boothby had been so confident that his newspaper tormentors were 'frightened to death' ever since Ronnie's visit. And it was the Nashes who had, it seems, leant on Bernard Black to provide the famous roll of film on that fateful Monday after the first story appeared. *Mirror* newspapers would be made to look like stooges in a gang war. In fact, they had been just that.

Reginald Payne was sacked. He became editor of *Titbits*. Norman Lucas kept his job. Boothby received letters of congratulation. The gutter press got the kicking they deserved. That's what people said.

\* \* \*

Fleet Street could not go after the twins again for a long time. And nor would the police. This was the real scandal. The top coppers had behaved appallingly. After MI5 had copied the Yard in on 24 July on what 'Source' had been saying, it was obvious that Lord Bob was making it up as he went along. Everybody knew.

Assistant Commissioner Bacon and his Home Office chums seemed to find that funny. But not so much Frederick Gerrard, who had shuttled in and out of 1 Eaton Square and been given notice of the Nash origin of the story by Boothby himself. 'Source' had been confirming the same to his agent runner from the start. The soon-to-retire Fred Gerrard was made to look an accomplice in the political bid to shut down the story.

The former DI Leonard 'Nipper' Read recalled in his memoirs how he was visited by Gerrard at Commercial Street Police Station to where he'd recently been transferred and told about a 'special job' to 'get a little team together and go after the Krays'. It was very conspiratorial. They'd work in as much secrecy as possible out of City Road nick.

'Fred Gerrard had decided to pre-empt directions from the Yard,' said Read in his memoirs. Simpson, Bacon and Millen had all been bypassed. It had happened on 27 July, the turning point in the Peer and a Gangster affair. It was also when MI5 made a 'look up' (went back to the file in their terminology) on the original report from 'Source' about the Boothby cheque affair.

Gerrard asked DI Read if he had any problem with the suggestion. Read replied sharply: 'No, of course not. I don't know them.' He knew why Gerrard was asking: could he be bought or intimidated?

The twins still had powerful patrons, but all of a sudden, they had their most determined pursuer.

# 13

## INVINCIBLE

Lord Boothby told anyone interested after the Mirror Group paid their giant out-of-court settlement that he'd used the money to buy a house in France. In fact, he passed much of it to Ronnie Kray. Alfie knew the truth of it: he was taking round money from Boothby so Ronnie would keep quiet.

Loads of money.

On two separate occasions Alfie was asked by Ronnie to go and get £5,000 from Lord Boothby for him. That was his share of the *Mirror* payout. The way he had to do it was very complicated, but Ron insisted. He had to walk from Vallance Road to Aldgate East, get a taxi down to Victoria Station, jump out and walk round to Eaton Square, a little way from Victoria.

He then had to go to Number 1, press the bell and go in and get the money, an envelope stuffed full of cash. The first time he went, Boothby asked if he'd like a drink, but Alfie told him: 'No, thanks, Ronnie is expecting me back straightaway.'

On the way back, he had to go through the same routine, all the while making sure he wasn't being followed – getting a taxi at Victoria to Aldgate, then walking down to Vallance Road.

And now it no longer need be a secret. The Peer and the Gangster seemed the best of chums. Boothby treated Ronnie to dinner at the House of Lords. Ron returned the favour with dinner at the Society Club. Doorman Billy Exley and Ronnie's good pal Charlie Clark made up the party with their wives. There is a snap to record the occasion. There were trips to Vallance Road and little chats with Violet Kray, who thought the famous peer off the telly was 'a real gentleman' so John Pearson recalled from a 1968 interview with her.

Boothby also felt pretty pleased with himself. His doctor recommended somewhere warm to get over bronchitis – he'd head for sunny Barbados that November. But not before he'd found time to write to the Prime Minister, Harold Wilson (who'd won the UK general election on 15 October 1964), to drop a hint that an ambassadorship might be in order. How about Paris? His letter is in the National Archives.

After the humbling of the *Mirror*, and he'd done down both the Yard and the Nashes besides, Ronnie really did seem invincible. His appetites just got wilder. When Alfie was driving him round, Ron used to tell him to stop the car in Piccadilly and go up to some boy on the 'meat-rack' (the railings by the tube entrance) and get him in the back of the car. Then he would take him back and sleep on the floor with him in the kitchen of Alfie's house in Millman Street, Holborn.

Alfie and his wife Wendy would sleep in a big double bed in one room with their two sons beside them, while Ronnie would order

Wendy to make up a bed in the kitchen for him and the boy. She hated it but they were too scared to refuse.

I was still driving Reggie's wife Frances Shea all around the place. The arguments with Reggie, if she dared to talk back, were getting worse. I saw Reggie once grab hold of Frances and shake her like a doll, kick her under the table in a club for not smiling when a photographer was snapping away. I've seen him so drunk, he could not get out of the car. He had a trick of getting me to pick her up, bring her to wherever he was and then order her to go back home and change her clothes and make-up. She would cry all the way. I couldn't talk to her when she was like that.

Reggie didn't care who knew. One night we were in the Talk of the Town. Shirley Bassey was top of the bill and the place was packed. Ronnie and Smithy were in, me and Christine, Reggie and Frances made up another table.

A few tables away a group of men and women were being a bit noisy. Reggie went over, picked up a chair and broke it over this geezer's head. He laid into two more of them. It was chaos. He strolled back as if nothing had happened.

Frances knew what to do: she ran to the Ladies. She just got up and ran. Reggie asked Christine to go and see if she was OK. Reggie got up and followed her.

The house lights came on full. Police were coming in the front door. 'Take Frances home,' Reggie ordered. 'She's not well.' I got her and Christine out of the club and into a taxi. Frances was crying and shaking: 'I've got to get away, how can I get away?' she kept saying.

Another great night out with the Krays for me and Christine.

Frances's father and mother, Frank and Elsie, couldn't stand the twins, either of them. When I dropped Reggie round to Bethnal

Green, I was not allowed to park outside her house. Reg had to wait outside because her father hated him so much – he wouldn't let him in the house even after they got married.

Reggie used to tell me to put Frances in the back of the car when I was picking her up, but sometimes she'd try and sit in the front with me. If she did, I'd get it in the neck from Reggie afterwards: 'I'm going to fucking kill you!'

Whenever we all got to Cedra Court, Frances would ask me: 'Is that pig there?' She meant Ronnie.

Ronnie just wound Reggie up as much as he could: 'You can't trust Frances,' he would say, 'she's going to cheat on you as soon as your back is turned. All women are bad, you can't trust them.'

Despite Frances's view of Ronnie, the twins weren't about to say goodbye to one another.

Esmeralda's Barn Club Limited was compulsorily wound up in September 1963 owing £4,400, most of it in unpaid tax. The 66 had shut down the year before. The Krays had found a new home. They set up operations at a place called the Glenrae Hotel, a big Victorian house in Finsbury Park, north London. It was at 380 Seven Sisters Road, not far from Cedra Court, and had a drinking club in the basement. It was owned by a woman called Phoebe Woods, whose husband had done a runner. A new bloke had moved in and, for convenience sake, called himself Mr Woods. There were two sons, Jeffrey, twenty-one, and Jackson, eighteen.

The twins had ordered the usual smash-and-grab takeover. That September, beer crates went through windows, heavies had gone in waving knives, the Firm were sent in as 'staff'. The old boxer and former doorman Billy Exley became the Glenrae's barman. Sammy Lederman, the showbiz agent, was his relief. The Woods didn't stand a chance. The regulars cleared off. The twins set up in two bedroom suites: they were back in the club business.

The day after the general election, 16 October,[24] Ronnie flew to New York in a bid to see a big middleweight boxing match. He was refused admission at the newly renamed JFK airport and his entry visa (who knows how he acquired it?) was stamped 'invalidated'. He took his anger at the establishment out on Boothby in an angry message. Goodfellow sent a spluttering written reply from the holiday isle of Barbados – 'No living man could have done more for you than LB has done'.

Something big happened that same day. The MI5 agent runner got a message that 'Source' had met Leslie Holt 'quite by chance' – who told him that the peer had sacked him in 'a very curt letter'.

Holt had been promised £2,000 out of the *Mirror* payout, but had received nothing. The election had been looming. Leslie Holt *was threatening to go to the press.*

That might have been very dangerous but Boothby, said 'Source', had got 'Ronnie Kray to threaten him that it would not be a good thing for him to do anything or say anything …'

The noble lord slipped him £200. Cheap at the price, Labour had won anyway.

So, according to 'Source', the TV-peer used threats by Ronnie Kray to tidy up the one loose end in the Peer and a Gangster affair. Leslie Holt did not tell his story, of course he didn't. MI5 knew about it, so did the Home Office. So presumably did the Yard pursuing related investigations of their own evidently.

---

[24] The incoming Labour Home Secretary who took office that morning was Sir Frank Soskice. He would be replaced by Roy Jenkins in December 1965.

And nobody said a word. It must have been quite a relief when it all went away, courtesy of state enforcer Ronnie Kray.

\* \* \*

The lovable twins wanted most of all to be back up the West End again with a big, celebrity-packed club of their own.

Their path to glory seemed clear.

# 14

## SOMEWHERE OVER THE RAINBOW

There was a face called Hew McCowan who had a big flat in Marble Arch: Flat 8, Number 23 Great Cumberland Place. It was very plush, full of fruit machines and antiques.

The music promoter Larry Parnes lived downstairs from McCowan. They'd been business partners briefly. Stars like the entertainer Tommy Steele and singers Billy Fury and Marty Wilde were in and out of there like it was a tube station – I used to see them on the way in and out.

Hew was the homosexual son of a Scottish baronet, living on a trust fund. He was dabbling in clubs and gaming machines, and of course doing that he was bound to bump into the Krays along the way. In fact, it was me who would make the first connection, via Charlie.

A small and insignificant man to look at, he always wore smart, expensive clothes. He was a right chancer. According to a press report I found, he'd got 'a talented army cook', Guardsman Eric Ash, out of Chelsea Barracks, round to his flat to prepare fancy lunches for his guests. The army did not object. Guardsman Ash, twenty-one, would serve cocktails from a 'quilted bar'. I remember that bar.

One time Hew had asked Alfie and me to go to his flat to ask us if we'd look after the security in a club he was going to open: fruit machines, something like that. McCowan was already in the Krays' sights because I'd introduced him to Charlie the year before. Charlie had told the moneyman Les Payne about this rich Scottish fun-lover he'd met and Payne just turned up at the door one day in September 1964 soon after the Boothby business. A businessman called Johnny Francis was with him. They had this investment proposal, about a housing development in Nigeria. According to a statement by McCowan that I saw in the National Archives, this face Francis would 'come round several times for a drink' thereafter.

One time he'd 'brought one of the Krays'. McCowan couldn't remember whether it was Ronnie or Reggie. That was the start of it.

There'd been a meeting in Payne's swanky office in George Street. McCowan – wisely, as it turned out – chose not to risk his family fortune on Enugu, whatever that was, without a bit more consideration.

Next, McCowan gets an invite to the Cambridge Rooms, the roadhouse club on the Kingston Bypass still just about holding off the creditors. He goes there with a party from the Colony Room – led by Alfie's friend, the famous Soho club chatelaine Muriel Belcher, and her barman, Ian Board. Off they went with McCowan to far New Malden to see the twins' suburban set-up for themselves. It was quite an outing.

I heard about that night. And I saw McCowan's version in the National Archives. The Krays were in. There were nodding acknowledgements. A number of 'untidily dressed young men were there', so McCowan could recall. He'd got very drunk, 'became objectionable' and the manager, an equally drunk Smithy – Teddy Smith – threw them all out.

According to DI Leonard 'Nipper' Read's memoirs, McCowan used to frequent a little club called the Music Box in Panton Street, off Leicester Square. It had featured in the Vassall tribunal and the Rickard murder case of two years before. McCowan would 'pick up boys there and take them back to his flat', so Read said. His visitors would nick stuff before clearing off, bags of coins from the one-armed bandits (he'd had them fixed to take half-crowns), antiques, which he would duly report to the police at Marylebone Lane. But he'd never turn up to give evidence, should one of the miscreants be caught and brought to court. He had good reason not to. A detective sergeant called John Donald dealt wearily with such incidents. They had an understanding – this would be important.

There was a club called the Bon Soir in Gerrard Street run by a face called Gilbert France, who also owned the restaurant Chez Victor in lower Wardour Street – it was a Soho landmark. A young man called Sidney Thomas Vaughan was his manager. McCowan had met Vaughan around the 'dilly (in the White Horse in Rupert Street, according to the *People*), who in turn introduced him to France at his twenty-first birthday party.

France and Vaughan had had a dispute and the Bon Soir shut in September 1964. It was agreed Vaughan could run a re-opened club however he liked, paying France's company £150 a week. McCowan saw a way into the club scene via his new friend. He would buy a half-share and put more money into the business to attract a smart clientele with young Sidney as his guide. McCowan gave Sidney a sports car (that was how it seemed to be with wealthy men and their boyfriends) and put him on a £40-a-week retainer – big money.

McCowan was planning to reopen at Christmas. He was going to rename it the 'Hideaway'. Vaughan had a friend living in a flat in Lisle Street, off Leicester Square called Peter Byrne (also known as 'Irish Johnnie'). He'd come to London from Dublin aged fifteen. Both young men would feature in the dramas to come.

Johnny Francis meanwhile had suggested that 'his friends' the Krays be involved in the new club, provide the money and get in the punters to put a casino in the basement, plus protection of course. But the price would be a big slice of the profits.

The twins summoned McCowan to the Grave Maurice pub in the Whitechapel Road to do a deal. Sidney Vaughan went too. I went to pick them up and drove them both there for the twins. It was early November 1964.

That first time, Johnny Francis did most of the talking. The suggested take was now 25 per cent of profits. The evening ended with more drinking at Vallance Road. The 'discussion was pleasant and business-like', according to McCowan. But not for much longer. As McCowan strung things out, the percentage being demanded went up. There was another meet at which 'tempers frayed'. Vaughan called Ronnie a 'cunt', which was not a good idea.

So, on 4 November, McCowan phoned his old pal Detective Sergeant Donald at Marylebone Lane for 'advice'. DS Donald went to his flat. 'I asked him who the men were and was told they were known as the Kray twins,' Donald would state. 'I told him to get every bit of information he could.'

Back at the station he phoned that old Kray aficionado, DS Tommy Butler, to tell him what had happened. I read Butler's response in the National Archives. Butler came over to Marylebone Lane on the 6th and promised to find out what he could from 'inquiries among his informants in the East End in as discreet a manner as possible'. He had never heard of McCowan. Should this complainant disclose more information, Sergeant Donald should pass it to Mr Butler.

From a statement he'd make some months later, Butler clearly knew nothing at the time about a discreet police operation to clean up clubland. Started the previous summer on the instructions of Frederick Gerrard after the Peer and a Gangster affair, it was being led by DI Leonard Read. The secrecy had clearly held, but not for much longer.

* * *

The twins' showbiz credentials got a big leg-up that autumn. Hollywood star Judy Garland was in town to do two shows that November at the London Palladium. Charlie had pulled an old Sammy Lederman favour to make sure Judy would take in what was left of Cockneyland. Ronnie said one night: 'This is great, we are going to meet Judy Garland!' Well, it didn't mean anything to me – she was more something for our mum.

'Oh, she's a star,' Ronnie told me.

It was in an old pub around the corner from Vallance Road, a small place with a piano and a jukebox. That night, it was full of real old East Enders. Then suddenly Judy Garland comes in with her husband or boyfriend at the time and someone puts 'Somewhere Over The Rainbow' on the jukebox. And she starts singing.

The place was packed by now and she came over to me and sat on my lap. The whole pub went wild. I was twenty-one years old at the time and didn't have a clue who she was.

Now it's a month later and the opening night at the Hideaway. The twins booked a table for ten people but failed to appear. But two nights later, 16 December, Smithy did show and bounced around the reception area, swearing at customers. He spotted a face he knew: 'Look who it is, Flash Harry!' he shouted. It was Sidney Vaughan. He 'punched him once or twice and kicked him'.

The doorkeeper, a Mr Collins, called for the boss. It was 2.30am. McCowan recognised the troublemaker from some recent encounter, somewhere out in the suburbs. New Malden, the Krays had been there. They'd all been very drunk. Muriel Belcher from The Colony had been with them, turning the air blue. They'd been thrown out. How could he forget it?

Smithy recognised him too. Waiters grappled him out of the door. It wasn't difficult, Smithy was slightly built, only five foot seven. Then he forced his way back in. 'Fuck you, McCowan!' he shouted. 'You know who I am and you know who my friends are …' Well, although he didn't mention their names out loud, everybody knew who he meant.

He went off in a taxi, still shouting.

Christmas came and went. On New Year's Eve, Vaughan took a call at the Hideaway. It was Reggie Kray – with an invitation for McCowan and his manager to a meet at the Glenrae in not quite so fashionable Finsbury Park. So off they went. I saw how it had gone in the National Archives:

'Have you had any trouble?' asked Ronnie.

'As a matter of fact, I have. One of your old friends paid me a visit and smashed the place up,' said McCowan.

'Who was that?'

'Ted Smith.'

'Well, he is a very violent man. Was he drunk?'

'Yes, he was.'

'Well, we dismissed him from the payroll months ago. He used to go around making trouble where we didn't want trouble.'

Employ a Kray doorman and there would never have been any trouble. The percentage was put back to twenty. The conversation continued:

'Are you busy?' asked Ronnie. 'Have you been full since you opened?'

'No,' said McCowan.

'Well, my brother and I can fill the place for you. We could guarantee you £1,000 every night and what's 20 per cent of that when you're taking that sort of money,' said Ronnie. There was talk of the Krays 'investing' in the club – with a proportion to reflect services provided. McCowan said he'd consider it.

There was something else: McCowan was into fruit machines. A change in the law seemed imminent which would allow one-armed bandits in public houses. McCowan supposedly had contacts with the big brewer, Courage. If he could get into a big chain of pubs, the Krays would make sure they were looked after. Could he set up a meeting? McCowan thought he could. They would all make a fortune.

It was agreed they would meet again at the Glenrae on the following Wednesday, 6 January 1965, at 8.30pm. They would discuss gaming machines and the proposed contract for protection of the Hideaway. The written contract would be ready after they'd seen the man from Courage Brewery. Then, for whatever reason, McCowan changed his mind. He had gone back round to Marylebone Lane Police Station, sometime on the morning of 6 January, and accused the twins of 'demanding money with menaces'. Yes, he would support police in any prosecution, recount the incident with Smith coming to the club, attend any court and say so in the witness box.

The next thing I knew, Charlie Kray was telling me the twins had been nicked and I had to go and visit Ronnie in Brixton remand prison. How had that happened?

It turned out a new copper was on their case. It all happened very fast. On the evening of 6 January 1965, Ronnie and Reggie had been nicked at the Glenrae Hotel by a Detective Superintendent called Leonard Read. We'd never heard of him. They didn't get bail and they were on remand. Billy Exley and the old boxer Tommy Brown had been nicked too. Of Edward 'Teddy' Smith there was no sign.

'Nipper' Read (we'd get to know him very well later) had already been on the twins' case for months, so it turned out. It had been a very well-kept secret as far as we or anyone else was concerned.

Read had set up at City Road Police Station with a team of ten – all of them fresh faces, none knew much about the Krays although they would soon learn. He'd started poking around and been amazed at the immunity the twins seemed to enjoy, he says in his memoirs. Read put it down to police laziness rather than corruption (he *would* say that).

In January 1965, he wrote a long note for his boss, Fred Gerrard, on progress (or lack of it). I saw it in the National Archives:

> There have been some efforts by officers of a number of Divisions including the Flying Squad. None of these inquiries bore fruit and nothing was gleaned that would determine the Kray connection with any particular offence.

DS Read had met the proverbial 'wall of silence which has proven impossible to surmount until the onset of the present case,' he wrote. He had begun the summer before with a visit to the veteran 'king of crime' Jack Spot, who was 'down on his luck and knew nothing.'

Spotty told him: 'He had tried to teach the twins to get plenty of money without violence, but they would not listen.'

Read had gone over old ground with anyone who'd speak to him. There were stories of buttock slashing (a Kray favourite), brutal intimidation, false tribunals and imprisonments, branding, cheek slicing, kneecapping. No one would make a written statement. West End club owners would say nothing except the Krays were 'good customers' or 'I'm too big for these people'.

Owners of betting shops were silent, so Read would say in his memoirs. The humbler end of London clubland was just the same. To begin with, Long Firms looked a better bet. Turning them over had been difficult. After six months of not getting very far, Commander Ernie 'Hooter' Millen wanted operations terminated. Hooter moved to do just that while Read's superior, Fred Gerrard, was on leave, so Nipper said in his memoirs: 'The object of the exercise had been to nick the twins and we were no nearer at the end of the day than when we started,' he wrote. Then, just when Read was being leant on from above, on the morning of 6 January, Hew Cargill McCowan walked into Marylebone Lane nick for the second time with a story to tell. This time DI Donald didn't bother getting Mr Butler agitated – after all, he had done nothing since that first call.

DI Donald rang Read at City Road pretty quick to tell him that he had a man in the station who was going on about demands for a percentage of profits by the Kray twins and his club being turned over. It had happened just over two weeks before.

Nipper rushed up west, put McCowan in his car and took him back to City Road. He gave a long statement. McCowan went through the meetings in the Grave Maurice, the role of Johnny Francis, the Krays suggested take for protection and their promises to get big celebrities through the doors of the Hideaway. Then he told the tale of the night when Smithy turned up, saying, 'Fuck you, McCowan! You know who I am and you know who my friends are ...'

The club manager, Sidney Thomas Vaughan, of Provost Court, Eton Road, NW3, who'd also been at the Grave Maurice meeting, said exactly the same in a statement he gave to Read.

Two potential Crown witnesses.

'McCowan is the son of Sir David and Lady McCowan and has access to a considerable fortune,' Read noted on the file. The fact he was homosexual with convictions for 'buggery and indecent assault on a male person' should 'not be too disadvantageous', he noted.

And yes, McCowan already knew the Krays, he said in that original statement to Read at City Road. He'd first met them and Edward Smith a few months before at the Cambridge Rooms, a roadhouse club on the Kingston Bypass. The evening had not gone well. After that, there'd been another meeting with the twins, Johnny Francis and Leslie Payne at his Marble Arch flat to discuss the Enugu scheme with its promised amazing returns on investment.

McCowan didn't fancy that so much, but he had mentioned to his visitors his interest in developing a new club in Gerrard Street out of the old Bon Soir. Gilbert France was selling him a half-share. There would be drinking and entertainment. That had been back in September, which was when Reggie and Johnny Francis first suggested a slice for protection and the whole Hideaway affair began.

Smithy was also in the frame. Nipper reported to Gerrard: 'Edward Richard Smith is very close to the Krays and more of a friend and companion than mere hireling.'

He had been 'living for some time in a flat leased at No. 8 Cedra Court' (Ronnie's old gaff). 'He went on holiday with Ronald Kray to

Spain in June 1964 [just before the Peer and a Gangster storm] and was acting as their business manager,' Read could report.

If Smith should claim he was pursuing some personal grudge when he 'menaced' McCowan at the Hideaway, there was enough to prove a direct link to the twins in court.

Where were the Krays now? Right then they were up at their new place, the Glenrae, in Finsbury Park. It was time to move. There was not even enough time to get arrest warrants. It all went down in a single day, that Wednesday, 6 January 1965. McCowan told Read in that breathless statement at City Road he'd be up there that evening for his scheduled meeting about the fruit machines and more besides. In the late afternoon, Read and Gerrard 'took up surveillance' outside the Glenrae Hotel with a DS from City Road. Just before 8.30pm they saw McCowan turn up in a 'white sports car' (a Kaiser Darrin, according to a file in the National Archives, a rare fifties Yank car, dead flash). They saw him leave less than an hour later.

DS Hall overtook the car and flagged McCowan to turn into a side road. 'Inspector Gerrard and I made contact with him a short distance away and had some conversation,' Read noted on the file.

It had all gone as predicted. What about evidence that would stand up in court? There was no signed contract for whatever might be called protection but Read decided they already had enough, they must move there and then. Five years before, Tommy Butler had sent twenty men to turn over the Double R. This time there were just three of them. The two senior officers went down into the basement clubroom. DS Sidney Hall from City Road blocked the door.

The arrest went 'quietly'. Reggie called out to Charlie, 'Get us a brief!' as he was taken away. Ronnie said, 'Alright, where do we go?' Reggie added, 'Can I say goodnight to my girl?'

He could not.

In the back seat of the squad car, Ronnie asked: 'Who's nicked us, Mr Read? I mean, who's this down to? Someone must have put the finger on us.'

That line would soon be in all the newspapers.

The twins were taken to Highbury Vale nick, then City Road, and charged with demanding money with menaces. Smithy was nowhere to be found – for now.

Cedra Court and three other known addresses were visited.

No Edward Smith.

Then the 'address of a relative', 151 Dartmouth Park Hill in north London, was staked out by Read's little squad. PC Breeze was advised to try the betting shop. Smith was arrested coming back the other way.

'What's all this about?' he asked the policeman.

'Detective Inspector Read would like to see you.'

'Well, you've got to be careful who's about. Lots of people could be looking to see me.'

He was taken to City Road and cautioned.

'I haven't been with the Krays, I'm a writer,' Smithy said. 'I manage a few singers for them.'

'But you were living with one of them.'

'That's right, Cedra Court. But I've got a lovely little place in Queen's Drive now. In Finsbury Park ...'[25]

---

[25] A little later, during the bail applications, Smithy would say he'd been at 109 Queen's Drive, N4, since May 1964, living with a man called 'Thomas Harris'. When the police checked it out, the landlady confirmed that Mr Harris lived in a room on the ground floor. She did not know a Mr Smith.

'I know what you're going to say. That's just around the corner from the Glenrae. But I don't do any villainy,' he insisted. 'The only time I get naughty is when I've had a few drinks. I did a club up the other day, it was the Hideaway. It was only a drunken brawl. I do these things and can't remember the next morning.'

Smithy was charged with demanding money with menaces.

A big pile of correspondence was seized at the Glenrae Hotel and hauled off by Read for investigation. The police found an address book, a Who's Who of the Firm, Long Firm fraudsters, solicitors and celebrities. A letter from Los Angeles showbiz lawyer Harrison Hertzberg congratulated Ronnie on his '$100,000 Boothby libel case win'. Hertzberg further assured Ronnie that he had given Hollywood star 'Zsa Zsa Gabor your name and number to call you. Hope you have a good time.'

I saw it in the National Archives. He'd sent it from Los Angeles addressed to Henry Granshaw, superintendent of the Cheshire Street Baths – Ronnie's discreet little mailbox round the corner from Fort Vallance.

Maybe Zsa Zsa did get in touch that way.

So now the twins and Smithy were in Brixton on remand. Bail applications began before magistrates. Ronnie's brief told the court that the Krays needed their freedom so they could find people to testify for their defence: 'We are dealing with Soho night life and it is extremely difficult to trace witnesses.'

Maybe so.

Celebrity barrister Victor Durand, it was him again, for the defence said the person or persons on whom the demand is alleged to have been made [McCowan] was 'quite unknown to the accused'. Well, I for one knew different.

Read had hoped, he'd write in his memoirs, for a 'snowball of witnesses' who would testify against the Krays – as long as they were inside with no prospect of coming out until the trial was over (and after which they were safely away). If nobody was coming forward, it was not just for fear of the Krays, it was because the prosecution case was so full of holes. Meanwhile, Charlie Kray was doing what he did best, scaring people off.

One time he used me to do it.

Like this …

One morning, Charlie came round the house and said: 'David, you've got to go up and see Ronnie in prison.' When I got up to Brixton, I was only allowed to talk to Ron through the glass at one of those prison visiting cubicles.

Ron leant forward and said: 'Listen, boy, you've got to go and see that cunt McCowan. Tell him to shut his mouth and say nothing happened. Tell him if he don't, we'll do him and all his family too.' I said, 'Ron, I can't. Please don't make me do this.' But he just answered: 'Go round and tell him!'

So that night I went to see McCowan at his flat. He had no police protection, although he'd been offered it by Read. I told him the twins had given me a message for him to drop the charges or he'd be in a lot of trouble. McCowan told me: 'I can't do that. I've got the police on to it now. I've given my evidence and that's the end of it.' He didn't seem to get it. Anyway, he was brave – but very foolish. I told Charlie, who passed on the message to Ronnie.

I can imagine what he thought.

Still bail applications were turned down. The 'severity of the charges', Charlie's bits of 'persuading' (Read knew about those from surveillance) and a 'kidnap' risk to McCowan were given as the reasons.

My visit (the coppers would have logged that too) to Great Cumberland Place with a message from Ronnie would not have helped. That and the fact that the mysterious 'business partner' Johnny Francis, who I took to the Grave Maurice, had cleared off to Spain.

Charlie was really going to work. He'd got to Sidney Vaughan, who was 'persuaded' to go to Vallance Road and make a statement to an inquiry agent. The local vicar had also been invited to ensure a higher authority would oversee whatever happened.

According to Vaughan, the twins had never asked McCowan for 'protection money'. He'd been forced by McCowan to lie. I saw what he said in the National Archives:

> The McCowan family are very powerful. They live in Loch Lomond castle and have £15m invested in Burmah Oil. They are the biggest manufacturers of sweets in Scotland!!! Hew McCowan has friends at Savile Row police station, he is a homosexual and drinks two bottles of brandy a day. He's been working on this case for five months with Inspector Gerrard and is telling everyone he's going to get a citation from the Queen and the OBE!

The Old Street Magistrates committal was a fiasco. Whatever Charlie had threatened or offered had worked. Vaughan, referred to in press reports as a 'tousle-haired youth', hadn't meant those original statements, he said. What he'd said to police was under pressure from McCowan. Johnny Francis (conveniently missing) had done that threatening talk about percentages.

Mr Edward Smith had had 'a fight' with him in the Hideaway club, that was true, that's what had caused the 'accidental damage'.

But he'd never been threatened by the Krays themselves. It was a journalist, Roy East of the *People*, who had put 'fear' in his mind that the Krays might do him harm.

Sidney had been turned completely. DI Leonard Read, so he would write in his memoirs, 'could not believe what was happening'. His case was in ruins.

Still bail applications were made and still they failed. Good old Lord Boothby famously asked a question in the House of Lords: 'To ask Her Majesty's Government whether it is their intention to keep the Kray brothers in prison for an indefinite period without trial.'

'I hold no brief at all for the Kray brothers, one of whom I have never met and the other of whom I have met on only two occasions in my life, last July,' he announced solemnly. Just so everyone was clear about that. They would be sniggering at Scotland Yard.

He didn't mention Teddy Smith.

Early that same day, 11 February 1965, McCowan phoned Read with the message that Sidney Vaughan had changed his mind about being part of the prosecution in the full trial. 'He's definitely going the other way,' said McCowan. 'He comes from the East End, like they do.'

McCowan had taken a long time working that out.

The trial would go ahead anyway even though the prosecution seemed doomed. It was set to start on 8 March at the Old Bailey.

Meanwhile, Charlie was keeping everyone onside with the Boothby cash off the *Mirror*. Vaughan had clearly been got at already. And there was another little Charlie stunt going down just to make sure.

On 1 March, someone called Peter Byrne phoned the Yard to say he'd been attacked by four men at his flat in Lisle Street, Soho. He said he'd been stripped to his underwear and socks, gagged, tied up and threatened with cutting with a big pair of tailor's scissors.

Read's original case notes in the National Archives describe his upstairs neighbour, a Mr Steve Brooks, finding Byrne (he knew him as 'Irish Johnnie') in this state on the stairs, his face bleeding. The neighbour thought it had been 'staged'.

Byrne had come to London from Dublin aged fifteen. He had worked in coffee bars and met men in 'dilly clubs like the Alibi in Berwick Street or the Mews Club in Duck Lane, he'd tell police in a rambling statement. Charlie had found Byrne somewhere along the way and got him to make a sworn statement to a solicitor about being attacked in his flat by four men who 'looked like guardsmen'. They said things like: 'No, McCowan only wants him frightened' and 'McCowan will see us alright'.

They seemed very keen to mention that name.

Things were made more complicated by the fact that, inevitably, Roy East of the *People* had been snooping round his old favourite, the Music Box. More of that later …

The trial began at the Old Bailey on the afternoon of Monday, 8 March 1965. The court heard a brisk outline from John Mathew for the Crown on the events which had led the owner of the Hideaway to find 'the courage to go to the police'.

On the second day, there was an attempt by Reggie's barrister, Paul Wrightson, to abort the trial and get a new jury. One juryman who had allegedly been discussing the case with a police officer was stood down. The trial would proceed with eleven.

Cross-examined by the defence on the 11th, everything was about the principal Crown witness's own character, how McCowan had been involved in four past cases of blackmail relating to his alleged homosexual activities. George Devlin, the private investigator hired by Sampson and Co., had been digging around.

McCowan agreed that he knew Detective Sergeant Donald at Marylebone, who had been involved in two other cases in which he (the witness) was concerned. As it was reported: 'Mr McCowan was then questioned about a Mr Peter Francis Byrne. He said he knew him as someone who worked on a postcard stand in Piccadilly Circus.'

'Is it correct to say that you have been to his flat?' asked Paul Wrightson, Reggie's brief.

'No, that is totally and utterly untrue. This is a diabolical frame-up.'

'You know that Byrne was beaten up in March and had to go to hospital?'

'I heard he had been slashed.'

'Have you threatened Vaughan similarly?'

'Never.'

Sidney Vaughan made an appearance the next day, 12 March. He was supposed to be a Crown witness but proved of far more use to the defence than the prosecution.

'The Kray twins never threatened Mr McCowan,' he said directly. 'Why should they?'

On the 15th, Nipper Read himself was cross-examined by the defence and had to say, 'There was no hate campaign against the twins.' Then McCowan was recalled to admit he'd been treated in a Glasgow mental hospital twelve years before, aged twenty, pending his trial for a homosexual offence in the Scottish High Court.

Now it was Peter Byrne's turn. He told the court how his room in Lisle Street had been burst into, how he'd been pinned in bed, tied up and slashed in the face by a gang who 'looked like guardsmen' making threats. The attack, he alleged, followed a visit from two other men, who asked him to 'forget something Sidney Vaughan had told him'.

He'd seen Vaughan and McCowan together in the Music Box and overheard McCowan saying 'he was going to get the OBE for nicking the Kray twins'.

John Mathew, cross-examining for the prosecution, teased out of the witness that he had been found guilty of blackmailing a probation officer by making allegations of homosexual offences a couple of years before. Byrne said: 'It was not blackmail, it was demanding money with menaces.'

There was a lot of that about.

Read knew of course that Charlie had got to Vaughan. Byrne's fantasy slashing, as it clearly was, would be irrelevant as it would turn out. But Vaughan's switching sides had been fatal to the Crown case.

In summing up, the judge said: 'If you think that Vaughan's evidence makes it impossible for you to rely on the evidence of McCowan then that is the end of this case. [But] do not make the mistake of thinking Vaughan has been got at by the defence. That would be quite improper. There is not the slightest evidence of that.'

Well, Sidney Vaughan had been well got at.

So, what would any jury make of that? One juryman could not agree with the others. Hours passed. The jury could not return a verdict. They were asked to try again but on 18 March, came back after half an hour with the same message. A retrial was ordered. The Director of Public Prosecutions, Sir Norman Skelhorn, chaired a meeting at which it was decided not to put up Sidney Vaughan again because he'd been such a disaster the previous time.

Charlie Kray's insurance policy of getting Byrne to come up with the 'guardsmen' yarn putting the frighteners on him wasn't needed in the end. Just as well ... There was no evidence the door to the Soho room had been forced.

The second trial began on 29 March. As in the first, the defendants gave no evidence themselves, but this time there were defence witnesses. Harry Beckett, a market porter and regular in the Grave Maurice, was put up to say he'd been in the pub when McCowan had expressed how 'disappointed he was when learning the Krays were no longer interested in his club'.

Vaughan and Byrne were not recalled. McCowan himself was the only prosecution witness. His own story was turned over again. He had been a psychiatric patient; he had been involved in a number of trials where in three cases he had alleged blackmail and demanding money with menaces.

Summing up, the judge told the jury the prosecution case depended entirely on McCowan. If they did not believe him, they should find the defendants not guilty and the trial would stop there.

On 6 April 1965, the jury gave their verdict after seven minutes: not guilty. Edward Smith: not guilty. Reggie, Ron and Smithy were discharged.

'For me it was a disaster,' wrote DI Read in his memoirs. The twins' solicitors issued dire threats about suing for false imprisonment and police harassment.

Reggie thought it poetic justice. In his 1991 ghost-written book, *Born Fighter*, he admitted 'corrupting some member of a particular jury [wouldn't you?] being totally innocent and having been fitted up by crooked police'.

That afternoon of 6 April, the courtroom victors all came back from the Old Bailey in triumph to Vallance Road to celebrate. There were photographers, reporters, it was a street party. 'Krays Back Home' said the evening headlines. About twenty actual East Enders turned up, as I remember. Frances Shea told reporters: 'Now I want to marry Reginald.'

As always, the twins had got what they wanted and that afternoon they took over the Hideaway the usual way through a holding company, with Charlie as the frontman. They didn't actually pay for it, of course. They renamed it 'El Morocco', like the famous showbiz club in New York. There was yet another big party. Lots of celebrities, the usual crowd but a bit more A-List, George Sewell, Victor Spinetti, the film actress Adrienne Corri, Barbara Windsor and her husband Ronnie Knight. The twin's mum, Violet, was there and Charlie's wife Dolly. Lots of the Firm. Alfie and I flitted about. It was as if the twins had really cracked it this time.

Ronnie pointed out to me the actor Edmund Purdom (very famous at the time in a TV historical romp called *Sword of Freedom* – like Robin Hood, but set in Italy).

'See him?' he said. 'I want you to meet him here tomorrow at ten and bring him over to Vallance Road.' He said it like it was the most normal thing in the world to pick up a film star and take him back to a little terraced house in the East End. Alfie and I got in trouble that night. In fact, we were barred for chatting up the cigarette girls. But it wasn't for long.

The next day I did as I'd been told and met Mr Purdom as arranged and took him over to the Krays' house. Ronnie called out, 'Mum, make us a cup of tea?' When Violet came in with the tray, she couldn't believe her eyes.

'Is that really him? In our house?'

Ronnie introduced them. When Violet had gone out, Ronnie handed the actor £200, saying: 'Give it back to me when you can.' I took him back to the West End.

But it wasn't just film stars I was driving. I was in the El Morocco a little while later when Ronnie told me to pick up someone the next day – someone who was to become far more famous than any sixties TV star, but only after he was dead.

'Right, Dave, go out tomorrow morning and pick up Jack "the Hat" at Aldgate at 10am,' he said.

The next morning, I found Jack standing on the corner, waiting for me. I picked him up by the jellied eels stall, Tubby Isaacs.

'Drive down Commercial Road, do a left and pull up,' he said. 'Don't move from here, I won't be a minute.'

Jack McVitie was an armed robber, getting a bit pissed a bit too often, taking too many of the drugs he was peddling, but otherwise inoffensive enough. He wore that trilby hat to hide a bald patch – he was very sensitive about it.

I waited patiently in the car, glancing up in the mirror a few minutes later to see Jack running towards me, a bag in his hand. 'Get off the manor, I've just done a bank!' he shouted.

Snatched a roll of notes from some poor shopkeeper paying in, more like. Anyway I did what he asked, got him out of there. Not too fast, not too slow. Jack was not a big-time blagger (bank robber). He was too drunk for that, too fond of a prank. James Morton tells a good story in his book *Krays: The Final Word* about Jack holding up a gambling club with a gun and forcing all the punters to drop their trousers. One time he dropped his own (he seemed to have a thing about it) to reveal a pair of 'striped underpants' in a drunken shouting match with the singer Dorothy Squires over her former husband Roger Moore's sexual prowess.

He was an embarassment. Anyway, Jack didn't deserve what was coming to him. More about that later.

* * *

The Hideaway trial over, the *People* newspaper could reveal its own part in the affair. The Kray twins and Mr Edward Smith had been found innocent, so it was no good trying to say they were not. But crime reporter Roy East had been co-operating with Hew McCowan from the outset. What to do? It was to blame the 'real' villains in the affair, Vaughan and Byrne, who had tried to pervert the course of justice. The story ran on 11 April.

Conversations on McCowan's phone had been tape-recorded, it could be revealed. There was a chat on 3 March between McCowan and 'a well-known West End character' called 'Johnny' (a cover for Sidney Vaughan, who was not named in the story), who McCowan first met in the bar of the White Horse public house in Archer Street.

It seemed 'Johnny' was offering money to McCowan not to give evidence at the trial, which was due to open in five days' time. Of the defendants, Johnny had said, 'They're bleeding good lads and they help a lot of people.' He was clearly a fan of the Krays.

With Patrick Byrne, it was easier. The '22-year-old Irishman' could be named outright. 'He confessed to *People* investigators that he had perjured himself in the witness box,' according to the story. 'Byrne, when seen by *People* reporters, admitted the whole affair: "I did tell lies at the Old Bailey about the slashing".'

According to Les Payne (though his account gets a bit confused): 'Byrne became a member of the Kray gang and one was not surprised to read in 1968 that he had been nailed to a wall in Soho and beaten with wires.'

\* \* \*

On 19 April 1965, Reggie married Frances Shea. It was the 'East End wedding of the year'. Fashion photographer David Bailey, another East End boy, took the snaps. The reception was up at the Glenrae, packed with celebrities. Tom Driberg was there, I know that. This time I wasn't – not because I wasn't invited.

The newly-weds were going to live up west to start with. A smart block in Marble Arch, near Hew McCowan. That lasted a couple of weeks before Reggie moved them to the flat in Cedra Court directly below Ronnie's, which he had specially done up with smart, modern furniture from the Harrison Gibson store in Ilford.

But Reggie wasn't happy, nor was Frances. As I saw it, Reggie would take Frances out at night to some club where the Firm were and all the talk was of villainy. She'd just stare into space. I thought she was permanently terrified. Reggie would come back to Cedra Court and leave her on her own while he went upstairs to where Ronnie was partying.

She cried her eyes out, night after night. Smithy could make her laugh and Alfie and me could cheer her up, but she hated the Firm and she hated Ronnie. The Shea family knew and they loathed Reggie for it. In the end, she left him after eight weeks.

I caught some of the storms. One night, Reggie came round my flat with Dickie Morgan for a drink. They came knocking on the door about two o'clock in the morning. I was asleep, but got up and found them a bottle of gin and sat down to talk. Dickie went home after a while, but Reggie and I sat up after he'd gone. Suddenly Reggie started to cry, saying, 'You know what, we're going to get a lot of bird when they get us.'

I told him, 'Look, Reg, why don't you get out of it? You're well set up, you've got a few quid, why don't you and Frances get away by yourselves?'

Reggie looked back at me and said, 'I can't do it, Dave. I can't. I'm a part of Ronnie, and he's part of me. I know it, I can see it. If he goes down, so do I. We're going to do lots and lots of bird. I know Ronnie's losing it, but I can't do anything.'

He stayed that night and I took him back to Vallance Road in the morning. Reggie asked me not to say anything about what had passed between us to anyone: 'Keep this just between us,' he told me.

But Reggie's marriage was over before it even started, Ronnie made sure of that.

# PART II

Me as a kid. The war was just over and times were hard.

We brothers worked a boatyard at Shanklin on the Isle of Wight in the summers. That's Alfie, our friend Bobby Quinn, me, Bobby, and our kid brother Paul. I met Christine on the island.

This is Christine (left) shortly after I met her, sitting with my sister Eileen.

The Teale family grew quickly. That's me on the left soaking up the seaside sun – with Dad, Mum, Bobby's new wife Pat, Bobby, Alfie's wife Wendy, and Alfie in front with our brother and sister Paul and Eileen.

And then Ronnie and Reggie Kray entered our lives. That's me in the grey suit, one away from Ronnie. At the time I was driving Reggie's new bride, Frances (left), around London.

The three eldest Teale brothers, our parents, and our wives.

Me and Christine at the Talk of the Town. We had a night from hell there with Reggie, Frances and Mad Teddy Smith.

The Boothby 'Peer and the Gangster' affair of summer 1964 put the twins in the headlines. Here's Lord Bob at the time looking shifty. Alfie took bundles of cash from him for the twins.

It's long been said that the Yard's C.11 (Intelligence) branch was about to pounce on the twins when the Boothby affair stopped their 'major' investigation. In fact, as I found in the archives, all that C.11 had come up with was a list of favoured Kray boozers, Kray motor vehicles, and mug shots cut from a press photograph.

The day the *Sunday Mirror* 'apologised', the twins staged a triumphant photo shoot at Cedra Court. The iconic snap was filed away by MI5.

Now Lord Bob could be as publicly chummy as he liked with the twins. Here he is at the Astor Club with Ronnie, Charlie Clark (left) and Billy Exley (right).

The Twins' next big rumble was the Hide-A-Way affair, the club in Soho where they and Teddy Smith were accused of 'menacing'. Nipper Read kept watch from a nearby phone box. I took threatening messages to their principal accuser from Ronnie when he was on remand in Brixton prison.

The twins and Teddy (centre) had a big laugh when the trial collapsed and Read was taken off the case.

And then the killings started, with the 9 March 1966 murder of George Cornell in the Blind Beggar. That's me and Alfie outside it, fifty years on.

That night, we all ended up in my tiny flat in Moresby Road (that's me outside the front door) for a terrifying week of armed siege for me, Christine and the kids.

The twins next holed up in a flat in Lea Bridge Road. Bobby tipped the Yard off where they were. They were nicked but the ID parade was a fiasco. Once cleaned up, they held a triumphant photo shoot there from which much quoted images were the result. We Teale brothers meanwhile were now in the gravest danger.

At the Bow Street committal, I said what I knew about the Cornell killing. 'Fucking liar,' Ronnie shouted. Bobby meanwhile revealed he'd been an informer. There was no press reporting, but word soon got out.

Nipper and his team outside Tintagel House after the trial. Christine and our daughters were given close personal protection.

And we were a family again. Here we are returning from our first holiday abroad. But our troubles were not over…

Debbie, to whom this book is dedicated, and who taught me to love again.

# 15

## DEAD MEN CAN'T SPEAK

That was the night it all happened. It was two days after my birthday, Wednesday, 9 March 1966. So, I still had a hangover and didn't want to do much. We were at my flat in Stoke Newington. It was downstairs in a two-storey house from which five tiny flats had been made. It wasn't much, a living room, a small dining room-cum-bedroom with a kitchen and bathroom plus WC at the back. As well as the one in our bathroom, there was a shared WC on the stairs.

It was £30 a month. I rented it as 'Mr Lee' because that's all I could spell. I'd got it because the kids were getting bigger and we'd moved out of Orde Hall Street in Holborn just before the previous Christmas. I didn't want Ronnie to know where I'd gone but of course he found out and kept ringing up, saying come out with them or he'd come round my place. He'd started using it for meets – Christine hated that.

Christine was getting tea ready in the little kitchen. Alfie and Bobby were with me in the front room, watching TV. I think it was the news, then *Crossroads*, something like that. We had just got back from work.

There was a coin box phone in the hall. It rang about 6pm, just after perhaps. I went out to answer it, but I already knew who it was. It was Reggie, very calm, very persuasive. His voice had the slightest edge of urgency: 'Come on over to the Widow's. No special reason, just get over.'

My brothers and I all looked at each other: better do as he says. My car was outside the flat – a grey, two-door Ford Popular. The three of us got in and started heading for Bethnal Green. I did the driving, with Alfie in the front and Bobby in the back. No big rush.

We got to the Widow's pub in Tapp Street, near Vallance Road. Also known as 'Madge's', it was all a bit confusing. Its real name was The Lion, but a lot of people called it 'Madge's' after the landlady, Madge Jacob, who had taken up the licence from her late husband. It was also known as 'The Widow's'. By now it was just gone 8.30.

I pulled up off Cudworth Street under the bridge. Opposite were big, old Peabody Building tenements. Madge's had a public bar on the right and a saloon bar on the other side. Anyone who walked in there was either an old-age pensioner, a policeman or one of the Firm. It was like a real hideaway near the twins.

Reggie was outside in the street with a bunch of the Firm, all of them milling around under the railway bridge beneath the street lamps. There was something funny going on, we could sense it. We all got out. There's Reggie walking towards us, saying to me quite matter-of-factly: 'Where's your motor?'

'It's just over there, Reggie.'

Then Nobby Clark, a founder member of the Firm, said to Reg: 'What motor are you going in?'

Reggie replied, 'I'll go with these.' He meant us. He was excited but spoke as if he was just arranging any other piece of business. Then he told me to drive to Walthamstow and not to panic.

We got back in the car. Reggie jumped in the front. He said to me, 'Come on, kid, we've got to get off the manor.' I stepped on the accelerator hard.

At first no one spoke, but eventually Alfie asked Reg, 'So, what's the matter?'

Reggie said, calm as anything: 'Ronnie has just shot Cornell.'

'Who the fuck's Cornell?' I asked.

Alfie had a bit more of a clue. George Cornell was some face who'd done rough stuff for the Richardsons, the scrap-dealing brothers who ran crime in south-east London with a ruthlessness that outdid even the Krays. His real name was George Myers. The word was he'd once beaten the shit out of Ronnie in a fist fight, the only one who ever had. The Christmas before, there'd nearly been a shoot-out at the Astor Club when Cornell was supposed to have referred to Ronnie as a 'fat poof'. For him to come drinking in Whitechapel, Kray territory, had been taking the piss.

Reggie was sat in the front passenger seat complaining about why Ronnie had to do Cornell. He was always moaning about what Ronnie had or hadn't done. The way he went on, it was like it was some domestic tiff.

*So where are we all supposed to go?* I was thinking. *Nobody's saying.*

I'm driving very carefully now, looking out for the Old Bill. Reggie says, 'Where are we going to go to now?' We all remain silent. Then he told me, 'Go up Lea Bridge Road way.'

The Krays had no hideouts, whatever anyone might have suggested later. It was all far less planned than that. We were heading out of the East End, up Cambridge Heath Road, back past Cedra Court and my flat in Moresby Road, past the dark Hackney Marshes and on into the suburbs. Nothing much else was moving, the streets were quiet as a graveyard.

I thought I knew where we were going. I'd driven the twins this way before. It was a place called the Chequers in Walthamstow High Street, a favourite of the twins, run by an ex-policeman called Charlie Hobbs. There was a poker club called the Stow round the back. A bookmaker's clerk and part-time house-breaker called Charlie Clark ran that. He'd do anything and everything for Ronnie.[26]

Reggie was still mumbling away, still complaining that Ronnie 'should have organised this better'. The twins never organised anything. Everything happened because there was no fear of the consequences. Both acted on their impulses.

We got to Walthamstow and went into the pub. The landlord glanced up at us, quickly opened a flap in the bar counter and we all marched into another bar room that wasn't normally used. Scotch Ian Barrie was sitting at a table, along with some other members of the Firm. Ronnie was already there too, they must have arranged where to go in Tapp Street. He came towards us when he saw us enter. It was all very chaotic, the calmest one was Ronnie.

'Do you want a drink?' he asked me.

I suppose at that moment, I could have used one.

While I'd driven Reggie, Ronnie had been driven to the Chequers by Scotch Jack (John) Dickson, so I found out a little later.

We all gathered in the back room. You could feel the tension and excitement fizzing in the air. Everyone was talking at once and

---

[26] Charlie took over the guns from the 'Beggar'. Ronnie's corroded 9mm Luger pistol would be found by a police diver in the Regent's Canal, Hoxton, in June 1968.

no one was making much sense. The radio or TV was kept on in the background so they could listen to the news. Somebody said: 'Sssh! There's a baby trying to sleep.'

A man called William Thomas was ordered by Ronnie to get hold of the croupier Bobby Buckley and get him over to, whatever this was, a party. Thomas rang him in the Grave Maurice and told him to get a taxi. He did as he was told – I saw that in the National Archives.

Ronnie went into a lavatory and changed his clothes then started to wash his arms and hands with Vim sink cleaner. When I first saw him that evening, he had been wearing a dark suit, shirt and tie. Now he looked more like a clown with a pullover too small for him and trousers too short. He had changed into Alfie's clothes and looked absurd. If Ronnie had been a woman, he'd have been a size sixteen, while Alfie would have been a ten. So now he looked like Max Wall in his trousers.

We heard off the telly news that someone was being rushed to hospital after a shooting. Over fifty years later, I read the transcript of the ITN 11.12pm bulletin in the National Archives:

Another London shooting. Three men walked into a public house in Stepney and shot a man twice in the head. They escaped before anyone else in the bar could stop them. The man's condition is critical.

There was laughing and whooping when they all heard that. The Firm were revelling in it. Showbiz agent Sammy Lederman was behind the bar and Harry 'Jew Boy' Cope, a fun-loving geezer who floated around the Firm, was fetching drinks. He was always the master of ceremonies whenever there was a party.

Ronnie said: 'I hope the bastard's dead.'

The whole thing felt surreal, overwhelming. It was hard to make sense of it all.

The actual news came on very loud (it was on the telly 11.25pm, BBC1; I saw that in the National Archives), telling us again that a man had been shot twice in the head. There were road blocks all over the East End. Everyone started talking excitedly and I heard Ronnie say, 'Always shoot to kill. Dead men can't speak.'

He'd get to like saying that.

So, what the fuck had actually happened? It came out in a lot of fractured conversations around me. It had started when Ronnie got a message that George Cornell was in the Beggar. *That's a bit of a liberty*, he thought. He got Scotch Jack to drive him there in his Cortina from the Widow's (it's under half a mile), along with Scotch Ian Barrie. He'd got a gun from Vallance on the way.

Ronnie had gone into the bar of the Beggar brandishing a 9mm Luger. Cornell sat on a barstool, sipping a light ale. Scotch Ian had his own gun and fired two shots into the air. Everyone dived for cover. And Ronnie calmly put a single bullet into George Cornell's forehead. We were driving over when it happened.

As I heard it later, the bullet went straight through his brain. He lay bleeding on the floor of the Blind Beggar. An ambulance came pretty quick and he was taken to the London Hospital just across the road. They had him transferred to Maida Vale Hospital which special-ised in brain injuries but at 10.29pm, about two hours after he had been shot, George Cornell died on the operating table.

The other drinkers legged it. The Beggar barmaid disappeared (she hid in the cellar apparently).

By now, it was well gone closing time at the Chequers. So, where were we going to go now? Around 11.30pm, people started moving out of the pub with bottles of spirits and crates of beer to a flat up the road above a row of shops, Palace Parade, rented by a regular at the Chequers. Turned out Charlie Hobbs had rung him and said, 'Ronnie wants to come round.' There was a hundred quid in it.

He was a brewery driver called Roland Tarlton. I'd never set eyes on him before. He'd set up a bar in his front room with space for revellers to carry on after-hours drinking. It was his idea of fun, especially if the Krays were in. That's where I started heading with everyone else. However, soon after a group of us arrived, Roland's wife Megan came in from her night shift (as a waitress at the Café Royal, it would turn out) at about 1.30am to find thirty or forty men and women cavorting in her flat. She also found a couple at it in bed – she soon turfed them out.

Then their daughter arrived back from her job. Young, early twenties, she started screaming at her dad: 'How could you be so stupid?' Mrs Tarlton done her nut again and started screaming for us all to get out: she was going to get the police. She went out to the phone on the stairway and someone from the Firm grabbed her and burned a lit cigarette into the plastic handset. Following this, she did not go near it again (her account is all in the National Archives). She went to live with her sister after that.

The party, if that's what it was, went on. It was the middle of the night. Reggie turned to me and said, 'Right, Dave, we're going to stay round your house. We can't go near the East End. You're a straight boy, the Old Bill don't know your place.'

'You can't,' I said. 'We've only got two rooms, a living room and a kitchen with a bed in it. My kids are there. And Christine has another baby on the way.'

I couldn't see any way out – the mother and daughter were still moaning and shouting, and Reggie would insist. We all packed into three cars, me leading, and headed back south.

Me, Alfie, Bobby and Reggie arrived first. A few minutes later, there was a knock at the window. I looked up and there was Ronnie with three more of the Firm.

Christine was asleep. The kids, Diane and Joanne, were in the back with her. I woke her up. Ronnie was actually quite nice. Christine had met him before round our Holborn flat. 'Isn't she lovely?' he said, and asked politely if it was alright for him to stay the night.

She looked at me and gave a half smile. I can't remember exactly what I told my wife about what was happening – I must have given her some old chat.

Alfie said, 'I'm off now.' Ronnie said, 'You can't go home, you've got to stay here tonight.' Alfie was angry. He said in front of Christine, Bobby and me, 'Who do they think we are, cunts?'

Christine started trying to get some cushions, sheets and blankets together, but it was ridiculous. There were so many of us, there was no room to move. There'd be about ten or twelve people sleeping on the floor. Alfie, Bobby, Ronnie, Reggie, Scotch Ian (Barrie), Scotch Jack (John Dickson), Nobby Clark ... The last three would spend the next day coming and going somewhere on the Underground. There was more of them in and out – Big Pat Connolly, Fat Wally Garelick, Bobby Buckley, Cornelius 'Connie' Whitehead, Charlie Kray, a little thin fellow called Frosty, a Glaswegian called Richie Anderson.

I think Harry 'Jew Boy' Cope and Sammy Lederman made appearances. It was like a tribal gathering.

Morning came. I was woken by Ronnie putting his head round the door and asking, 'Can Christine make me some tea?' He'd been up with the sparrows. I don't think anyone had actually been asleep. Christine got a kettle going.

The 7am radio news was on. It said that a 38-year-old named George Myers of Camberwell (George Cornell's real name) had been shot in the Blind Beggar. He'd died on the operating table overnight. There was a link to a similar shooting in Catford (I saw the BBC transcript in the National Archives). It was the same at 8am. There was whooping and cheering when they heard.

So, we all got up and had some tea. Bobby was sent out to get the papers. Not much in them, the radio had more; there was a radio report at 6pm that evening actually from the Blind Beggar.

It named the landlord, Patrick Quill, who had heard the shots and came running down from his flat upstairs. His first thought, he told the reporter, was that the man on the floor was drunk and then he saw blood. He rang the nearby hospital and the ambulance arrived within minutes. Then the police took statements from the three customers, he said. No one had seen the killer of course. I saw the transcript in the National Archive: the reporter's name was Jack Pizzey.

Ronnie didn't even seem to notice. Then he announced, 'I want to have a bath.' I told him my wife was back in bed and he'd have to walk through the bedroom to get to the bathroom. I then explained that we had an old-fashioned heater that would take a while to warm up. Ronnie put half a crown in the slot and waited to have his bath. Then he demanded: 'Can't she get up and make us some food? I'm starving!' Realising then that for Ronnie this was just an ordinary night, I asked Christine to make us some cheese sandwiches. And she did, I think she must have thought that would make them go home sooner. Well, they didn't.

Alfie wanted to go home, he asked me to drive him. Ronnie forbade it, but let him go home and come back in a taxi around lunchtime to get clean clothes. Alfie got it from his wife Wendy for doing another disappearing act.

What could he tell her?

Alfie was sent out to get more booze. He'd done that a lot over the last few years, coming back from Madge's way after hours wherever we might be, with crates of the stuff – gin, whisky, beers, tonic, cigarettes. Madge told him one time: 'Where's the money? What does Ronnie think I am, a fucking charity?'

Ronnie and Reggie started arguing so badly that Alfie and I had to dive in between them. Eventually Reggie said, 'Fuck you, I'm going!' and went out with Nobby Clark. It wasn't very long before he came back.

People were coming and going after that. Ronnie came back in after his bath and after Reggie had returned with Nobby, he and Ron started arguing again. It was like we were dreaming.

There was a very tense moment when former boxer Billy Exley got tooled up with a couple of shotguns. Cornell had been on the Richardson Firm, that's why he got done. The Richardson brothers, Charlie and Eddie, the scrap-dealing and fruit-machine merchants from south London who took a perverse pleasure in extreme violence. Wouldn't they hit back where the twins were now, round my house or at Fortress Vallance? Billy and Scotch Pat Connolly were despatched to stand guard over Vallance Road, 'in case the Richardsons come round'.

The *Mirror* had something big on the morning of Saturday, the 12th:

Detectives led by Scotland Yard's ace gang-buster, Detective Chief Superintendent Tom Butler, were last night hunting for a missing key witness in the London pub shooting. The man, who was not named, has vanished from his usual haunts [That was Ronnie]. There are strong reasons for believing that the shootings spring from the activities of 'protection' gangs.

Butler was famous – he'd nicked the Great Train Robbers, back in 1963. A chastened Ronnie said to me: 'We're going to have to stay here for a bit longer.'

We needed more supplies – cups, plates, food, everything. Christine and I were allowed out to the shops in Upper Clapton Road but not without one of the children staying behind as a hostage. Every time we went down the shops with one of the children, we'd see one or two of the police standing outside, pretending they were buying fags.

'They won't come in while the kids are here,' Ronnie said, meaning the police. He said that twenty times at least – he was clever like that.

Ronnie was always very polite to her, but Christine was terrified. And now she knew exactly why they were all camping out at our place: that there'd been a killing. She was scared I was going to be arrested for a murder along with the rest of them.

Then our 11-year-old younger brother, Paul, came round the next morning from our mum's house nearby to see Christine and the kids without knowing what he was walking into. He wasn't going to be allowed to leave.

One night, they even had their old mother, Violet, come over to bring them some clean clothes. Ironed shirts, as always. Otherwise it was Billy Exley running the laundry service. Ronnie told Violet that the police had fitted him up, that someone had done Cornell and the Old Bill were trying to make out it was him. Ronnie sent for his doctor at one point, and he duly came round. It was Morris Blasker.

The strange thing was Ronnie seemed to be in his element, enjoying every minute of it. Occasionally, he and Reggie would start whispering to one another about 'getting a few quid' to this or that officer in Scotland Yard. That was not just myth making to keep grasses in order, it seemed real enough.

During this time, I saw some list Ronnie had drawn up of all the people he wanted to get shot of. He'd just take a pencil and piece of paper from one of my kids' little notebooks. He was constantly revising and changing it. There was a firm in Clerkenwell, the Nashes, someone from that was going to go. Leslie Payne, who used to advise them and ran Long Firms of his own, but who the twins had fallen out with, he was on the list too. There were also people from south London. He'd leave the list around for a day, then tear it up the next morning and start again.

If one of us didn't turn up for a day or two, Ronnie would want to know the reason why. Bobby was acting very subdued, but following his own agenda. He seemed quite relaxed on the surface.

It's obvious now that the local police knew something was going on almost from the beginning. About three days after the shooting, a copper came round and knocked on the door to ask if we, my wife and family, were 'alright'. Ronnie was in the bath while this was going on. When I asked Ronnie what we were going to do, he told me: 'Don't worry about it.' He was so confident, so sure they wouldn't come in if my wife and the children were there. In fact, Smithy – Teddy Smith – came in and told Ronnie to stay in the flat.

Ronnie sat talking in my front room like he was some uncle at a family get-together. There was no panicking because he wasn't scared of anyone, he knew exactly what the police were doing all the time. He wouldn't allow Christine and me and the children all to go out together without one of the children staying behind as a hostage. When anyone other than the police came to the door, and there were lots of comings and goings, none of us was allowed to answer. It was always one of the Firm and we were kept out of sight in the kitchen.

Our daughters, Diane and Joanne, were doing OK because they had no idea of what was going on. The same couldn't be said for their mother who was looking more drawn and terrified by the day. She was not getting any sleep and the fear that something might happen to one of our children was constant. But I thought that, young and in love as we were, if we could just get through this bit, we were going to be alright.

The neighbours were getting cross at the noise and strangers using the toilet on the stairs. Mrs Gillian Pellegrini lived in the flat upstairs. I found her statement made later to Nipper Read's men in the National Archives. She did not know the Lee family (that's the name I'd signed the tenancy agreement as – it was all I could spell) that well but remembered 'David' (me), who was about '24 years old, slim build, light brown hair, pale complexion'.

David Lee's wife, she could not remember her name, was 'slim build, long blonde hair, pale complexion'. They had two small children. There were 'parties' there till early morning, she would tell the police in 1968 when they'd come to check up on my statement.

She remembered 'six men, two of who were extremely fat and greasy-looking'. 'The Lee family stayed a few months then left suddenly.'

A man from the letting agency came round and there was apparently an angry scene with me, Alfie and Bobby. I found his statement too in the National Archives. Mr Ronald Powe of H & H Holdings, his name was. He thought we were 'undesirable characters' and he phoned 999 on three occasions (he did not give his name). He was watching the house. One evening, sometime in March 1966, he saw 'five men leave the flat in an old car', the police arrived and 'an officer went into the flat'.

I remember that moment. One evening, Christine heard a knock at the window and opened the door to find a policeman standing there. Ronnie, Reggie and some of the Firm were all standing out of view in the front room, ready for a shoot-out. Someone had a shotgun – well, there were quite a few guns. It was like something from a film. Ronnie started gesturing at Christine to get rid of the policeman. The policeman told her that they'd heard there'd been a robbery in the area and were just checking up that everyone was safe. 'You alright?' he asked my wife. Christine must have been terrified but answered, 'Yes, I'm alright. Everything's fine.'

The policeman said: 'Well, we've had a report but as long as you're OK, I guess that's it.'

Once the policeman had gone, Christine started to break down. Turning to Ron, I said, 'Look, you just can't stay here anymore.'

So, he left – only to come back two days later, telling me that he 'felt safe here'. 'Ron, Ron, Ron, don't do this to me!' I said, but he wouldn't listen. This went on for about the next ten to twelve days, the Firm constantly coming and going. Occasionally, Ronnie would send someone out to buy toys or treats for the children, trying to make himself look good.

By now, Alfie was allowed to go home at night if he wanted to, going back to his wife and returning during the day. He told Wendy what was going on and he told our parents too some of what was happening. But, as he was to tell the police a lot later: 'I think all my family knew what would happen if anyone started talking.'

Like I said, Bobby seemed calm enough. Like Alfie, he was also being allowed to go out. About the third day of the siege, he told Ronnie mid-morning he was going to Cedra Court to see if our mum was alright. Ronnie looked suspicious but mother love conquered all: he told Bobby to hurry back as Reggie might have to leave later in the day.

So, out goes our Bobby.

Bobby came back from seeing our mum – Cedra Court wasn't that far. As he would one day tell how it happened, when he got back, he tapped on the window and a face peeked out so fast, he couldn't see who it was. Christine – 'who didn't say a word but gave a look of utter helplessness' – let him in.

'The place stank of booze, smoke and sweat,' Bobby would one day say. 'After being out in the fresh air, I wanted to get out again straightaway. But I knew I couldn't. I was back in it, I would have to stay in.

'And there's Ronnie, sitting in one of our chairs: "Hello, Bobby, had a nice little outing, have you? How's your mum?"'

That's what Ronnie would say.

# 16

## STEEPLE BAY

Those last days at Moresby Road were the most chaotic – and the most dangerous too. I said to Ronnie, 'This is the last night. I can't stand any more and my wife can't either.' Ronnie said, 'Listen, Dave. Dead men can't speak, can they?' as he'd said in the flat in Walthamstow. It was like his new catchphrase. I took that as a threat and went to the bedroom.

What was this, a hostage siege or a big piss-up? There'd be trips out to boozers as if we didn't have a care in the world. At first, we went to a dreadful place in Clapton filled with pensioners sipping stout. We called it the 'Dead Pub'.

We'd go to the Harris Lebus furniture factory, a huge place in Broad Lane, Tottenham. The Firm would have their meets at the social club, which had a big bar and a boxing ring (the old boxer Tommy Brown knew the people there and maybe all that furniture made it handy for a sit down). Anyway, the Lebus management got uppity and told Ronnie that was enough. He didn't put up a fight. A note in the National Archives from the security man says Reggie used to come into the sports club with 'a blonde girl aged about 20'.

After that, we started going back to Madge's or the Grave Maurice, where the twins were greeted like long-lost friends: 'Where've you been, Ronnie? There's all sorts of talk about you.' Well, you can imagine how it went.

Then we'd all been in the Dead Pub. The police had come back again and Christine had let them in to look round, so she told us when we got back. I think they'd been getting sightlines for coming in tooled up, making sure my kids weren't in the way of a shoot-out.

Reggie told Ronnie, 'We can't stay here, the Old Bill knows.' How they knew he didn't say, but it was more than just neighbours complaining this time.

'We're going over to Scotch Jack's,' Ronnie announced. He turned to me to say, 'You're coming with us.' He meant just me, not Christine and the kids. Every day for another two weeks, I'd be forced to go over there to this flat at the top half of a house in Clissold Road, Hackney, with a minder from the Firm.

There were more comings and goings. For some reason Eddie Pucci, who was supposed to be Frank Sinatra's bodyguard, turned up at Scotch Jack's. Sinatra was doing a personal appearance at George Raft's Colony Sporting Club in Mayfair at the time. They took Eddie to The Albion pub on the corner of Clissold Road – Frank couldn't make it.

I was with them one time, they wouldn't let me go. Reggie and Ronnie had a heated conversation. There was someone down the West End called 'Harris' who had upset them somehow. Ronnie said to Reggie: 'Do I have to do all the fucking work? I done Cornell, now you do Harris.' They'd hole up there in the day then I'd be allowed back to my place at night with a minder. It went on like this for about a fortnight.

At last the twins and the rest of the Firm finally left – I think they wanted their old mum back, washing their shirts. More important, by then they'd got word that nobody who'd been in the Blind Beggar that night was talking.

The flat was a wreck. I was skint, I just wanted to give my family a break. What could I do? Christine wanted to go to her parents in Birmingham. So did I – I could do some street trading, get some money. But in the end we didn't go, there was somewhere closer we could all stay.

* * *

There was a caravan site in Essex called Steeple Bay. Ronnie and Reggie had a caravan there that they used to take their mother to. At weekends, I would run her down there sometimes with the old man. Charlie later got a caravan with his old woman, Dolly, on the opposite side of the bay. I liked Dolly – she was a nice woman, strict perhaps, but otherwise OK.

Ronnie had said to me one day the year before, it was during the McCowan thing: 'Get a caravan, Dave. I know the fella down there, I know the geezer on the site, he'll get you one.' I'd taken his advice and in summer 1965, I got a caravan at Steeple Bay, a great big brand new one they put right next to Ronnie's parents. It was like a matchbox next to mine. Ronnie and Reggie had come over to admire it. Reggie said: 'Look at that, Ronnie! We've got another caravan. Isn't it great?'

So of course, it wasn't my caravan. It was in my name and I had to pay for it, but it was their caravan, the twins' possession, just like everything else. But at least it was somewhere to go. It might have seemed crazy looking back, but after the time in Moresby Road, a caravan holiday with the Krays looked like a welcome break. One day, I'd tell the police how it happened. I found a copy in the National Archives after fifty years. This is what I had said:

> Reggie said I better go down to the caravan with my wife and children. He gave me £40 to go with. Someone took us down. I came backwards and forwards with various minders. I think little Frosty [see p. 174] took me down. I went in a van which Reggie arranged. My wife and children stayed for a fortnight. Then the minders started to ease off on me, but I was left in no doubt that if ever I said anything to anyone, I would be for it.

We used to go to the clubhouse and have a drink, while Christine would sit and chat with Mrs Kray. I remember Charlie coming round one night. It was pretty late and then Reggie and Ronnie turned up too. I thought, *Oh, no*, because we were all tired, but got up and got them a drink.

We couldn't stay in the caravan forever. 'Don't go back to your flat,' Ronnie and Reggie warned. Well, I had to one last time. I packed up our clothes at Moresby Road, switched off the lights and just left. The furniture had come with the flat or was on HP. I took some bits of it, I didn't pay the rent.

The car, the Ford Popular I'd driven Reggie to Walthamstow in, I left in north London somewhere and walked away – it's what people did all the time, doing a moonlight flit. We moved into my brother Alfie's at 30 Millman Street, Holborn. I got back to work as a street trader.

\* \* \*

So, Ronnie was still moving around: Scotch Jack's place and Steeple Bay. Nobody was saying anything about Cornell. The local 'Divisional' cops didn't have a clue. The barmaid of the Blind Beggar had said out loud that Ronnie had done Cornell apparently but was too scared to tell the police. There'd been others in the pub, all too terrified to say anything. The man who fired the shots into the ceiling was a mystery. His description featured a burn mark on the right side of his neck. I knew who that was, it was Scotch Ian Barrie.

Olive Cornell, George's widow, would tell anyone who'd listen the twins had done her husband. She even went round Vallance Road a couple of times to shout it out loud outside Number 178. She told Violet her sons were 'puffs' (that's what it says in her statement in the National Archives). Billy Exley got an earful from her when he was on guard duty there.

Ronnie found a new gaff, a bungalow in Loxham Road, E4, behind Walthamstow Greyhound Stadium. It was more like Chingford. He moved in with Scotch Ian Barrie. The place was owned by Charlie Clark, who was the manager at the Stow Club – a spieler, which had become a Kray regular. His wife had twelve cats.

Charlie had several more properties: a bigger house nearby, 24 Marlborough Road, and a flat above a hairdresser's in the Lea Bridge Road called Adams Barbers. All handy for ducking and diving around. My brother Bobby went to at least two of Charlie's places on his adventures, so I would one day find out. He would describe one in a statement to the police that I saw in the National Archives. There were 'lots of cats', he said and there was 'a fish-pond in the garden'.

Charlie told police that he was a bookmaker's clerk but he's most often described as a 'cat-burglar' – he must have been getting a bit old for shinning up drainpipes by now. Much later, Charlie Kray would write that Clark had to pack it in after a fall.

I saw a statement made by Charlie Clark in the National Archives, dated June 1968. He made up a lot of things, lied outright about more but it was very interesting to me, nevertheless. He'd fitted Ronnie up with a room 'free of charge' in late 1965, he said, and he'd lived there with him and his wife 'as one of the family' for a few months. Ronnie's friend Teddy Smith had stayed there too, he said.

In their time together, Ronnie once confided in Smithy: 'The tragedy of his life was that he was the twin who was born the wrong way round sexually. He cried inside to himself every day.'

Charlie had been in the Chequers, Walthamstow, on the night Cornell was shot, he said. After it closed, Ronnie came back to his house with him and he 'was there the morning when I read about it in the paper, I'm pretty sure'. According to him, the siege of Moresby Road had never happened, and that is what would be repeated by Kray chroniclers until our own first book appeared.

Ronnie stayed there for three months after that, Charlie said. Lots of the Firm had been around, but also, as he told the police, actors George Raft, Judy Garland, Diana Dors, Barbara Windsor and Frank Sinatra junior had apparently been in and out of his feline-filled house in Chingford.

They never came round my place.

\* \* \*

So, nobody was talking about who done Cornell. Ronnie was getting his confidence back: 'I'm the Governor round here,' he'd suddenly shout in that squeaky voice. 'I'm the Colonel and whatever I say, goes! Fuck everyone, the police, the government!' He couldn't give a monkey's about any form of authority, except occasionally perhaps his mum.

It was as if he knew the Yard weren't going to come after him, like he was being told something. That he was safe from arrest. The twins always put it out that they had police on the payroll. I'd seen it myself from the 66 Club days, it was their way of keeping any grassing buttoned up. But they did have an intelligence service as good if not better than the honest cops. I'd seen that happening, it went to the top.

By now, Reggie's renting a third-floor flat off a Jewish bird, Ana Kerin, who worked at the Le Monde Club in the King's Road. She didn't need the flat right then because she was in prison. I don't know why. It was in a new block of flats, Flat 6 Manor Lea, 295 Green Lanes.

He got it fitted out with contemporary furniture from the Harrison Gibson store in Ilford. Alfie went there to order it – it cost £100 on account. Frances Shea had lived there very briefly before she ran for cover. By now, my brother Bobby had split with his wife Pat (Reggie paid for the lawyer) and seemed very well in with Reggie.

For a time, Bobby took up residence in Reggie's new flat. As far as Alfie and I knew there was nothing funny about it. Reggie got a new girlfriend, a 21-year-old croupier called Christine Boyce. There were birds going in day and night – a non-stop party, four in a bed sometimes. The Firm were over there all the time, of course, and so was Ronnie. Then the twins got jumpy again – they couldn't stay in the same place for long.

I didn't know much about it at the time but that April 1966, Ronnie went to Saffron Walden in Essex, to see Geoffrey Allen the insurance fraudster, his old friend who'd got him out of trouble plenty of times before. He had a big old house called Hempstead Hall and seemed very wealthy. After that, they stayed at some hotel which Allen had booked them into, the Saffron. It was supposed to be some kind of holiday. The manager recognised the two of them as the Kray twins from newspaper photos (the Hideaway, presumably). After two nights, they were kicked out for general mayhem and went to another hotel in Cambridge, the Garden House – I've seen the file on it in the archives.

Albert Donoghue, the Dublin-born Kray enforcer, was there, Scotch Ian Barrie and Scotch Jack Dickson. They all scrawled false names in the register. Local coppers took an interest – they thought they were professional bouncers. Bobby went along too for whatever reason. I saw his name, R. Teale of 4 Millman St Holborn, recorded by the police in the file on the Cornell investigation, fifty years later in the National Archives.

Then the twins moved to a flat on the Lea Bridge Road, Number 471, one of Charlie Clark's various hideaways. It was above a hairdresser's. Scotch Ian moved in, so did Bobby – apparently for a few days at least before doing a runner. That's what I knew at the time anyway. I'd find out much more of what was really going on a lot, lot later.

# 17

## THE MAD AXEMAN

That spring of 1966 was the start of what would come to be known as 'The Mad Axeman' affair. Way back, Ronnie had met this Frankie Mitchell in Wandsworth Prison. He promised to help him after he came out. But it looked like Frankie, who was now in Dartmoor, was never coming out. He had a form sheet as long as your arm, had been in Broadmoor special hospital, escaped and got life for attacking someone with a hatchet. He kept budgies in his Dartmoor cell apparently.

Even banged up, Frankie was the newspapers' number one celebrity bogeyman, while his sufferings were an affront to the criminal fraternity. By now he'd calmed down a bit and was allowed on outside working parties. The twins used to send him little treats, like a woman to have sex with in the back of a van.

Ronnie wanted Alfie to go down to Dartmoor and sort of bump into Frankie Mitchell on an outside working party. Two of the Firm, Tommy Cowley and Fat Wally Garelick, a mini-cab driver, had already been down to see Mitchell a bit before he did. Alfie couldn't quite believe what he was hearing.

'You want me to plan Frank Mitchell's escape?' he asked Ron.

'Well, yes. If we don't get him a date for a release, then you'll be the one to go down and get him out and fetch him back to London,' Ronnie told Alfie.

So, it's down to Alfie to go and see Frankie Mitchell and tell him what the twins have in mind. He would go there with Wally Garelick in his big Rover 3 Litre and they were to leave that same night.

They were pulled by a police patrol on the way, but got to see Frankie Mitchell alright. They marched right in and Alfie signed the visitors' book as Mr Walker.

'Tell the twins that once you get me out of here, I can get a machine gun and kill anyone they want,' Frank told Alfie. 'When you leave here, I want you to stop at the phone box you passed on the way here and wait there for me. I want you to take me to London now!'

That wasn't Ronnie's plan – Alfie had to leg it out of there.

About three months after the Cornell shooting, Ronnie was still lying ever so slightly low, no street parties or charity stunts, but he could still show who was boss in the West End. And it was his way of showing he was untouchable by the coppers.

One night, we were down the Astor Club at about two or three one morning when Ronnie asked if I was going home and would I give him a lift. Tired and half-pissed myself, I said I would (I had begun to realise how dangerous it was to drive after so much to drink). So, I started saying to Ron: 'This looks bad, Ron. If we get pulled, I'm going to be done. I'm getting a taxi.'

'Don't worry about it,' he answered. 'You drive, boy. I'll look after you.'

By some miracle we managed to get to Vallance Road without being stopped. I was a lot less drunk by now. Ron said, 'You might as well stay here. You were all over the place driving back here, you'll get nicked if you don't.'

I didn't want to stay but had to agree that Ron was right. I told him I was going to kip on the couch but he insisted I sleep upstairs in his bed to avoid disturbing his parents, Violet and Charlie, who were sleeping downstairs, next to the kitchen. The toilet was out in the backyard, so you had to make sure you used it before you went to bed or you'd wake everyone else in the house.

Ron told me to go into his room and I asked him again where he was going to sleep. He kept telling me, 'Don't worry, you just get into bed. I'll just get in with you.'

Of course, I knew Ronnie was that way. He once told me he had liked women when he was younger, but that one experience had put him off. He'd taken a young woman back to Vallance Road with him one night. After having sex, he'd fallen asleep, only to wake the next morning and find himself, the woman and the bed all covered in her menstrual blood. He'd gone over to the bath-house six times that day to wash himself. He said he couldn't even speak to his mother for days.

That was in my mind. So, I said, 'Ron, no funny business. I'm not like that, Ron. I don't want any of that.'

'No, I know you're not. I promise I won't touch you, it will all be OK,' he insisted. I thought he would keep his word.

So, I crept downstairs to use the toilet, then went back up to Ron's bedroom and climbed into his very small bed on the side next to the window. I put my head down on the pillow and went spark out.

All of a sudden, I woke to find Ronnie playing with me, sucking my cock. I couldn't believe it, I thought I must be dreaming. But there he was, crouched over me – more and more insistent, wrestling with me in the bed and using his weight to force me down, telling me, 'Just try it.' I kept saying, 'No, no, Ron, get off me!', struggling against him for all I was worth and shouting for Violet and Charlie to come and help. No one came. Ron kept telling me, 'Shut up, me mother's downstairs!' In the meantime, he seemed to be becoming stronger than ever.

I knew he fancied me, but I never dreamt he would do something like this. He held me down and forced my legs apart. At one point he put his arm round my neck in an attempt to strangle me. In the end, he overpowered me.

To my lasting shame, Ronnie Kray raped me.

After it was all over, I sat on the bottom of the bed all night, shaking with cold and shock, while Ron slept, oblivious to everything, in a drunken stupor.

I managed to get away and ran down to the toilet to throw up. I felt sick and ill, and just wanted to be out of there. Ronnie woke up and came after me, whispering: 'Be quiet, be quiet!' I went back up to bed, but was awake all night after this.

About six in the morning, I had to go downstairs to use the toilet. Ron stirred then and told me: 'Don't say nothing' (to his mum and dad). They must have heard, I'm sure of it. I was screaming and shouting loud enough to wake the dead. I then threatened not just to wake his mother, but also to tell her what he'd just done. By now the morning sun was streaming in.

'You open your mouth one word about this and you know what to expect. You won't have a family anymore,' he told me.

We went downstairs like nothing had happened, with Mrs Kray fussing round with the tea and toast. I didn't have anything, just some tea. Ronnie was blustering, but I could see in his face that he might be remorseful, embarrassed even. He looked like he was thinking, *What the hell did I do that for?*

Inside, I was so angry, I wanted to kill Ron then and there. I'd never felt like this about anybody. I knew I couldn't fight him as he was physically much larger than me, but I felt I had to get my revenge somehow. Forgetting all my fear of him, I told him I was going to go straight to the police and 'get him nicked for this'. Even though that was ridiculous, Ron looked worried and started insisting that he'd been drunk.

'Ron, you weren't that drunk,' I told him. 'You knew exactly what you were doing. I'm going to tell your mother and make sure everyone, all the chaps and all the villains, get to hear about this.'

'Don't you ever say a fucking word!'

If I ever said anything, I was dead, he told me. And my wife and kids.

'I will know, you see,' he warned.

He phoned Smithy – Teddy Smith – and told him to come over straightaway. Violet brought us another cup of tea. Ronnie and Smithy led me to the bath-house across the road. I heard Smithy whispering, 'No, no, Ron! No!'

Coming home to Christine the morning after was terrible. All I really wanted to do was run and hide. And I did. I got to my car and drove, shaking, back to where we were living in Millman Street. I felt so ashamed as Chrissie asked me, 'Where've you been all night?' when I got home.

I couldn't tell her, I just couldn't. Nor could I touch her sexually for months after that. All my confidence as a man had gone completely, destroyed by Ronnie in that brutal attack.

If only I had been able to talk to Christine about it I am sure it would have helped her as well as me. But I couldn't do it, I was too ashamed. Afterwards I avoided Ronnie completely. I didn't see him or any of the Firm until inside a court room two years later.

And I didn't say a word for a very long time. I didn't tell my brothers, nor my wife. I felt too frightened, too humiliated. I told Nipper Read some of it when he took my statement in Tintagel House in January 1969 on the brink of the big Kray trial – but he seemed keen to keep it under wraps, unless they really needed it. They didn't. The first time I ever spoke about it properly was when I told Alfie more than forty years after it happened.

\* \* \*

And still, no one would talk about George Cornell. My family and me certainly were not about to. But, according to a file I found in the National Archives (it's only a few pages long), around this time the law thought they might have discovered a breakthrough.

There was a conference on 29 July between Superintendent James Axon of H Division (Whitechapel), Tommy Butler, Ernie 'Hooter' Millen and Mr David Hopkin from the office of the Director of Public Prosecutions. It was decided that there was enough evidence 'to put Ronald Kray on an identity parade', if not enough for outright arrest on a charge of murder.

Hopkin at least thought they might get enough witnesses to say what they saw that night in the Blind Beggar. The police were reluctant – an 'unsuccessful prosecution of Kray would only inflate him in the eyes of the underworld', that's what the top policemen thought.

'But other matters are in the melting pot which may come to a successful conclusion,' said Mr Butler. What did he mean by that? He was sure all along that Scotch Ian Barrie was the second gunman, but nobody knew where the suspects actually were. Then somebody told him ...

Their hiding place had been put 'under observation', the file revealed, Superintendent Butler 'having learned that was where Ronnie Kray was living'. 'Information was later received,' one document said, that the 'Kray brothers intended holding a drinking party there'.

What happened next was in the papers: 'Yard Swoop on Party in Big Gunmen Hunt' said the *Mirror*'s front page on Friday, 5 August 1966.

'The Kray twins were having a party at their flat when Scotland Yard's Flying Squad called early on Thursday asking if they could help with their inquiries,' it said. The 'raids were organised by Chief Detective Superintendent Tom Butler'.

It was the first time that anyone knew that the 'Yard's Ace Gangbuster', as he was called in the story, was back on the case. As I heard it, the coppers hit the place early in the morning of 4 August 1966. They went in at 1.50am, well tooled up. This is what I found in the National Archives. Detective Inspector Michael Hyans was duty Flying Squad officer at New Scotland Yard that night. Two years later, he would give a statement:

I received information as a result of which pistols and ammunition were drawn and I went to an address at 471 Lea Bridge

Road. I ordered other officers to surround the premises. After knocking at the door, it was opened by a man named Smith who immediately started to struggle with us.

Smith was arrested and I entered the flat with other officers. Reginald and Ronald Kray were both undressed. I saw [Scotch Ian] John Barrie, Thomas Cowley and a young fair-haired youth who was on leave from an Approved Nautical School.

Ronnie was taken to the Yard to be interviewed 'briefly' by Butler, then along with Scotch Ian early the next morning, he was taken back east to Commercial Street Police Station. Reggie was taken to Leyton nick with the others. There was an outstanding warrant for that old friend of the Yard, Edward (Teddy) Richard Smith, 'writer' of no fixed abode, for inflicting actual bodily harm. He was whisked off to West End Central with an order to pay a £20 fine or do three months in prison.

The 'fair-haired youth' – his name was Patrick Saman – was released.

Next morning, the identity parade was a farce. Ronnie refused to remove his horn-rimmed spectacles. It was all a big joke, they had briefs scuttling everywhere. The Blind Beggar barmaid failed to show altogether and the two witnesses who did turn up would not say anything except 'maybe' and 'I'm not sure'. One 'witness' (it was a set-up) identified a bloke dragged off the street to make up the numbers. The fact that the parade had taken place was in the evening papers.

Ronnie and Scotch Ian got out the next morning, Friday, 5 August 1966. Fleet Street was tipped off. Reporters and a snapper got down the Lea Bridge Road pretty quick for another police screw-up victory celebration.[27] *Mirror* journalist Brian McConnell recorded what happened in a book rushed out after the big Kray trial called *The Evil Firm*, published in 1969:

> A minder on the door pointed up the stairs and said, 'The Colonel's up there, he'll see you now.' Upstairs was Ronnie, not smartly turned out as usual, but dishevelled and wearing a grubby white shirt tucked into slacks, looking as if all the laundries were closed. To those surprised at his appearance, he said that was what he was wearing when he went to Commercial Street police station and he had not had a chance since to bathe or change.

Reggie arrived a bit later. There was a change of clothes and the snapper got a big, low-angle pic of the twins in suits, ties and pleated trousers, buttoned pockets held up by braces and a woodland scene wallpaper in the background. The next day, it was on the front page of the *Mirror* – it's been used over and over again in Kray accounts.

'The first we knew about [Cornell's] death was when we read about it in the newspapers,' Ronnie told reporters. 'Mr Butler came to see me – I don't know what they wanted to charge me with. It may have been murder, they didn't tell me. They looked after me alright. I had sausages and mash and another time, beans and chips and there was tea when I wanted it.'

---

[27] The press call was typical Ronnie 'cunning' according to the twins' cousin Ronnie Hart, who would explain it one day to Superintendent Harry Mooney. 'If they were rearrested at any time, Ronnie could plead that any witness who identified him as the man wanted for murder could be said to be doing so because he had seen his picture in the paper,' he said.

The *Mirror* reported:

Before he left the police station, brother Reginald saw the Flying Squad boss, Chief Detective Superintendent Tommy Butler. 'Mr. Butler told me that me and my brother were being released along with the other people because he was satisfied that we had nothing to do with the shooting in the Blind Beggar,' Ronnie told reporters.

'Our Mum's getting distinctly worried about all this,' he said. 'And today's her birthday. So, we're going to have a little drink and cheer her up.'

How very nice. But nobody's laughing when they're in private. As soon as the press is out the door, they're angry as fuck. How did the Old Bill know when and where to turn them over? Who's the bleeding grass?

I saw what Ronnie Hart, the Krays' cousin, had had to say about what went on in the National Archives. There was a man called Tony Dove, who ran the Cubana Club in Ilford. He was moaning to Hart about paying 60 per cent of the take on Kray-installed fruit machines. Hart gave him Ronnie's number at Lea Bridge, LEY[tonstone] 3778, to tell him about it himself and was there in the flat when Tony Dove rang. Ronnie flew into a rage, shouting, 'Who gave you this fucking number?' and slammed down the phone.

'It was decided that Dove would have to go because he'd tip off the police,' Ronnie Hart would one day explain. That was actually before the big raid. After the Flying Squad knocked on the door, it was decided the complaining club owner would 'definitely have to go'. But Tony Dove remained unmolested. The tip-off as to where to find the twins had come, as I would discover, from much closer to home than Ilford.

Anyway, the next thing I know at the time is that Ronnie Hart and a Kray hanger-on called Frosty have turned up at Steeple Bay, looking for my brother Bobby for some reason. It wasn't to invite him round for a drink. Christine was there with the kids.

She told me later that they'd come down on the Sunday night after that 'raid' that was in the papers and searched all over the caravan – in the cupboards and under the trailer – and wanted to know when she last saw Bobby. They were not exactly polite about it (she told me that she thought they were going to beat her up). She told them she had not seen him for a few days. They were searching late into the darkness, calling, 'Bobby! Bobby!' Then they left.

What the fuck had Bobby done?

So, we know, as the whole world knows by now, that once again the twins had got away with it. Of course they had, they really were untouchable.

Ronnie had got himself into a new bit of bother meanwhile. There were rumours at the time, but I'd only find out what was really going on when I visited the National Archives five decades later and read the file on it.

It's complicated. Holed up in Charlie Clark's place, Ronnie could not resist going on little outings, just like it had been at Moresby Road. There was a pub – the Bakers Arms, off Mare Street in Hackney. The landlord was called Eric Marshall. The Firm started using it for meets. On 25 July, the landlord told the local nick about his new customers. He knew exactly who they were. A certain Detective Sergeant Leonard Townsend out of Hackney nick picked up on it, but rather than tell the Yard, seemingly saw a little money-making possibility.

Ten days later, the raid on Lea Bridge Road went down. After the ID parade fiasco, they were all arrest-proof. Ronnie, Scotch Ian, Smithy (he'd paid the fine at West End Central and been released) and Harry Jew Boy Cope went back to the Bakers Arms. Two plain-clothes police arrived (DS Leonard Townsend and DC Peter Barker), all a bit obvious.

Ronnie and the Firm left for another pub, the Kenton Arms, but Harry Cope stayed behind long enough to be told by one of the coppers: 'You can drink here as long as you "play ball".' They suggested a meet with Ronnie on the evening of the 11th, two days' time.

This is how it seemed to go. When Ronnie heard all this from Harry Cope, he got very animated. No surprise there. The Colonel having to pay coppers to drink where he liked. Ronnie arranged for a private detective to go to the pub and tape any conversation he would have with this cheeky bastard.

George Devlin, the private inquiry agent who'd been so useful in digging up dirt on McCowan in the Hideaway trial, would do the business. Devlin worked very fast. They met at lunchtime outside the Stamford Hill Odeon – Billy Exley did the driving in his minivan. They went to Charlie Clark's place in Chingford, I know that.

Devlin had got a Mini-fon tape recorder from a Tottenham Court Road radio shop and fitted it up in a shoulder holster with a tie-pin mike.

*Very* MI5.

Smithy tried it out a few times, he loved this kind of thing. Devlin also that afternoon had put a hidden mike in Eric Marshall's office at the back of the pub – the landlord had chosen to stay in with the Krays.

So, wired-up Ronnie in a big overcoat (it was a summer's night, but no matter) went into the Bakers Arms, Northiam Street, accompanied by his fan club for a little chat with whoever it might be. Devlin is lurking incognito with a female assistant, a Miss Langland. One of the coppers beckons Ronnie over. They go to the landlord's office for a talk. The tape is running.

So, the coppers left and so did Ronnie and company. The intrepid Miss Langland collected the tapes. They all went to the Kenton Arms for a celebration drink and then to the Krays' favourite solicitor, Jacob Sampson's house in Finchley, to put the tapes in his safe. The transcript from the landlord's office is in the National Archives. Townsend supposedly began the conversation:

'You can use this pub. It's on my manor.'
'What is this? Well Street?'
'It's Hackney. All we're asking is a little bit of rent.'
'Yes, how much?'
'Well, there are two of us. A pony a week each ...'
'A pony a week? Well, I'll have to discuss it with my brother. Because everything I do I do it with him, you know ...'

So, what Sergeant Townsend seems to be saying is that Ronnie could continue to drink there without anyone troubling him, but it was going to cost him fifty quid a week, to be handed over to Mr Marshall in an envelope full of readies. Ronnie's brief Jacob Sampson made a formal complaint the next day to a DCI Fletcher at the Yard.

It must have all been a bit of a surprise: Ronnie Kray, exposer of supposed police corruption. And the voices on the tapes really seemed to be those of Ronald Kray and DS Leonard Townsend.

Three days later, the copper did take a sealed envelope with £50 in it off the landlord – it was an attempted Ronnie sting.

Townsend had been put under surveillance by Ronnie's new friends in the police, whoever they might have been. Quite a step that. Townsend made a run for it, throwing the packet into the road. He was caught, but not with any evidence on him. Later, he explained that he thought the envelope contained information about a crime about to be committed.

On the 19th, Smithy told the police what happened on the nights of 9 and 11 August. His statement was taken down by a DS Leslie Emment – I saw it in the National Archives. He was not a local copper. Scotch Ian Barrie made an identical statement to the same DS four days after that.

\* \* \*

So, there's Ronnie supposedly cleaning up police corruption, but when a summons arrived, ordering him to attend Old Street Magistrates as a prosecution witness, it didn't seem such a good idea anymore.

Ronnie had changed his mind, as did Scotch Ian and Smithy, who promptly went to the solicitors to say they were not going to give evidence either. Ronnie actually went into hiding in a flat in Finchley and some other places, like Earl's Court, apparently – he'd be there for months. I'd only find out about this a lot later. By which time it didn't really matter to me and my brothers what Ronnie Kray was up to.

I didn't know anything of this 'bent copper' hanky-panky in Hackney. It happened that just as Ronnie and Smithy were getting ready to go scampering round with tape recorders, the three of us – Alfie, Bobby and me – were all in the Rugby pub in Holborn one night.

It was 8 August 1966. We were discussing a stall we wanted to buy in Chapel Street Market, Islington. The man who owned it wanted £900 and we were trying to see how we could come up with the money. We were just deciding it was too much when Bobby said he knew a wealthy man called 'Wallace' who lived in Dolphin Square, who might be able to help. He'd met him a few weeks before and there'd been some row, now resolved, over a sports car Bobby said this geezer had let him borrow.

So, Bobby phoned up Wallace from the pub call box: 'Yes, I'd love to meet your brothers. Why don't you come over and we'll meet for a drink?' he said. That's how it went. So, we all went down the West End, taking in a few pubs with this geezer. In his late forties, he was clearly homosexual. Afterwards, we went back to his flat in Dolphin Square on the Thames Embankment.

We went up in a lift. There was a long corridor leading to his flat, I remember that. It was small and neat, decorated in a fashionable, expensive style. Bobby's idea was that there was going to be a party, that other people were going to turn up and join us and have a drink. But, it never happened like that – there's just this Wallace geezer.

'Working-class people like you are the salt of the earth,' he said (or that sort of thing.)

'What's your name?' I asked. Or maybe it was Alfie who asked him.

'Call me Wallace,' he said.

'What Wallace? Wallace what?'

'Just Wallace will do', he said.

We were all quite drunk by this stage of the evening and when we told him about the stall we wanted, he said, 'I might be able to help.'

Bobby offered to write him a receipt for the £900, confirming that we would repay it within a month. By now it was one in the morning, so Wallace asked if we'd like to stay the night. Alfie slept on the small sofa while I slept on the floor. Wallace went to his room.

Well, about seven thirty the next morning, the 9th, the doorbell goes. I can't remember who opened the door, but it wasn't Wallace – he wasn't even in the flat. In marched six plainclothes policemen, with Wallace coming up behind them.

Wallace was blustering and claiming that he'd left in the middle of the night via the rubbish chute because we'd been 'holding him hostage'. We had woken with raging hangovers, so Alfie volunteered to make tea for us all. It was funny really, at the time, the coppers drinking tea and Wallace going on about how we'd demanded money from him. What a load of nonsense! It was a joke.

The police didn't think it was funny – they said they were going to take us to Rochester Row Police Station. Alfie kept saying, 'I can't believe this.' Bobby seemed less indignant. Looking back, you might think he was expecting something like this to happen.

We were separated and put into three different cells, then brought in, one by one, to be interviewed. Subsequently, we were charged with 'demanding money with menaces', booked by a police sergeant called Maidment ready to be carted off to Bow Street Magistrates' Court the next day.

Detective Sergeant Maidment was in charge of our committal. After a few hours, the police asked us who they should contact for us, who were our next of kin? So, they got in touch with Christine and Wendy. I don't know what Bobby did about that. He didn't seem as bothered as Alfie and I, he seemed to think it was all a big police balls-up and we'd be released at any moment. Christine came up that night. She was frantic. I couldn't tell her what the charge was because I didn't understand it and still don't to this day – I didn't know what 'demanding money with menaces' meant. It was all a load of cobblers, I told the police.

All three of us were put up at Bow Street and charged. We were remanded in custody and sent to Brixton Prison. It was 10 August 1966. HMP Brixton was so crowded at that time that there were people sleeping in the corridors, even in the chapel. We were going to be there for the next eight weeks.

We were then told we were being provided with a legal aid solicitor, only one between the three of us. The solicitor claimed as we were all on the same charge, we only needed one legal representative. Alfie got cross, but at the time he was so convinced the charge was going to be dismissed that he just let it go without insisting on a separate brief for each of us.

At the end of the eight weeks, our brief arrived in Brixton to tell us that our trial had been set for Court Number One at the Old Bailey. What was that about? Court Number One was usually reserved for the worst criminals, the gravest crimes.

We were there so that we would be found guilty. That was clear as soon as His Honour Alan King-Hamilton[28] took his place on the bench and looked us up and down. Mr John Leonard led for the prosecution – we'd be meeting him again one day.

On the first day, the judge announced: 'Before we begin today, a very serious allegation has been made to me in my chambers by a reliable source that one or two members of the jury have been

---

[28] Described as 'one of Britain's toughest judges', he was famed for his hatred of homosexuality.

approached. Now, in cases of blackmail, people do get approached. I am going to ask you one at a time to stand up and to tell me if you have been approached.'

One by one, the jurors denied having been threatened so the judge then instructed them to 'wipe this from your minds and continue with the trial'. We had been branded as jury nobblers, real villains. What the judge should have done after making such an allegation was to dismiss the jury and start again. There should have been a retrial on those grounds alone. But there wasn't – we were already guilty. I called our brief over to complain, but all he said was: 'Don't do anything yet.' Back in Brixton, we arrived to a stone-cold dinner.

The next day, the geezer I knew as 'Wallace' was put in the witness box and referred to as 'Mr X'. He was asked whether we had demanded money with menaces. 'No,' he replied. The prosecution then asked whether we had tried to blackmail him. Again, he said: 'No.' When asked why he had made the accusation against us, he finally answered: 'I was frightened.'

It would be enough to put us away.

We were sent back to Brixton each night during the trial in a prison van with little cubicles. You couldn't talk. Anyway, Bobby was very quiet, keeping himself to himself all the time.

Three coppers gave evidence, how Mr X had come to get them at the nick in the middle of the night. How a cheque had been produced for £900 drawn on the account of Mr X at the National Mercantile Bank. I'd never heard of it, I'd never seen it. All I remember is this cheque being waved around at the trial. There you are – hard evidence. Otherwise it was all just the word of Mr X.

Two weeks later, we came to the judge's summing-up. It was relentless. Our defence offered nothing by way of explanation or excuse. Wendy and Christine were in the gallery. The jury returned with the verdict of guilty: 'I am sending you to prison for three years,' he said. 'Take them down.' There were gasps from the gallery at the severity of the sentence. Christine hid her head in her hands. Wendy stood up, open-mouthed as if she simply couldn't believe it.

The screws said: 'You two, David and Bobby Teale, in this cell. Alfie Teale in the other.' We gripped one another's shoulders and sang 'You'll Never Walk Alone'. The screws actually clapped. It was the last Alfie would see of me and Bobby for two years. He told me later, he went back into the cell and cried his eyes out.

On the way to the Scrubs, I remember looking out of the prison van through the tiny windows, knowing the route through Holborn and recognising the streets I'd grown up on. The van stopped at some lights. I looked up and could just see the flat my mum and dad had moved into two weeks before. How was my wife going to live, what about the kids? I was the money-getter. Who was going to put food on the table, get clothes, pay the rent?

We got to the Scrubs about seven at night and were told to take off our clothes, put our belongings into boxes and put on the prison suits. It was very busy, with everyone jostling and being sent off in different directions. I remember looking at Bobby as if to say, 'This is awful.' He looked back at me as if to agree.

The next day, we saw the Governor, who allocated us jobs and gave us a release date: two years' time, calculated on the length of time we'd been held in remand and on condition that we behaved ourselves. Christine would be allowed to visit, briefly.

When she did, it was like we were discussing a death in the family. Her face was stricken white and I didn't know what to say to try and make it better. She looked so sad I could hardly bear it. I couldn't explain because I didn't understand it myself. Nor could I explain it to anyone else on the inside.

'So, what you done?' I'd be asked on the landings.

'I've been fitted up, I was verballed,' I told them.

Who was the jury going to believe? Those police witnesses, nice, respectable Mr X, or a young scallywag like me?

About a month into our sentence, Bobby and me were told we were being transferred to Maidstone Prison. I didn't know it quite yet but Alfie would be going to Lewes Prison. It was the same routine when Bobby and me got to Maidstone, kind of like Russian dolls, one nick inside of another. Our building was called 'Thanet'. This block is for the high-security prisoners or the nutters – and that's where they put me.

There was a red security light on in the ceiling twenty-four hours a day so they could keep a watch on me. When I asked them to turn it off, the screw told us it was high security and asked how long I was sentenced to.

'A lagging, got carpet for three years,' I replied.

The officer seemed puzzled: 'I don't know what you're doing in here then. This is for lifers ...'

Christine used to come up and visit me. It was never easy. I'd ask my friends to write letters to her for me. Around this time she gave birth to our third daughter, also called Christine. Some of the prisoners made some hooch in the toilets so I could celebrate.

And where were the Krays? While we were having our little adventure with Mr X, the word was they'd flown off to Tangier in Morocco to live it up in the sun with the old villain, Billy Hill, and his wife Gipsy. They'd got out of the country in a private plane on 13 September 1966. Ronnie would have plenty of boys to entertain him there.

Scotch Ian went with them. God knows what he made of it. After a while, the Moroccan authorities threw them out for being 'undesirable aliens'. They flew back under their own names on a regular airline flight apparently. Maybe they knew the coppers wouldn't come after them. Maybe someone in the Yard tipped them off.

That winter and spring, I was getting loads of messages from the twins – notes and little parcels, cigarettes, Scotch, lots of things. Then I started getting more direct messages from Ronnie. I was approached in prison by a geezer, a messenger from the twins apparently. He warned me the Old Bill were snooping about and that if they came to me, I was not to say a word about the twins. My wife and kids were on the outside, don't forget, and I'd be doing myself a favour to keep schtum.

I had at least five heavy messages sent in from Ronnie warning me not to say anything. He particularly didn't want me talking about any of the personal stuff. I knew what he meant. And that was not the end of it.

I used to get called into the Governor's office: 'You've had some people try to visit you, Teale, but I'm afraid under the Home Office rules we can't allow it.'

'Why, sir, who was it?'

'[Dickie] Morgan, Smith and [Connie] Whitehead. All of them have form.'

'Never heard of them,' I said. I was lying of course,

I knew, without seeing them, exactly why they had come: to tell me if anyone asked about Ronnie or Reggie to tell them I didn't know anything.

We'd all of us pick up rumours on the prison grapevine about what was going on outside. That Reggie's wife, Frances, had attempted to gas herself in the kitchen oven at her parents' house a week or so after our arrest. Her father found her just in time.

We also heard that when Reggie and Ronnie had been thrown out of Morocco and flown back to London, they got through Heathrow like any old tourists and the Yard had shown no interest. Then Ronnie had gone to ground again in north London somewhere. Wherever he might have been hiding, Ronnie was getting messages out. Apparently, he'd been mixed up in something to do with a corrupt copper. Teddy Smith had been involved, but then Smithy was always involved.

There'd been an inquest on George Cornell in November. The result was a verdict of 'murder by person or persons unknown'. So that was that. The Coroner, the Old Bill, the Department of Public Prosecutions, the newspapers, everyone had given up – or so it seemed.

# 18

# RUMOURS, STORIES AND HAPPENINGS

A couple of months into our sentence, Bobby started acting very oddly. Every evening, around six, the prisoners were allowed a period of association where they could go into one another's cells, watch television or play pool or cards in the association room. So, each night I'd go to Bobby's cell, only to have him kick the door closed and tell me he wasn't in the mood to chat. I didn't know why, but I do now.

Instead, he would often sit practising his guitar without saying a word. When I asked him, 'What's the matter, aren't you coming out?' he'd just make some excuse or say he 'didn't feel like it'. I'd go down to the association room and the others would ask me about him, unable to believe that he was my brother: 'Have you had a row?' 'Don't you speak?' 'Aren't you close?'

As mystified as any of them, I would answer: 'Yes, we are close.' I really couldn't understand what was the matter. Other times, he was missing altogether. When I asked a warder where he was, I was told he'd hurt his back and was being taken to the general hospital for treatment. These visits to the hospital soon became a regular pattern to the extent that I began to worry there might be something seriously wrong. The only times we saw one another were in the carpentry workshop and even then, he hardly talked to me.

What had I done? What had *he* done?

Christine would be allowed to visit, but not for very long. She looked pale and stressed. Talking was not easy. I tried to explain over again that we hadn't done anything, that the charges at the Old Bailey had been a fix. Me, a blackmailer. Really?

Chrissie knew me well enough to know that wasn't my style. But did she believe me? I couldn't tell. Nor could I bear to see what all of this was doing to her and the kids – with a new baby daughter I had yet to see.

I wasn't long inside when suddenly there was something new about the Krays going round the landings. It was to do with Frankie Mitchell. As I heard it, that December 1966, Smithy and Billy Exley had sprung him off an outdoor work party on Dartmoor and driven him back to London. That was what Alfie had made a dummy run for in the spring. Now Mitchell was hidden away somewhere.

Letters in Mitchell's name started appearing in the *Daily Mirror* and *The Times*, saying the Home Secretary (it was Roy Jenkins) must give him a release date: 'If I must be buried alive give me some reasons to hope. I am ready to give myself up if I can have something to look forward to.' It was pathetic. Smithy wrote those, like he did all the Christmas cards for the twins. That's what I was thinking and I was right. Then the letters stopped appearing.

All we knew was that Frank was sprung out while we were in prison. And we're all thinking at the time when we first heard about it – that's nice, at least Frankie Mitchell will be out for Christmas, the first time for years. Well, it didn't quite work out that way.

We're hearing that Frankie had been brought to a flat in Barking, east London, and kept prisoner there by the Firm (after Moresby Road, I knew how that felt). He got very difficult. Reggie and Albert Donoghue 'persuaded' a hostess from Winston's Club (she was known as 'Lisa') to provide some company, but Frank just didn't know how to stay quiet.

Albert Donoghue would tell me that when he visited Frank wherever he was in hiding, Frank told him: 'Go back to the twins and tell them if Ronnie doesn't come to see me straightaway, I'm leaving here, that's it.'

When Albert took the message to Ronnie, Ronnie told him, 'We've got to get rid of him, we can't handle him anymore.' Frank was as strong as a bullock and the twins knew the only way to get rid of him was to shoot him. So, they arranged with whoever it was who shot him, some say it was Albert, others that it was Freddie Foreman but that's all hearsay. All we know is Frank was sprung out while we were all in prison and apparently shot in the head and the heart in the back of a van sometime in late December 1966. His 'freedom' had lasted a couple of weeks.

New rumours about the twins kept coming. The big shocker was Frances's suicide. She'd made at least two attempts already. This time she had succeeded. She'd taken an 'enormous overdose of phenobarbitone' at her brother Frank's house in Hoxton.

I heard about it from the guy who acted as the twins' messenger when I was in Maidstone. He said she'd done herself in, but all the chaps were saying Reggie did it. We all knew he'd wanted to get back with her, and when she wouldn't, it made him really angry.

We had heard that Kray hanger-on Frosty was on the missing list. Then we heard that Smithy had disappeared. They did Smithy down the caravan, or so I heard. At least that's what the police and screws were saying too.

Anyone seen Teddy? It was funny at first. Not now. We were having a chat in my cell about it. Someone said: 'I reckon one of those twins has killed him,' and we all knew it was true. No one ever found Smithy, although word went round he went into the marshes at Steeple Bay, right where Ronnie used to talk about getting rid of a body. That's what we all thought.

The Richardsons – the 'torture gang' – were taken down on 7 June 1967 after a trial that lasted forty-two days. That was big news on the wings. They got twenty-five years for fraud, extortion, assault and grievous bodily harm.[29] And there was more. Despite Ronnie's continued absence, the alleged bent copper Townsend case went ahead. DS Leonard Townsend claimed he'd walked into a trap, the tapes were fakes. After two juries disagreed, on 18 July 1967 the prosecution offered no evidence on the third attempt at the Old Bailey. No disciplinary proceedings were taken against Townsend. Ronnie re-emerged from hiding.

And Lord Boothby got married! In September 1967, to an Italian bird, thirty-three years younger than him – that must have been nice for her. Boothby's manservant Gordon Goodfellow legged it soon after that. But the really big story doing the rounds inside was about Jack 'the Hat' McVitie. There was a contract on the moneyman,

---

[29] The investigation was led by Assistant Chief Constable Gerald McArthur of Hertfordshire Police, who led a combined squad of Home Counties, Regional Crime Squad and Metropolitan Police officers. The Met were always touchy about the out-of-towners' involvement.

Leslie Payne, who I'd run into during the Hideaway affair. The twins had fallen out with him big time. Jack and Billy Exley were supposed to carry out a hit. I heard that Jack had gone round with a gun then bottled out on Payne's doorstep in Tulse Hill when his missus answered the door. But Jack kept the money, so they killed him for that.

Word went round the landing, round the whole nick. I was shocked and saddened too. Jack didn't deserve that. He wasn't a gangster, he was just a thief. A thief who liked a drink, that was all. Ronnie and Reggie took a liberty to do him, especially the way they did it.

The story went like this: the twins gave Jack the ready-eye and they'd all gone back to Blonde Carole Skinner's for a drink. Or something like that. What I was hearing inside was all garbled up. I hardly knew Blonde Carole. She was a hairdresser's model who'd met the twins along the way. She did some hostessing at the Starlight Club in Highbury, a Kray favourite. She had two small children and a basement flat at 97 Evering Road, Stoke Newington, which according to Kray historian James Morton writing many years later, the twins had asked quite nicely at first if they could use for meets, and then had just taken over.

After Moresby Road, I knew how that felt. 'She would come home and find dozens of empty glasses and overflowing ashtrays,' apparently.

This time the twins ordered Carole and her friends out altogether and took the flat over 'for a party'. It was 28 October 1967, a Saturday, late at night by now. Jack was drinking in the Regency Club when a couple of the Firm who he trusted, arrived to invite him to join the swinging scene in Evering Road. He went along willingly.

Reggie was going to shoot him when he came in the door but the gun jammed. Ronnie grabbed him and started screaming, and Jack gets it from Reggie with a breadknife in the stomach. When I heard about it, to be honest, I thought, *Thank God I'm in here.* Safe in prison, I mean.

Jack's body vanished. There were plenty of rumours. It was in the concrete foundations of a supermarket, it was in a motorway flyover, it had been fed to animals, burned in a hospital incinerator. One story had it dumped over a railway line near Cedra Court.[30] It was like Frankie Mitchell, where was his body? Our mother Ellen had heard something about that – I'd hear about it later.

Almost New Year … I'd been inside for fourteen months. Going round the landings is a tale that after Jack 'the Hat' McVitie got done, there's a new broom at the Yard been ordered to go after the Krays. His name was DI Read – the same Leonard Read who got burned in the Hideaway affair when I was taking messages from Ronnie out of Brixton to put the frighteners on Hew McCowan.

This time, so we'd find out, he'd got a team working outside of the Yard, away from the old faces. If that was true, the twins had a problem. And since the previous summer there'd been rumours about a cozzer (policeman) called Henry Mooney going around the East End, talking to people about the Blind Beggar. And the Widow's and the Chequers. He wanted to know the names of everyone who'd been there the night Cornell was done – they still wouldn't leave it alone.

Read would make it clear in his autobiography (*The Man Who Nicked the Krays*, 1991) that from the start the high-ups in the Yard

---

[30] Nipper Read thought Jack McVitie's body might have gone into the furnaces that heated Cheshire Street Baths, near Vallance Road.

(the 'fifth floor,' he called them) were not at all keen on going after the Krays. He'd insisted on secrecy, but somebody was trying to get what he was up to out there in big headlines.

There'd been a Norman Lucas exclusive in the *Sunday Mirror* in June 1967: 'Net draws tight around the Gangs', which could reveal that after the very recent conviction of the Richardsons, top Yard men, Brodie, Millen and du Rose, were after a gang of 'well known criminals in a bid to clean up the West End'. Lucas reported in July and again in August, that 'Chief Supt Ferguson Walker and DS Hemmingway' were 'probing the finances of a London gang'. It was very clear who.

Then, on 7 January 1968, the *News of the World* had 'Gangbusters Move in On the Top Mob', which identified Nipper Read directly as the man in pursuit of an unnamed gang. He was being helped by Gerald McArthur of the Richardsons fame, so it said.

Well, that bit was wrong.

In this new reign of terror, one man had been nailed to the floor of a club, so the paper reported. There had been 'brutal assaults on boys with homosexual tendencies'. The newspaper could not resist a re-run of the Peer and a Gangster affair of almost four years earlier and those 'sinister rumours':

> A complicating factor has been the background of homosexuality of some members of the gang. This has given them introduction to spheres of influence which they could otherwise never have had.

Norman Lucas was back in the *Sunday Mirror* on 18 February 1968 with another story: 'Murder for Silence by Big Time Racketeers', with the news that DI Leonard Read was investigating the murders of Cornell, McVitie and Frankie Mitchell. No suspects were named, but with the Richardsons behind bars, that could only mean Read was after the Krays.

'This ruthless mob's terror is spreading into jails,' Lucas reported. 'One man in Maidstone Prison is under special protection.' That was Bobby – how did Norman Lucas know that?

Read was furious. He would later say the information had been deliberately leaked (he wouldn't say by whom). Whatever, it meant his investigation wasn't a secret anymore: 'Any vestiges of cover had been well and truly blown by our own side.' There was, he said, *an enemy within*.

So, how had all this come about, a whole new team going after the twins after Tommy Butler walked away? Well, Mr Read wasn't about to tell me or anyone else the details right then, but he would put it down on paper one day in his memoirs. I'd find out a lot more when I came to read his book, even if there were whole episodes in it when I can say out loud now that Read was bending the truth.

Read's book explains how he would have to get evidence from convicted criminals (like we were) to use in court. Home Office and police lawyers were dubious. And this bit seems real enough. On 18 September 1967, almost a year after we brothers had been sent to prison and a month before the McVitie murder, Leonard Read had been summoned to a meeting at the Yard with the new Assistant Commissioner Peter Brodie, who told him: 'Mr Read, you're going to get the Krays.' He was to report direct to Commander John du Rose, the head of the Murder Squad. Frederick Gerrard took a step back. In fact, he'd retire before too long, as would Butler.

Another published account from 1972 has Read being told by Brodie 'that he wanted him to take over a top-secret investigation, started some months earlier by a Superintendent Ferguson Walker', That's what John Pearson said in his book, *The Profession of Violence.*

'Walker was being promoted and Read was the only man available to take his place,' the author said. There would be a cover story about it being an 'investigation into police corruption'.

No one would be surprised at that.

This Ferguson Walker seems to have taken over from Tommy Butler in summer 1966, with a DS called Leslie Emment under him. A 26-year-old DS called Alan Wright was assigned in March 1967 as 'record keeper'.

Emment was soon replaced on the team by a DS Algernon Hemmingway. Wright would stay on. Then Henry Mooney replaced Walker himself, who had been 'promoted and transferred'. This rearrangement of the deckchairs on the Yard *Titanic* looks a little obscure, but it would be important in maybe explaining what had happened to me and my brothers.

Read was dreading it. He was 'absolutely pissed off', as he said in his memoirs, but could not say no. 'My only concern was about the enemy within,' he said.

Bent coppers. Kray informants on the take – in local nicks and at the Yard.

In fact, that's what he told Peter Brodie – who merely nodded, but 'understood what I meant', said Read. Not once in his book does he mention Superintendent Ferguson Walker and his 'top-secret' pursuit of the twins.

It's as if Walker and his investigation never existed.

It's very hard to find evidence of the Walker episode in the National Archives, but I did come across this little item. Someone (name redacted) gave a statement that he had gone into the Old

Horns in Bethnal Green, a Kray favourite, and seen Ronnie and Co. in their special Firm-only section of the saloon bar. That's how it worked.

He mentioned the 25-year sentence the Richardsons had just received and said it was 'excessive'. Ronnie had said: 'Don't worry, that won't happen to us. We've got too much help.' He didn't mean local coppers, he meant help from inside the Yard.

Read would also write:

I received my first shock when I discovered the Criminal Intelligence (C.11) Branch files contained not one single item added to the wealth of stuff I had put in during my own Commercial Street [and City Road] days.

That was when he was told by Inspector Gerrard to first go after the Krays in summer 1964 in the wake of the Boothby affair. And he had done so. There'd been no politics or MI5 subplots, it had been good old-fashioned detective work. For months, he and his team had worked on Long Firms and protection rackets in the long trail that would lead to his humiliation at the Hideaway trial. That was all on file.

After the McCowan fiasco, Read had been sent off on a police 'middle management course'. From that point on, through the Cornell murder and its aftermath, when he came to look, the cupboard was bare: 'Not one item'.

Why would that be?

# 19

## 'HOSPITAL'

I myself had been trying meanwhile to get to an open prison in order to get easier living conditions – it was very strict in Maidstone. But each time I put an application in, the answer came back: 'Never'. I couldn't know it at the time, but the Krays and everything to do with them was getting more sensitive than ever at the Yard – no one was going to risk losing sight of me.

But there were little clues that the twins were getting jumpy. Around a year into my sentence, the twins' messenger warned me once again that if the police did come sniffing round asking questions, I was to stay well schtum – not to say a thing or ask for my lawyer. That was a message from the twins.

I told him directly: 'Fuck them and their message! You've told me this about five times, I don't need you to tell me what to do.' My cellmate, a face called Terry Millman, even offered to put him down the laundry chute if he didn't stop.

I had tried again for a transfer, expecting another knock-back. Then around April 1968 I was called in by the Governor and told I was going to Ford Open Prison in West Sussex. It was 6am a couple of days later when they picked me up, no farewell to Bobby. When I got there, there were about twenty of us in each dormitory. It was huts like a war film. I'd have preferred to be back in Maidstone, back in my old cell. They gave me a job, to break the tarmac of an old airfield opposite the prison with a pickaxe. We called it the 'Burma Road', like we were wartime prisoners of the Japs. It was good exercise, but I'd have terrible blisters by the end of each day.

By now, it was May 1968. Then there was the really big news going round Ford: the twins had been nicked. They'd lifted Reggie and Ronnie together in their parents' new council flat in Finsbury. It was Number 43 on the ninth floor of Braithwaite House, 6am, 7 May. Charlie was arrested at his flat in Poplar.

It was to be famously reported that Reggie was in bed with a girl, Ronnie with a boy. Their names and ages are on file in the National Archives in a statement by DS Hemmingway. To me, it doesn't feel right to reveal them here.

Ron and Reggie had been in the Old Horns in Bethnal Green, then the Astor Club up west the night before. The rumour was true, it *was* in the papers – they really were on remand. Read was putting together the charges for a full trial. *Well, he'd better not come round me*, I thought. I wasn't going to grass, nor would anyone in my family.

Alfie, I'd discover later, was down for home leave when he heard in Lewes Prison about the arrests. He had wanted to go to the police right then, so he would tell DI Henry Mooney (who was acting like Read's chief of intelligence) a little later, but was afraid his pending home leave would be stopped.

He did get out for a weekend, on 16 May, and told our parents what he knew. The Krays were all over the newspapers by then. Alfie said he'd tell the police about it all later, but he couldn't right now because he was 'frightened of Scotch Ian being free'.

A little later, Alfie would tell Henry Mooney in his formal statement, 'by the way, I had asked my deputy governor to get in touch with Superintendent Read to tell him all of this', but only when the time was right.

The Sunday papers of 30 June 1968 reported the arrest of Scotch Ian. There was no doubt left for Alfie, he wanted to see Read immediately. The Deputy Governor at Lewes put in a call to the duty officer at Tintagel House. Read must have made a decision on the spot. The next morning, Monday, 1 July, Alfie was brought from Lewes to Tintagel House to give a statement.

I've seen what my older brother had to say in the National Archives, just as I saw my own and Bobby's statements. Alfie explained to Mooney how it all began, how the twins had come to like the Tudor Club and they'd go out to charity shows and boxing matches with him and me. He explained how Bobby had started up a boat business on the Isle of Wight and how he'd go down there for the summer season and how he and I acted as street traders the rest of the time.

The night Cornell was shot, Alfie described how the phone had rung in the hall at my flat and Reggie had said come over to Madge's, how we'd driven there to find Tapp Street full of the Firm milling around as Reggie gave orders to drive to Walthamstow before he got into my car with him and Bobby.

Alfie described the arrival at the Chequers pub to find Ronnie already there – and knowing someone had been shot, he 'gained the impression that Ronnie Kray or Scots Ian had done the shooting'. To some remark, Ronnie had said, 'What's done is done.'

Mooney wanted to know especially about Harry Jew Boy Cope and Sammy Lederman. Then they'd all gone back to my flat when I got Christine out of bed. She'd come into the living room and didn't look best pleased, so Alfie said. Ronnie had told us, 'You must not tell anyone, you know what will happen.'

The next day, Alfie saw two shotguns at the flat – one was a pump-action repeater. He thought Scotch Pat Connolly or Scotch Jack Dickson had been sent out to get them. They were for fear of reprisals by friends of Cornell, so Alfie thought.

Alfie began giving his statement to DI Mooney at 2.30 that afternoon and was still talking at 7.55 that evening. Alfred William Teale, butcher's assistant, CRO number 48109/5, it turned out from Criminal Records Office, was doing three years for having demanded 'money from a homosexual and threatened to expose his activities if he failed to pay', so it said on his form sheet. That was the 'Wallace' set-up.

He had two brothers, David Charles and Robert Frank, arrested the same day, all serving the same sentence for the same crime.

Well, that was a coincidence.

What was known? They had Alfie's statement. Next thing was to take statements off me and Bobby. At least Nipper would know where to find us and we weren't exactly going anywhere. He moved very fast.

Since their arrest, the twins had been on remand in Brixton on holding charges. Whatever Read could put together to get them arrested. Charlie too. It wasn't much. Bail applications were expected next. In fact, to general surprise the main defendants didn't make any. The twins stayed inside, declaring through their lawyers they were innocent of all charges.

Read meanwhile fretted about how to keep his witnesses safe: 'In the whole investigation it was this which gave me the most headaches,' he would say in his memoirs. The suspicion that there was a Kray informer within made it all the more dangerous.

Read said he was concerned about witness safety. Well, he needn't have worried about me – I was safely tucked up in Ford although it wasn't exactly high security.

Every lunchtime on our outside working party we would have a parade so the screws could count the number of prisoners and make sure no one had run away. First, you heard your name shouted out and written on a board up in front of you. You then had to get into working party lines, as instructed. They would then tell us which amongst us had visits or appointments of any kind.

All of a sudden, one afternoon, I heard my name: 'Teale! Hospital, over there.'

I didn't have a clue what they were talking about. I'd nothing wrong with me and hadn't complained of anything. 'Me? What for?' I asked, and the two screws who were with me told me it was a check-up. 'What's happening? What have I done?' I said.

They told me I had to go over to the hospital. When I asked why they wouldn't tell me, just told me a car would be coming to pick me up. Shortly afterwards, a car pulled up at the gates driven by a screw. Once we were in the car together, I asked again: 'Where are we going?' But he just replied: 'I don't know.'

After about half an hour's drive we pulled up at the back of a police station in Littlehampton, taking the lift up quite a few floors until we reached a large room with a huge window, like a great wall of glass, where you could see the whole of the South Coast spread out below. The screw stayed with me.

Suddenly, two plainclothes policemen came in, full of apologies and strangely polite. It was: 'Sorry we're late, Dave, only we got caught up in traffic on the way from London. Do you want a cup of tea and something to eat? Some fags?' One threw a packet of twenty fags down on the table. 'Do you want anything else?'

They were acting like we were mates.

They were two detective sergeants – Read's men, as I later found out. Their names were George Ness and Anthony Story. Then it started:

'You know that the twins have been arrested?' one of them said.

'I had heard that,' I said.

At that, the screw left the room and one of the detectives told me: 'So you know the twins have been nicked and are going to go away for a long time. What do you know about them?'

I didn't know what to say, I'd had that warning: 'Not a lot,' I answered.

The officer replied with heavy sarcasm: 'Oh, you don't, do you? And you don't know anything about the Cornell murder either, I suppose?'

'No, I don't,' I said.

'Well, there are lots of rumours flying round, I suppose you've heard … When we asked Ronnie Kray about it, he said that all he knew was that "the Teales were involved". That's what Ronnie told my governor.'

'You've got to be joking!' I said. I couldn't believe even Ron would try a stunt like that, but I still stuck to the line that I didn't know the Krays and had nothing to say. He then started asking me to write a statement; he was very insistent.

'I can't do that. I've told you, I've got nothing to say. I don't know what you're talking about, leave me alone,' I said.

Finally, they agreed to take me back to the prison. It was late by now. Returning to my cell, I didn't sleep a wink, worrying what this was all about and what was going to happen.

Next day, 2 July, at about ten in the morning came the message that I had to be sent to the 'hospital' again. At least this time I knew what to expect. On arrival at Littlehampton nick, I was given a fag and a cup of tea.

'Right, Dave,' the officer said, and pulled a load of photos from an envelope in a desk drawer and laid them on a table.

They were of me, my wife Christine and our children, of Alfie, Bobby, Ronnie and Reggie Kray, all going in and out of my flat in Moresby Road. Me and Christine were going shopping, getting in and out of my car, going to Vallance Road, different pubs; lots of us at Steeple Bay, the caravan site. They were surveillance photos and had clearly been taken when half the Firm was camped out at my place after the Cornell killing. I don't know what chilled me more, the memory of that time two years before or the fact the coppers knew all about it. How did they know? Why hadn't they stormed the place?[31]

'So, you don't know the twins?' he asked again.

'Well, I do know them … They used to go up my mother's club in Islington.'

'But you still don't want to make a statement?'

'No.'

---

[31] Later on, in a talk at Tintagel House with Nipper Read and his deputy, DI Frank Cater, Read told me: 'When the police surrounded your flat, it was a spin-up on a coin as to whether we [he meant the police at the time] were going to come in guns blazing or leave it. The only reason we didn't was because of the kids, because we thought that the Krays were capable of using the children as shields to get out.'

At that moment, the phone rang in the room at Littlehampton nick. Picking up the receiver, the officer answered, 'Yes, he's here. Do you want to speak to him?'

Passing the receiver across the table to me, he whispered conspiratorially: 'It's the wife!'

I felt myself starting to sweat with anxiety. 'Hello, love. You alright? Where are you?' I said.

'Hello, Dave. I'm in Albany Street Police Station. They brought me here. They've been round a few times, asking about Ronnie Kray and the Cornell murder. They've taken the photos of us and the Krays, the ones that were taken down at the caravan. I had to give them to them.'

'That's alright,' I said, 'don't worry about it. Where's the kids?'

'They've got a policewoman looking after them.'

After telling Christine not to worry about a thing, I put the receiver down with a shaking hand.

'Listen, Dave,' said the officer now. 'I'll tell you what you're going to do. You and your wife are both going to make statements. You know your mother has been nicked?'

Well, I didn't know. I just sat there with my mouth open. What the hell was this? It had to be some kind of trick, just a crazy story to make me say something, surely?

'It's true,' said the copper, 'and just to prove it, if you like we'll show you the court papers.'

'Nipper Read is working on all this in Tintagel,' the other policeman told me. Whatever 'Tintagel' was. 'You're going to be doing a lot of bird [time] if you don't tell us what happened on the night of 9 March 1966 when you drove Reggie Kray from Bethnal Green to Walthamstow.'

'Alfie and Bobby have made statements,' the copper continued (I later found out that Alfie already had in fact, but Bobby was only just in the process of making one at Maidstone). 'I suggest you do the same. Do you realise you could be charged with harbouring a murderer? If you don't play right by us, you'll be looking at twelve to fifteen years, your wife and mother could both get five and your kids will end up in care.'

There was no way out. Stuck between the twins and the police, I was now completely cornered. I answered: 'You've got a deal.'

So, I made a statement that afternoon and on into the evening. On 2 July, I told them how the twins had moved in on the 66, how Ronnie had pursued me and used my flat as a meeting place. I told them about the night of the phone call from Madge's and how I'd driven to Tapp Street with my brothers. How Reggie had got in my car and told me to get them 'off the manor', the drive to Walthamstow and who'd been in the Chequers – Bobby Buckley, Sammy Lederman, Scotch Jack, Fat Pat, Harry Jew Boy, Nobby Clark, Charlie Kray, one of the Barry brothers from the Regency Club – the drive back and the days of mayhem in my flat that followed.

The next morning, I was back at Littlehampton. I told them about the trek to the nearby flat when the Chequers closed, with the improvised bar and not-very-happy wife and daughter. How Billy Exley and Ronnie Hart had been there. I told them more about Moresby Road and how Christine and I could only sleep for a couple of hours between five and eight. How Connie Whitehead [an East End-born comparatively younger member of the Firm] had come in with a pistol and Reggie had brandished a shotgun and a bandolier of cartridges.

I told them how they decided after two weeks to go to Scotch Jack's place in Clissold Road and sort of abducted me to go with them, because, as Reggie had said, 'If the Old Bill come here, it's better if your wife and kids are on their own.' The reason I never contacted the police was because I was frightened of the Krays and their friends, I said.

I was very, very frightened.

I didn't know it then but Christine was making a statement that same afternoon. Henry Mooney came round the same day to her council flat, Number 8 Hawkshead, in Stanhope Street, near Euston Station. She'd got the place when I was away.

I found out something of what she told them a little afterwards. And I would see it all in full, nearly fifty years later, when I held her typewritten statement in my hands in the National Archives. She'd given them lots of family photographs of us with the Krays at Steeple Bay (I'd love to know where they ended up, I've asked loads of times). She said I'd come home that night two years earlier 'with some friends' who she recognised. Ronnie had asked 'permission' to stay (hardly) and said: 'Isn't she lovely?' to the Firm when he saw her.

Well, that bit was true.

She'd told them how there had been all sorts of comings and goings, how Alfie hadn't been allowed to go home on his own. How Alfie had said: 'Who do they think we are ... cunts?' She named the Firm members who'd been there: Exley, Connolly, Jack 'the Hat' McVitie, Albert, 'a very large American' and the Nash brothers.

'There were a few drinking parties held at the flat. I think Madge's daughter came to the flat one night, she was friendly with Bobby Teale,' so Christine told them.

On the last night before they finally all left, Ronnie, Reggie, Scotch Ian Barrie, me and my brothers had all gone out to the pub they called the 'Dead House', she told them, when a policemen knocked on the door, asking about a suspected burglary at the flat. She had shown him round.

I had bought a caravan at Steeple Bay after all of this, so she had said, where we'd all gone down (in fact, I'd got it the year before). And I did have a car, a grey Ford, which in the end had either been stolen from outside the Regency Club or repossessed by the finance company – more likely, the latter. So, as far as the coppers were thinking, all I'd said checked out.

The next day, or maybe the one after – 4 or 5 July – I got another summons to go to the hospital wing. I was assured it would be spread around Ford that I was being taken in for an operation. In fact, I was put in the back seat of an unmarked car. Soon, we were moving fast up the A3, then heading through south-west London – but not to New Scotland Yard. Instead, we went to a big new office block on the south of the Thames, opposite the Houses of Parliament. I would get to know it as Tintagel House.

I recognised Leonard 'Nipper' Read from the time at the Hideaway and the McCowan business. And he recognised me. He could not have been friendlier.

A couple of police officers took me downstairs to the canteen to have something to eat before taking me into a large room, where one wall was completely covered in pictures of the twins at Vallance Road, Steeple Bay, everywhere, with all the members of the Firm. My brothers and I were in loads of them.

Just to make the point, they showed me a statement Ronnie had made sometime, claiming: 'All I know about the Cornell killing is that the Teales were involved.' I recognised his childish scrawl from the letter and cards I'd seen him write in Vallance Road, so I knew it really was his statement.

Although he didn't explain to me then, Read had gone for the Long Firms first, picking up where he left off, before the McCowan thing had stopped the show. Since then, moneyman Leslie Payne[32] had had a very big falling-out with the twins – I'd only find out about all this properly from his memoirs, *Nipper Read, the Man Who Nicked the Krays*, where Read said that Payne had had enough of the violence and just left the Firm.

Nobody did that.

Over the next three weeks, Payne made a statement 146 pages long. Here's a snippet from the National Archives:

One day the three Krays arrived at the office and asked me for money. I explained there was no cash. They all began to rave and shout. Ronnie said: 'we aren't going to walk around fucking penniless when you've got money up here.'

So it went on. Read called him the 'first supergrass'. Payne gave leads and more leads. Read's team had begun to grow, but still the three murder cases were full of holes.

---

[32] Les Payne would be sentenced in 1972 to five years for conspiracy to pervert the course of justice. Read was a defence witness at his trial. Payne would say in his own book (*The Brotherhood*) thereafter: 'Perhaps as many as a quarter of [detectives] dealing with serious crime are willing to take a pension. In return for a quick chat six times a year, a man in the fraud squad or the flying squad might earn £1,000 a year.' I'd say myself back then, up to half of them were on the take.

My two days of statements at Littlehampton had filled in some of the gaps on the Cornell killing. Now up at Tintagel House, Read asked me to go through them again as if I might have been asked to say it all in court. He loved it – 'That's good, David, that's great ... and then what happened ... ?'

The inspector told me how he wanted it all to go: 'What we want you to do is to go to Bow Street first. That is where the committal proceedings will be before the main trial. The prosecution is going to ask you some questions and you've got to tell them everything you know,' he said. The prosecution, he did not need to remind me, were the good guys.

I agreed to everything.

# 20

## CROWN WITNESS

I saw what Alfie and Bobby had said in their statements at the same time as I saw my own and Christine's in the National Archives. It was over forty-five years since they'd been taken down.

They were both full of detail about the night of the flight from Madge's to Walthamstow, the coming and goings in Moresby Road, shotguns, Ronnie's threats. But they checked exactly with each other and with what I had said.

No wonder Nipper had been so pleased.

Alfie also said he'd been on a Ronnie-ordered mission to Dartmoor to see Frankie Mitchell in May 1966. That would cause him some grief when it came to the full trial.

In the statement Bobby had given at Maidstone Police Station, he mentioned showbiz agent Sammy Lederman saying to Ronnie in the room at the Chequers, 'Ronnie, you're a cold-blooded murderer.' And he said how, when the radio or TV was switched on and Ronnie made out that he wanted to hear the football results, there was a newsflash about the shooting in the East End and that the victim had been rushed to hospital. And then it appeared that there was a carnival: 'Ronnie almost jumped for joy.'

He mentioned his own movements, going to Suffolk and Cambridge, and how he'd briefly moved in to the flat at Lea Bridge Road.

'After a while I left them and moved away from the area,' Bobby had said. 'I know they were looking for me [at Steeple Bay] from inquiries I now know they made for me. By them, I mean the Krays. I have not seen the twins or Ian [Barrie] since I left the flat.'

Bobby also kept a much bigger admission out of that statement he gave at Maidstone nick on 2 July. But more of this later ...

So now I'm in the National Archives, looking at stuff taken down four decades before. It's like I'm back there again. I could see the way Read must have been thinking: what sort of charges could be brought out of all of this? A defence might say the time in my flat was all a great big party – dancing, drinking, Zorba routines, outings to pubs, all of which was true. That the police had come around to Moresby Road because of neighbours complaining about the noise. In fact, that's exactly what the twins' briefs would say.

I was taken up and down from Ford to Tintagel House a couple more times. It was something that had to be done. I didn't want to be a grass, but didn't feel I had a choice. I'd also sworn to Ronnie that I would one day tell everyone how he'd raped me. I would have my revenge, not in a fight because he'd have wiped the floor with me, but one way or another. But I never could tell my wife – I felt horrible. Ronnie said at the time: 'They won't believe you, I'll just say you were drunk.'

I didn't know much about what had been happening with the Krays since their arrest but, as far as I could remember, I picked up what I could from what the police were telling me in our little chats and rumours going round the huts at Ford.

The twins had been nicked on what were 'holding charges', a lot of guff about stolen bearer bonds, the Mafia and Long Firms. That had come from Leslie Payne and his epic statement. Then there was more to come, a 'conspiracy to murder an unnamed man', something about the United States Secret Service and assassination plots that Read had cooked up somehow – I'd hear about all that much later.

And looking at the mass of files, of the investigation of summer 1966 into who done Cornell, no one seemed to have been spoken to formally by Read's team. No statements taken off James Axon in Whitechapel or Tommy Butler. Of Ferguson Walker there seemed to be nothing – funny that. But Sergeant Joe Pogue was tracked down and gave a statement to Henry Mooney.

Nipper went back to the Esmeralda's Barn days. I saw the evidence collected that autumn and spring of 1967–8 in the National Archives. The Long Firms, boxes of accounts for sweets, shampoo, stair rods, crisps, whatever, they didn't tell me much. Hundreds of witnesses were interviewed, their statements typed up. Lots of tales of villainy, with violence woven all the way through – a lot of the files are still closed.

And gossip about things I could not possibly know about and were not in published Kray histories. Little scraps, like an interview with an informant called John Ivor Coles, who had heard prison gossip about where Frankie Mitchell's body ended up (in a pre-dug grave in an east London cemetery, he said, but there were loads of theories), so he told one of Read's team in July 1968.

Then this snippet from the same source: 'I got to know a man named Leslie Holt in Pentonville Prison. He used to get mail from

Lord Boothby and told me when he got out, he was going to black-mail the Kray twins and Lord Boothby because he knew a lot about them.'

It was a bit late for any of that.

Or a Nipper interview with the wife of the wealthy arsonist Geoffrey Allen, who told him on 3 July 1968 how her husband had sold the twins a cottage in the Suffolk village of Bildeston for their mother, Violet. She'd met them there in autumn 1967 in company with 'an editor and two writers'. One of them was the *Sunday Times* writer, John Pearson. He remembered being offered light ale to drink. The McVitie murder had been just eight days before.

Then there was another Nipper talk with the company secretary of Blackwater Holidays, owners of Steeple Bay caravan park. There were lots of rumours about the Krays, but they had never given trouble. Large quantities of concrete had been delivered as footings for caravans in 1967, but there was nothing sinister about that ... Probably.

Read's digging would go on relentlessly like this until the main trial opened in January 1969 at the Old Bailey – and after that too. But now it's midsummer 1968. Thus far, he's got his best break about Frankie Mitchell from the old boxer Billy Exley, who'd helped with the escape.

I found a statement from Exley to Read in the National Archives about how he'd hired a car, a Humber Hawk, given his licence and a bank reference and passed it over to Teddy Smith at Vallance Road. Smithy, he was sure, had used the car to pick up Frank Mitchell from Dartmoor. The car was getting very late to return to the hirer, some-one would come looking. 'Don't worry,' said Teddy – Exley had to sort it out somehow.

One time, he had gone with Lisa, the nightclub hostess hired by the twins to keep Frank Mitchell company, to collect her clothes from her flat somewhere off the Bayswater Road. After a few days, Teddy had told him to go to the flat from where Frank had 'gone' – 'He was very insistent everything be wiped down, the walls, everything.'

\* \* \*

Frankie Mitchell would be the first murder charge to be brought. Committal proceedings had begun on 26 June 1968 at Bow Street. Back in March, Read had also got a slender lead on Jack 'the Hat' McVitie's demise with an indication where the killing had happened: it was Blonde Carole Skinner's basement flat in Hackney. Still in Ford, I'd have to catch up on all this later.

Read was still trying hard to get the Blind Beggar and McVitie cases to stand up. Charges had yet to be brought. That's why he moved so fast when he found out about us Teales. To do that, he not only had to get witnesses who'd talk, but as he said himself, keep them physically safe. More to the point, he had to keep his witnesses believing they were going to stay safe, that in the end he'd nick the twins and they would stay nicked.

Charlie was inside as well as the twins. Hardmen like Albert Donoghue were in custody, as were Connie Whitehead, Scotch Jack Dickson, Big Pat Connolly and some more who'd been involved in the killings of Frankie Mitchell and Jack 'the Hat' McVitie. There were no immediate applications for bail for the twins and Charlie but most of the Long Firm fraudsters were bailed to reappear whenever – they were not killers. Scotch Ian Barrie was still outside.

To begin with, there were no restrictions on reporting at Bow Street. It so happened there'd been a change in the law the year before.

239

Up until then, all committal procedure evidence, not just the names of witnesses, could be reported in detail. It was what court reporters lived on – petty crime, indecency. Now the law was that proceedings could only be reported if the defence said they could be. And if a press ban was lifted for one defendant then it had to be for all defendants. Otherwise it was to be what they call 'in camera': No Publicity.

Reggie's solicitor, Paul Wrightson, had asked for the ban to be lifted right at the start on 17 May during applications for bail – well before the murder charges were brought. It might be that Reggie thought the charges would all collapse, just like the Hideaway trial. Well, that had been a big laugh. Let it all be open. Reggie would later say that he 'wanted the public to see the diabolical liberties the law had been taking'.

So, for the next few weeks, the committal was all in the papers although it was very hard to follow what was actually going on, especially for someone like me, hearing about it second-hand in prison. The stolen bond stuff was incomprehensible, the conspiracy to murder an unnamed man charge was pathetic. It was a Maltese club owner called George Caruana, irrelevant as it happened to the outcome of the trial.

To begin with, the press seemed to be expecting another walk-over. When exploding briefcases and deadly syringes came into the testimony, plots to assassinate various African leaders, to kidnap the Pope, to kill the Hitler-worshipping Colin Jordan on contract for a Jewish villain, Reggie had asked, 'When is James Bond going to give evidence? This is ridiculous!'

Then it got more serious. To start with, it was all about the disappearance of Frank Mitchell, 'The Mad Axeman', about which I knew not very much. Alfie knew a lot more – although we'd both been in prison when Frankie went on the missing list at the end of 1966. Billy Exley gave evidence on the escape and harbouring of Mitchell in which Teddy Smith had been involved.

Nipper Read was able to bring specific murder charges on that one (even if there was no body) on 31 May. The hunt was still on for the girl who'd been persuaded to comfort Frankie Mitchell: 'Lisa'. Committal proceedings in the Mitchell case began on 26 June.

The day before that, Ronnie was charged with doing Cornell. Reggie was charged as an accessory in acting 'to impede the apprehension of Ronald Kray and [Scotch Ian] Barrie'. Ronnie's brief said: 'My client is not guilty and reserves his defence. He has a complete answer to the charges.'

Maybe he would have.

Having been too terrified to attend the disastrous identity parade two years before, the barmaid from the Blind Beggar had been won over by DI Henry Mooney into making a statement. Then, after Scotch Ian Barrie had been arrested (not until 29 June), the barmaid said she would identify him as being the second gunman in the Blind Beggar. Scotch Ian's arrest was the trigger for Alfie to make his statement in Lewes. My coming over had quickly followed.

An eyewitness to what actually happened to Jack 'the Hat' McVitie in Blonde Carole Skinner's basement in Evering Road, Hackney, came over to Read, but that would be after my little time in the testimony-giving spotlight at Bow Street.

His name was Ronnie Hart. He was the twins' second cousin, roughly the same age as me, and he was on the run from an open prison. In fact, it was he and Frosty who'd gone after my brother Bobby at Steeple Bay in early August 1966. He heard he was 'being plotted up to get done' (Read's words) and would give himself up at Tintagel House on 2 September. The full details of how Jack had been butchered by Reggie came out, who was there, who cleaned it all up.

He had a girlfriend, Blonde Vicky. They were quite a pair, liked to think of themselves as Bonnie and Clyde. Anyway, Ronnie Hart would not stop talking, apparently. He'd spend three days giving a statement the size of a novel. After the trial, he'd give a lot of it to the journalist Norman Lucas on which he based his 'quickie' but very informative book *Britain's Gangland*. Hart would not be one of those charged for Jack's murder or anything else. Read would give him money after it was all over.

Again, in the Jack 'the Hat' McVitie case there was no body, but no matter. On 19 September 1968, Reggie would be charged with the murder of McVitie, but that was still a way down the line.

\* \* \*

While we'd been busy making statements, being shuffled from our various prisons, Mum and Dad were having their own little brush with the law. Alfie would tell me (when we both got out of the nick in September 1968) how he was told in HMP Lewes that there were whispers going round that our mother had been arrested for 'conspiring in a robbery'. The victim was Lady Violet Hamilton of 8 Russell Court, SW1, who had been employing Mum as a housekeeper. Ronnie had fixed it up apparently, I don't know how – I can't see him reading the small ads in *The Lady*, I think he must have heard about the job from Boothby. We'd been in prison when all this happened.

Back in March, our father had been interviewed at West End Central. They'd let him go, but told him: 'We're not charging you, but we're charging your wife.' Mum and Dad were then remanded. In fact, Mum's committal would be postponed until after I'd given my statement on 2 July.

Alfie would later tell me that Read's team started putting pressure on him in little trips to Lewes soon after he'd asked the Deputy Governor to make contact and that his visitors would tell him our mother 'looks like getting five to seven years' and that she would be put in 'Durham jail with the likes of Myra Hindley'. Unless, of course, he and the rest of us brothers should decide to help with the investigation into the murder of George Cornell and other things about the twins. It had been just the same for me.

So, what happened? I sort of worked it out later. One day, in early spring, our mum Nell was in the posh house alone when there was a knock at the door and there's Leslie Holt. Charlie Kray is just up the road in Jermyn Street. Leslie pushes Nell down on the couch and tells her: 'Don't you say a word!' Then Charlie comes in.

Then they rob the place. They take it out the front door in suitcases. When the Hamiltons return and call the police, Nell doesn't dare say who it was she let in – she's frightened for herself, much more for us. So, the police nick her for the burglary, or being part of it. Charlie meanwhile fences all the stuff.

At this stage, Mrs Ellen Teale, née Bowden, born Lambeth, 1922, former joint licensee of the Tudor Club, 66 Upper Street, London N1 (that's what it says in her police file) has no connection with the Kray investigation. Then Read discovers her pending court appearance just as he's discovered us Teale brothers tucked away in three different prisons. After the Krays are arrested, Nell can say what really happened, but going after Charlie for thieving candlesticks isn't the best use of this opportunity to advance the course of justice.

As long as it looks like she would be found guilty, he's got leverage over all of us. If we agree to give evidence, he'll get Mum off – that is, make sure she doesn't actually go to prison. Inspector Read got a message to her (I'm guessing it went like this): 'Listen, plead guilty on this and I'll get you off with a suspended sentence – as long as your three boys go into the witness box to give evidence on the Krays.'

Well, it wasn't Mum herself who'd be striking that particular bargain with us, but Read's men would make it very clear that was what was on the table. That's what Alfie was told in Lewes and I was told in Littlehampton Police Station. How could we say no? It could not be part of any formal statement. And if the defence got hold of it, they'd claim anything we said as prosecution witnesses had been to keep our mother out of prison – that's exactly what they would say.

So now Read's got to start playing his witness cards, one by one. It was my turn on 16 July 1968. I was collected at Ford very early to be driven to London to give my evidence at the committal being held at Bow Street Magistrates' Court. Two plainclothes officers, I think I knew one of them. We were very well looked after.

We were in a squad car driven fast. I was in the back under a blanket. Each day, the twins were being brought this way over the river from Brixton, in a prison van at high speed. It was all a bit of theatre – that was Read's idea apparently.

The Krays were top of the pops. The trendy Carnaby Street boutique, I Was Lord Kitchener's Valet, was selling David Bailey portraits of the twins for 'three bob' a time, said the *Mirror*. 'They were outselling the Beatles.'

I bet they were.

The Magistrates' Court was in Covent Garden, an area I knew well from when we were kids, nicking flowers from the market for the altar in St Joseph's in Macklin Street. At that time, early in the morning, the market was very crowded and I knew a lot of the porters who worked round there. The police told me to 'put this blanket over your head'.

I was in the back of the car just near the Opera House when I peeped out from behind a corner of the blanket and saw a face I recognised in the crowd – a family friend called Johnny Cracknell, a market worker known as a 'cart finder'. Johnny was directing the traffic around Bow Street as there was quite a back-up by then.

I thought to myself: *If only you knew it's me in the police car!* We then went through the big gates, into the back of the yard behind the court. The place was packed. It was overrun with police, a lot of uniform, but even more in plainclothes. I'd been this way before when I was fined for obstructing the footpath in my fly-pitching days.

Well, this was a bit more serious.

I was bundled into a crowded room at the back, where we waited for about half an hour and they gave me a cup of tea. When I glanced round, I thought I recognised the barmaid from the Blind Beggar or assumed it must be her. Also, Leslie Payne. Then I was sort of pushed into a smaller room, all separate rooms so we couldn't compare stories. Christine wasn't allowed to be in with me. Bobby was in another room and Alfie kept apart from him as well. I wasn't allowed to hear what my wife said.

Nipper Read came in and said to me: 'Just say exactly what you've been telling us and confirm that you are prepared to go to the higher court and say the same.'

I would be known as 'Mr D'.

Well, that wasn't much protection. I was to go on the stand at Bow Street as a Crown witness and tell the world about what happened the night George Cornell got shot. The newspapers would love that, surely? Turned out, they would not know about it.

Not yet.

I didn't know it, but five days before, on 10 July, the Chief Metropolitan Magistrate (his name was Frank Milton) had ordered restrictions be put back on reporting because 'a completely separate set of committal proceedings [concerning Ronald Kray] was beginning'. There was no objection from the defence. The three sessions about the Cornell indictment to be held between 11–16 July would be conducted in secret.

That might be good for my survival prospects, but how long would Mr D's testimony stay secret? About ten minutes, as it turned out. Nipper, meanwhile, wanted as many villains as possible to know what was being said. He'd find his own way of making sure it got out.

Ronnie and Scotch Ian Barrie were put up on 16 July charged with murder, with Reggie an 'accessory after the fact'. Alfie had been on that morning as a witness for the prosecution. He was announced as 'Mr A'. I didn't have a clue what he said and wasn't about to ask anyone. He'd been taken straight back to Lewes.

And then me and my minders were heading into the court. And there was my brother Bobby, coming the other way, having said what he'd had to say. He was smiling, looking pleased with himself.

'Are you OK, Bob?' I shouted out.

'I'm OK, Dave. Just tell them everything you know,' he shouted back.

That's what Mum had said when I was on home leave.

'What did you tell them, Bobby?'

But Bobby couldn't answer. Already he'd been propelled outside in short order by four armed guards to be whisked back to Maidstone.

All of a sudden it was my turn to talk about Cornell. Read had told me to say what I knew – and I was prepared to do so.

The witness box was surrounded by armed police. The court was so crowded, at first it was hard to make out what was going on. The twins themselves were in some sort of open cage watching the proceedings as we were taken through our depositions. I tried to 'front it up' the way I always used to, to act tough even if I didn't feel like it, but inside I was absolutely petrified. Until I looked across the court at Ron, that is. Staring me out, hissing, muttering, he seemed especially angry.

'Grass,' he whispered, 'fucking Teale grasses.'

All I could see in my head was the face on top of me in Vallance Road when he sexually assaulted me. Suddenly I felt a tremendous rage for all the damage Ron had done, not only to me but to all my family. I didn't have the strength to beat him physically in a fight, but now I did find I had the courage to tell the truth about him. As I caught his eye, I saw that he was scared too.

I was so nervous as I began to give evidence that the magistrate had to stop me and ask me to 'speak up and also speak more slowly' so that the shorthand writers could get everything written down.

So, I made my statement. I went through the night of the Cornell killing and the drive to Walthamstow. I said how Christine had reacted when we all got to our flat. I told them about what happened there. How after it was over, my wife had wanted to get away and live in Birmingham where she came from, but instead we'd gone to the caravan in Steeple Bay. After that, we'd stayed at Alfie's place in Holborn.

I remember the magistrate asking me: 'What guns were in the flat at the time?' I got some black looks from Ron across the court as I told them about the guns.

'Fucking liar!' he shouted out.

Then Scotch Ian's brief had a go at me: If what I was saying was true, why hadn't I gone to the police? 'I was too frightened for myself and my family,' I explained. The first time I'd said anything to the police about any of it was two weeks before, on 2 July, in Littlehampton Police Station when they had offered me and my family protection – and we needed it.

It was over. My time in the witness box had lasted just under an hour although it felt like ten. After I'd done my bit, I was escorted out. And there was Christine coming the other way! I tried to run towards her but was physically held back. I could see her after she'd given her evidence, that's what I was told. For now, I mustn't speak to or touch her.

Christine made her statement. I wasn't allowed in court to hear it. I could gather afterwards that it was pretty much as she'd told DI Henry Mooney on 3 July about the time the Krays set up camp at Moresby Road. I don't know what she said under cross-examination and how tough it might have been for her. And she was in no mood to tell me even if she could and there was nothing in the newspapers. I just hoped facing Ronnie and Co. hadn't been too much of an ordeal, although I suspected it was.

Back in the big room, I waited for what seemed like ages. After a while Mr Read came in, thanked me, shook my hand and said I could see Christine – but not until later. After what seemed like hours, I was taken in an unmarked car to the flat in Stanhope Street, behind Euston Station, where my wife now lived with our three kids and to where she'd been taken after her testimony. I'd not seen her outside of a prison for two years.

It was so wonderful to be able to hug her and the kids again properly in our own home, rather than surrounded by screws on one of those awkward prison visits. It all just felt much more natural – we were at last a proper family again. Both Chrissie and I got very emotional, it was a terrible wrench to have to say goodbye.

It was getting late.

'Come on, David, time to go,' said one officer (Frank Cater, I think it was). Then we were in the car going through south-west London, heading down the A3 back to Ford. There were two detectives minding me.

'Well, David, what did you make of that?' the second copper asked. I don't know his name.

'Make of what?'

'That's right, you don't know. Well now you've given your evidence, there's no harm in telling you. Your brother, Bobby, being a police informer. Inside the Firm. He just told everyone in open court. Nipper is well pleased with him, I can tell you!'

'What are you talking about?'

'Well, turns out he went to the police right at the beginning of Moresby Road, right after the Cornell killing. He was with Butler.'

I didn't even know who 'Butler' was.

'Better let the prison governor tell you all about it. You'll be on Rule 43, special measures.'

\* \* \*

I'd seen Bobby for only a few seconds, coming past me as I myself went into Court Number One – I didn't know what he had said. He was able to recollect in detail almost fifty years after he'd been on the witness stand that summer morning in Bow Street. Like me, he'd been woken in his cell before dawn and brought in a fast convoy from Maidstone Prison to London. This is how my brother remembered it when he told his story to the journalist and author Clare Campbell in 2011:

I told the court about the night of the drive from Madge's to Walthamstow and the arrival at the Chequers pub, where Ronnie had washed his hands with Vim sink cleaner.

I told the story of Moresby Road in a kind of matter-of-fact way without too much detail. And I explained what happened after it was over – my time on the Firm in summer 1966, my trip to Cambridge and Saffron Walden, the flats Reggie and I had shared in Green Lanes and Lea Bridge Road.

After I'd finished, Reggie's brief lays into me. He says I'm being paid to say all this.

'That's lies,' I replied.

Then Scotch Ian Barrie's barrister began his cross-examination for the defence. 'When did the witness,' meaning me, 'first consider giving evidence?'

That's a good question. I'm under oath, after all.

'I first considered giving evidence in this matter just after I realised [Cornell's] murder had taken place and I did something about it then. I gave it some thought. It was obvious to me that my brothers were terrified, so to speak, so I got in touch with Scotland Yard. I met a man by the name, I think, of Arthur Butler.

'I was then put on to another chap, Tommy Butler, and through him a man named Joe Pogue, who is in the Flying Squad. I kept Tommy Butler up to date on everything that was happening ...'

So that was a bit of a shocker. There'd been a spy in the Firm, a grass. And what had the police done with the information? Nothing. Nipper Read must have been astounded (unless he sort of knew some of it already. Bobby thinks he did, he'd tell me later). Tommy Butler wasn't about to say anything and nobody was bothering to ask him. He'd not be appearing in these proceedings or any other. Bobby continued:

Then I explained how Butler & Co had not asked me at any stage to make a statement, an official statement that could be used to bring a prosecution, I mean. In fact, I had first been asked to make a statement very recently – only two weeks ago. I told the court that I'd been in touch with the police for about six weeks to two months after the shooting, till after I'd left the flat in Green Lanes [and gone to Lea Bridge Road] at which point I'd stopped all contact. I deliberately did not put this in my statement of 2 July made in Maidstone Police station.

I was taken back to Maidstone. I could not believe how fast word got back to the nick that I was the grass. A friend who I trusted in told me: 'Bobby, watch your back, the word is out on you and you are going to be hit.'

The Governor knew about it. I was put in solitary for my own protection. All kinds of threats were fed to me from crooked screws through the prison-cell door. I would get a banging on my cell door in the middle of the night and someone would call out, 'Bobby, Bobby!' in a deep voice until I answered.

'What do you want?' I'd say, and the voice would reply: 'You are a dead man and all your family are going to be poisoned.

You can still stop all this if you say that the Old Bill put you up to it using your Mum to make you tell lies about the Krays?'

Then I was shipped out of prison in the middle of the night because a gun had been smuggled into the prison to kill me, or at least that's what I was told by the Governor.

The news I was an informer had reached Maidstone even before I'd arrived back there on the afternoon of 16 July.

And it had got to Brixton just as fast as it took a prison van to get back there from Covent Garden. And to Ford. And to Lewes and to Maidstone. All the nicks that mattered. Bobby Teale had been informing since summer 1966. No wonder Ronnie had been so fucking angry.

We must all have been grasses, we were all in grave danger.

The head of Read's witness safety team, Sergeant Bert Trevette, must have briefed the Governor by phone. We'd got back to Ford late at night and I'd been driven straight to the hospital wing. It was clear I'd be staying there. I fell into a troubled sleep, dealing with the emotions of seeing Christine and the kids again, the threats from Ronnie, trying to get my head round this crazy story that Bobby was a grass.

What had really been going on?

It was straight into the Governor's office next morning. He explained a bit more about what Bobby had said, what he revealed in his evidence in open court about meeting Mr Butler during the time the Krays and others had been staying with me and my family.

I would be on Rule 43, something you could either ask for yourself or it was put on you by the authorities. So, at first, I was kept in a little room by myself so that they could see how the rumours went around the prison and whether I would be at risk.

He couldn't help asking: did I have any idea that my brother had been in contact with the police? No, I did not, it was a total shock.

I think he said the Home Office had been in touch. I wasn't to worry as my wife and children were still under police protection.

Well, I *was* worried.

So, what the fuck did it all mean? Bobby had been staying in the flat in Lea Bridge Road while, according to what he'd apparently just said in the magistrates' court, he was getting messages about what the Firm were up to to Mr Butler at Scotland Yard. Then there was the raid on the flat above the barber's shop in which Ronnie, Reggie, Scotch Ian and Smithy had all been nicked. Had Bobby told Butler somehow that's where they'd all be? It looked overwhelmingly as if he had.

Then Ronnie Hart and Frosty had come looking for Bobby at Steeple Bay. Christine had been roughed up. And then we'd all been arrested in that flat in Dolphin Square for getting pissed with some geezer Bobby says he met in a pub. Result? Three years in prison. Was that all part of it? You bet it was!

As for me, I was more vulnerable here in Ford than walking the streets of London.

'I think for your own safety, it's good you stay in the hospital wing,' the Governor said. 'We'll need to see how the land lies.'

A week later, I was put back into the system. I volunteered to go back on the Burma Road, breaking up the old tarmac runway of Ford airfield. Things were rocky anyway. The Kray fan club has its members everywhere. I had been a prosecution witness and my brother was a bleeding grass all the time! Were we Teale brothers all grasses?

There was sneering, hissing, like I'd had from Ronnie in court. I'd been paid to tell lies by the Yard. I had a couple of fist fights. I didn't want to blow any pre-release home leave (I'd get five days in July). So, I'd been a Crown witness against the Krays, a pack of murdering, raping, scumbags.

So, what?

Right then, all I wanted was to survive and get back to my wife and family alive.

# 21

## YOU CAN ONLY TELL THE TRUTH

It was all working out as DI Read had planned it. Even though there'd be nothing in the evening or the next day's papers about what Alfie, me and especially Bobby had told the court in Bow Street, it was all over all the nicks that mattered. It had got back to Ford quick enough.

The Teales were singing; the wall of fear was crumbling. Look what Nipper wrote in his memoirs:

Things were moving behind the scenes. On 16 July [the day Alfie, I and Bobby gave evidence] I had the biggest break of all. While I was at Bow Street dealing with the Cornell committal proceedings, I received a note.

This is what happened. Albert Donoghue's mother had come herself to give the note to Nipper Read after she'd been handed it by her son in Brixton (she'd visited him earlier that afternoon). Mrs Donoghue 'pleaded with me to see her son, saying it was a matter of life and death,' Read wrote. He had got down there fast to see Donoghue in the prison hospital early that same evening.

The 'sullen, defiant man' he had first encountered was now very different, so Read said in his memoirs:

> He came straight out and said: 'It's been put to me to volunteer for the Mitchell business [confess to killing him] and, if I do, my wife and kids will be all right.'

As I myself would hear it very much later, there had been a meeting in the solicitors' rooms in Brixton. The twins told Donoghue he should take responsibility for the Mitchell murder and that their cousin Ronnie Hart would put his hand up for the Cornell killing, thus leaving Scotch Ian Barrie free of charges. Reggie would plead self-defence for doing Jack 'the Hat' McVitie.

Big Albert was not happy, he wanted to make a deal with the prosecution. If the murder charge against him was dropped, in return he would tell Read the lot. Over the next three days, according to Read, Donoghue did just that. So, the next day he was spirited out of Brixton to Winson Green Prison in Birmingham and his wife and family were put under guard.

It was the same with Scotch Jack Dickson. He'd tell how it happened when it got to the full trial. When they were in Brixton, the twins were leaning on him to cook up an alibi. Then he said he wanted to change his brief, get a new one, not the twins' brief. Suddenly he gets transferred to Wandsworth and asks to see Mr Read. On 16 July 1968, late in the day he made a statement about how he'd driven Ronnie to the Blind Beggar.

It was the twins' defence who screwed up this time. Their solicitor had shown Scotch Jack our statements – Alfie's, Bobby's and mine (they were allowed to do that) – and leant on him to say: 'Why have these three brothers said all the things they must know are not true?'

But it went wrong. Read in turn came down heavy on Scotch Jack and got him to change sides, using our statements as a way of persuading him that the Krays' influence was crumbling and that he needed to switch so as to avoid being dragged down with them.

Funnily enough, immediately after our in-camera appearance, the full Kray read-all-about-it works were turned on again. The next day, 17 July, Ronnie and Scotch Ian Barrie were formally committed for trial for the murder of George Cornell. Reggie was charged with 'acting to impede their apprehension'.

Reporting restrictions were lifted at Bow Street for that big bit of news. And for the depositions heard the rest of that day. More loopy stuff about poison syringes and crossbows. Presiding magistrate Mr Kenneth Barraclough admitted he didn't understand a word of it and threw it out. But that stuff didn't matter anymore, the tide was already turning. I'm sure it was because of what we brothers had had to say at Bow Street on 16 July about the night Cornell was done.

But Nipper Read needed more if this (as yet) single murder charge was to be wheeled into the Old Bailey for a full trial. What was going to be a big problem was what Bobby had said in open court (even if it was in camera) about Tommy Butler and Joe Pogue in the committal – a defence could rip into that.

Well, that had been a shock for Read (apparently) and indeed anyone who heard it. Bobby was due for pre-release home leave. In fact, he was going to have a sit-down with DI Henry Mooney in

London for a bit of urgent clarification – I saw it in the National Archives.

Bobby had been in Charlie Clark's bungalow in Loxham Road and heard 'Ronnie saying that Reggie should kill someone to prove he was just as good as Ronnie', so Bobby said. 'The words used were, "Why don't you do something? I have done one, you don't do fuck all."'

'Reggie used to say, "Don't fucking tell me what to do," and he often said he would prove himself in time.'

Well, he would, with Jack 'the Hat' McVitie.

'There was a list of people to be executed. There were about ten names on it, one being a fellow connected with blue films in the West End,' Bobby said. Reggie had staged a mock execution of a small-time villain called Bobby Cannon with a muffled revolver 'at a party in Hackney Road. I think it was the flat of Blonde Vicky [Ronnie Hart's girlfriend].' Bobby had intervened to effectively let Cannon escape.

Bobby described a visit to the Regency Club, where Reggie had demanded £1,000 before shooting a face called Jimmy Field in the leg. He'd heard four shots. Scotch Ian had also been there.

Bobby ended his statement saying: 'I kept in touch with police after the Cornell murder. The officer I dealt with was Pogue. I used the name of Phillips. I was arrested on 9 August 1966. (Signed) R. Teale.'

We'd each done well at the committal – the prosecution would want to use us again. It was decided there would be two trials, Cornell and McVitie on the same indictment for murder, and a separate one for Mitchell. Security around witnesses would be extra-tight while there was time to test prosecution evidence already given for chinks the defence could prise open. They would do their best.

I was really shaken down. A finance company had a record of a car registered as 6544 MF, the grey Ford Popular in which I had driven from Madge's to Walthamstow. It was down to a Mr David Lee.

And when the twins were nicked, Ronnie and Reggie's address books were taken from their parents' seventh-floor council flat in Finsbury. There was a phone number in both, UPP[er Clapton] 4014. A GPO official could confirm that was the number for a subscriber at 51 Moresby Road, E5 – that was me.

Ronnie had me down in his book as 'Dave Tiel' aka 'Dave Lee'. I'm in there on the same page as 'Kenny Lynch, entertainer' and 'Eric Lubbock MP, chairman of the parliamentary civil liberties group' – I saw it in the National Archives.

The landlords of Manor Lea, 295 Green Lanes, confirmed they had rented Flat 6 to a Miss Kerin and a Mrs Marshall. Emmanuel Ackerman, manager of the Green Dragon, was the guarantor. Neighbours had complained about noisy parties and owing rent, the ladies had quit the flat and moved out all the furniture on 18 June 1966.

So that was Bobby's statement stood up.

They even got a statement from our mother, Ellen Teale. It was on 24 July, the week after we'd given evidence. I've seen it in the National Archives. She called the Krays the 'Craigs' throughout apparently. Good old Mum! It was taken down by Detective Sergeant Story, the same DS who had interviewed me in Littlehampton.

Yes, Charlie, Ronnie and Reggie had been members of the Tudor Club, they were extremely well behaved and never gave any trouble, she told DS Story. They promised to look after her sons and not let them drink and drive too much (!?!). She and Mr Teale never visited Moresby Road or knew who was there. After we'd been arrested and were on remand, one of us had told her that the Krays would help pay for our defence, but they hadn't. Bobby had said, 'They must think we were right mugs, we've never had anything off them.'

She'd heard from one of us that Reggie or Ronnie had tried to visit either Bobby or me in Maidstone, but the Governor would not let them in.

Alfie had been on a pre-release home visit to see her and Mr Teale. He knew about the arrest of the twins. Her eldest son had said, 'If I'm asked about them, I shall tell the truth.' Bobby had more or less said the same on a similar visit home, said Mum.

I myself had done a home leave visit. There'd been some joking with me apparently. 'You can't believe these things being said about them [the Krays], Mum,' I'd said to her. 'But you can only tell the truth,' she'd replied. 'Alright, Mum, I will tell the truth, only kidding ...' I'd said. That's what she told the police I'd said, anyway.

As a cheerful little sidelight our mum told DS Story that she'd 'heard a woman at the Odeon Bingo in Hackney Road talk about someone straightening the man at Hackney General Hospital's waste incinerator to cremate Frank Mitchell's body'.

# 22

## THE BIG TRIAL

On 13 September 1968, I was let out of Ford prison after doing over two years for something I did not do. When I walked up to the prison gate at about 9am, Christine was waiting in a car outside with a policeman and woman in the front.

Was I really being set free of anything?

By then, I'd given plentiful statements to the police and live evidence in the magistrates' court. Even if there'd been a press ban on my big day at Bow Street, what I'd said had come out within hours. That was Nipper's intention.

It felt strange to be free but even odder to be kissing and cuddling my wife in front of my new minders. I asked where the kids were and Christine said they were being looked after by a friend. So, the copper, who was named Dick De Lillo, said he'd got a horse to back and suggested we all go to the races.

Christine and I found ourselves along with him at Sandown racetrack. We didn't get back until the evening and there wasn't much time to talk about anything intimate with Dick around us all the time. Christine, too, had a policewoman with her so it was virtually impossible for us to be natural with one another.

By the time we got back, at about seven, her friend had brought the children home. I rushed into the house to see them, picking them up and cuddling them, hardly able to believe I was really home again.

Bodyguards were with us all the time. The police who looked after us used to take us out to eat, Alfie as well because they were on expenses and wanted to go somewhere nice. They particularly liked the restaurants along Southampton Row and round Queen's Square, Italian restaurants like the Mille Pini. They really couldn't care less what we did and were not bad company. They were meant to stay with us in the flat or in a car outside, but in fact we told them we'd be OK and so they used to go off and sleep in the Section House across the road and come back in the morning.

It was the same for Alfie. He was 'released' only to be whisked off to Tintagel House for another run-through with DI Nipper Read of what he should say in court, how the defence might try and get him. That's what he'd tell me. At the end of the interview, Nipper had said, 'Right, Alfie. You can go home now. You and David, and Chrissie, have each got a police officer looking after you. They'll keep you safe.'

We could only hope.

Christmas was coming, but things weren't altogether festive. Mum's case came up at the Old Bailey on 28 November 1968. There were two charges, housebreaking, in that she 'broke in and entered Lady Violet Hamilton's house and stole three paintings, jade jewellery, candlesticks, chain, enamel, crystal, clocks, boxes and ornaments to the value of £25,000'. And count two, conspiracy to steal, in which she conspired with persons unknown to steal property at 8 Russell Court, SW1. She pleaded guilty to count one – she wasn't going to say anything about Charlie Kray and Leslie Holt. She was sentenced to two years in prison, suspended for three.

She passed out in the dock. I was there but not allowed to go in the court because of being a witness at the forthcoming Kray trial. She had been told to plead guilty by Read because she let the thieves in and had no proof that she was not involved in the robbery.

Alfie and I knew we'd got to start earning a living again so we went out fly-pitching with our minders in Strutton Ground in Victoria, near New Scotland Yard. It was one of the funniest things you'd ever seen: we had the police looking out for the police. We worked Oxford Street, two plainclothes men telling us 'Up!' and 'Quick!'

It was like the old days. Strutton Ground was lunchtime trading, but the council man would come along to move us and we'd tell the police to order him to ignore us. We made a lot of money and used to give the police some to get the drinks in for all of us at the end of the day. Eventually, we had to stop as the police were worried it would come out in the *News of the World*.

\* \* \*

The start of the big trial was just a few days away. Then, just after New Year in January 1969, I visited Tintagel House for a last-minute briefing – I had something very personal to say.

I talked to Nipper Read and his number two, DI Frank Cater. I told them how Ronnie Kray had forcibly raped me at Vallance Road in the summer of 1966. It wasn't easy, I stopped and stumbled several times. As soon as they realised what I was saying, they asked me to 'put it all down in a statement'.

A week later, they told me they would keep my statement safely, but that they had so much on the Krays already, they would not need to use it in open court. But they would if the other charges failed. Meanwhile, I was advised not to mention Ronnie's sexuality. I was OK with this as at the time I wouldn't even have wanted what I'd told them about being raped to be printed on a toilet roll, let alone a national newspaper. They said not to worry, that the Krays were 'not going to see daylight for a very long time'.

Maybe so.

* * *

The time had come. The newspapers were full of it, the opening of the full trial was just a few days away. I'd been inside one or two courtrooms in my not very long life, always on the wrong side of the law, always with some dock brief to 'defend' me.

Unsuccessfully.

This time, the defence put together by the solicitors Sampson and Co. was the enemy, hiring the best barristers the Krays and the other defendants could afford, ready to tear into the testimony of police and civilian prosecution witnesses. Three war babies from Holborn, street traders with dodgy form sheets, looked easy enough.

It was kind of class war. Nearly all the Crown witnesses had criminal records, weren't educated, barely literate like me. Kenneth Jones, QC for the prosecution, gave it away when he called the characters involved (and I'm sure he meant all of us, not just the defendants) 'absurd creatures from the underworld'. And the defence briefs could hardly disguise their contempt for those of us Crown witnesses who had been suckered into testifying by the do-anything-for-a-prosecution police and bribed with the prospect of a softer sentence.

It was Scotch Jack Dickson who would say it best: 'Someone had got to have the guts to come forward and tell ordinary people what cruel bastards [the Krays] were ...'

\* \* \*

The order of witnesses was to be Alfie, me, Christine and then Bobby. The defence meanwhile had clearly spent a lot of time finding out what we might say, what we might know, all about our mum, our backgrounds, our sex lives, our wives, our kids, our weak points. Any way we might be attacked had been trawled through, our CRO records from the age of ten picked clean.

When it came to the trial, they knew the inside on our fitted-up trial of summer 1966 (how did they get that?). They had the depositions and cross-examination from the committal proceedings. They'd seen copies of the statements we made to the police with plenty of time to go through them.

It was Tuesday, 14 January 1969. The trial had begun on the 8th. At the start there was a big row apparently about the defendants being ordered to wear numbers on ribbons round their necks. Ron tore his up. The judge backed down and the numbers were stuck on the front of the dock.

I was woken very early. So too, I know, was Alfie and we were taken under separate guard from our homes to the Old Bailey with another extra police car behind us. Alfie and I were not allowed to see one another or speak. I didn't have a clue where Bobby was, but I could guess he'd be putting in an appearance sometime very soon.

Alfie was on first. I could not see him or make contact, or even hear the proceedings. I'd find out much more later in conversation and almost fifty years after it all happened when I saw the transcript of what Alfie (and indeed, what all of us) had said that day, just as it was taken down by the court stenographers at the trial. It's all in the National Archives, fresh as the day it was typed.

The junior counsel for the prosecution, John Leonard, led Alfie through the testimony he'd given to Read's team and a reprise of what he'd said at the committal when he'd appeared as 'Mr A'. It was a detailed account of the night of the phone call from Reggie and the days of mayhem that followed.

Alfie was on again as 'Mr A'. Ronnie's defending counsel John Platts-Mills let rip with an attack on him as to why he might want to conceal his identity. It could not be on account of fear of his peaceable, law-abiding client. It could not be to protect his children, aged four and nine. Alfie said his youngest had been told when he was in prison that he'd been away in the army.

It was 'imperative' that Mr A's real name be revealed, said Platts-Mills, 'so that past or present blackmail victims might be emboldened to come forward and reveal his full character'. The judge allowed it. Then Platts-Mills really started sneering.

'Are you accustomed to cases where men wish to call themselves "Mr A" or "Mr X"?'

'No, I am not.'

'Because you are accustomed to blackmailing cases, aren't you?'

'I don't think so.'

'Your way of life is the most sordid known to British crime, is it not?'

'You seem to think so.'

'Are you homosexual yourself?'

'No.'

'Any tendencies that way?'

'None at all,' Alfie replied.

'You seek out older men who have respectable positions in life and have homosexual tendencies, then you blackmail them,' he persisted. 'Isn't that your way of life?'

He'd clearly got hold of the trial transcript of our appearance in Court Number One two years before. Mr John Leonard had prosecuted that case. Strange that. Who had conveniently made that available to the Krays' defence? We'd be none the wiser.

Alfie got a lot of questions about Tapp Street and just where and at what time his brother (me) had supposedly stopped his grey Ford Popular to be met by Reggie shouting: 'Get us off the manor!'

The defence's claim was that Ronnie had never been in the Blind Beggar. There had been no siege of Moresby Road. There might have been a party there, which Ronnie had attended much later, but that was all.

It turned into a second day of questions.

'Do you remember singing and dancing?' Platts-Mills asked Alfie.

'No, I remember drinks there – nearly every night there was a drink.'

'And some girls, people's wives and so on?'

'I don't remember no people's wives.'

'Dancing going on?'

'No, there was a record player.'

'One of your favourites is "Zorba the Greek"?'

'You cannot sing that, it is music, there are no lyrics to it.'

'The neighbours sent for the police that night because of the row you were making, singing "Zorba the Greek".'

'What night was that?'

'About a week to ten days after the night when Cornell was killed and the uniformed police came in and conveyed the protest of the neighbours.'

'Well, I cannot remember it.'

'You mean it is the kind of thing that could happen any night at David's?'

'No.'

'The impression you sought to give yesterday was that David's flat was used as a hideout for a week?'

'Yes.'

'And I suggest, the only occasion Ronald came was either at the end of that week or at a later stage when there was quite a noisy party, far from being a discreet hiding place ...'

'No, that's not true.'

Then they opened up on Alfie about Bobby. The defence clearly knew a lot – from someone on the inside or worked it out from what our brother had said at the committal.

'Did you know there were identification parades in August 1966?'

'I did read something about it.'

'And you were not asked anything before these identification parades?'

'No.'

'If Bobby had a meeting with Chief Superintendent Thomas Butler before September 1966, he managed to conceal that from you?'

'He did.'

'And neither Chief Superintendent Butler nor anybody else came to ask you any questions?'

'Nothing at all,' Alfie said.

\* \* \*

They were trying to make out that we three brothers were good friends of the twins. But we had no reason whatsoever to fear them. We were saying all of these lies because of police pressure or because we were being paid to say them, they suggested.

Then the defence opened a new line.

'The [Krays] were great people for going to a caravan ... Mother Kray had a big caravan on a site?'

'Yes, she did.'

'Where?'

'A place called Steeple,' Alfie said.

'And you went frequently to the caravan at weekends, with or near the Krays on the same site?'

'No, I went with my wife and children.'

'You have, have you not, been yourself a party to the taking of a number of photos showing you and the Kray families in very happy domestic friendship? [the pictures the police took from Christine. How did they know about those?] That was all under compulsion, was it?'

'Well, up to a certain point, yes.'

Then the defence got to our mum – you could see this coming.

'Your mother is Ellen, is she not?' he asked. 'At about the time you first gave a statement to the police, June [sic] of 1968, had your mother been arrested?'

'Yes, she had.'

'[She worked at] a house of titled people?'

'Yes.'

'I think ennobled people?'

'Yes.'

'Was there £25,000 worth of jade involved?'

'I don't know how much was involved,' Alfie replied.

'Mother was alleged, as housekeeper to this house, to have opened the doors and let the burglar in?'

'That was what they said.'

'And Dad, so it was suggested, was the burglar ... ?'

'Well, why wasn't he arrested?'

'I am going to ask you that in a moment. Is this the bargain that was made with you: you help to put the twins inside, Dad will be let off [and] Mum will plead guilty and get off with virtually nothing?'

'No, it was not.'

And then it was over. There were no more attacks on Alfie's character or our mother's. Nipper Read came rushing up to Alfie, who asked him: 'Was I alright?'

Placing his hands on Alfie's shoulder, Read stood back and told him, 'Alfie, you were absolutely brilliant! You didn't let them get away with anything.'

Then it was my turn. It was the second day for us at the Old Bailey: Wednesday, 15 January 1969. I don't think I've ever been so scared before in my life – I had a couple of stiff drinks before we went in.

It started even before we'd got into the main court. The police put me in the same room as Scotch Jack Dickson when we were both waiting to give evidence. Jack came over and shook my hand, telling me: 'You're doing the right thing.'

But I didn't trust him. I gave him some fags – he'd run out as he was smoking like a train, he was so petrified. We both were. He kept asking Nipper's men for more.

The time had come. I crept into the court like a little weasel, hearing Ron and Reggie and others all hissing at me as I entered.

I kept remembering what Ronnie had said to me when I'd said I was worried about my wife and kids at Moresby Road: 'Dead men can't speak.'

I didn't know then and still don't, whether Ronnie meant Cornell was dead and couldn't speak, or did he mean if I said anything either about the murder or the night he'd raped me that I too would be dead? He kept spitting 'Liar!' at me each time I spoke, hissing and glaring at me in an attempt to put me off. So, I looked straight at him and said, 'You know the truth, Ron,' referring both to Cornell and the rape that, as far as he was concerned, only he and I knew about. I said it quietly but I felt like screaming at him.

It began as it had for Alfie with a rake over of juvenile misdemeanours, robbing gas meters, Approved School, what a right little tearaway I was. And this was the prosecution asking the questions! Then the demanding money with menaces in October 1966 for which I got three years. No mention of wealthy homosexuals, mind you. They wanted to get the CRO stuff out of the way.

Then the junior counsel, John Leonard, got pretty smartish to the evening when the phone rang out in the hall of my flat and the drive to Tapp Street. There was a lot of trying to be precise about where and how I'd parked the car.

I went through the story of the night of the Cornell murder and the Firm coming back to the flat. When I said that Reginald Kray had passed a gun to Cornelius Whitehead, Ronnie shouted out, 'You fucking liar!' and had to be restrained. I just answered: 'Ron, the truth hurts ...'

It wasn't over. I had to go back in the afternoon. During the lunchbreak, I started to worry more and more, feeling I was betraying my family as well as the code I'd always lived by, never to grass.

Even with police protection, I wondered whether my wife and children would ever be safe.

Platts-Mills was on next for Ronnie. He went on and on about how I parked the car at Tapp Street, could I tell left from right, up from down, east from west, and what car Nobby Clark had been driving. Was it a green Rover or a green Vauxhall?

The judge got cross.

Then he got to a tougher bit: had I been in a common jail with one of my brothers? Was it Alfie or Bobby?

'It was Robert, sir.'

'And where was that?'

'Maidstone, sir.'

'And Bobby was the one who first gave evidence to the police?'

'I don't know.'

'Do you not know?'

'I know now, sir, but I didn't know then.'

And I did know. I knew Bobby had been an informer since the Governor at Ford had called me in after the Bow Street committal to put me on special protection. And that was it, no more questions on that tricky little topic. No more Bobby and Butler.

I went through the drive to Walthamstow, the cramming into the Chequers pub while Ronnie's brief was trying to trip me up on details. Was the broadcast news that 'a man called Cornell has been shot and died on the way to hospital' on a TV bulletin or on the 'ordinary radio'? I was asked. In fact, as I found in the National Archives, it was on the TV news, not the radio – which hadn't said Cornell was dead, just 'critical'. Anyway, I survived that ambush.

It was the same for the Moresby siege. There might have been one night when Ronnie and Reggie had stayed, he said, but no more than that. It was just a big party. And when I suggested I'd gone back for the last time, 'it was to collect your and your family's clothes and do a midnight flit, dishonestly dodging the rent, not because you were suggesting to the jury, you had to leave for some such reason as the ghastly experience you had had with the Krays, wasn't it?'

That's what Ronnie's brief might think. He got rapped by the judge for putting words in my month. Then he implied that I had given Inspector Read my statement in a bid to get myself off a charge of harbouring a suspected murderer (to my knowledge, not suspected, an actual murderer). And here it was again, I was saying all these untruths to get my mother off a serious criminal charge in a bargain I'd made with the police.

\* \* \*

Christine was up after me for a grilling by the defence. My wife kept her dignity and answered bravely to everything. John Leonard for the prosecution led her through her evidence, who'd been there in the flat, what they did, what she remembered. She picked out Ronnie, Reggie, Scotch Ian, Charlie Kray and Connie Whitehead, all with their identifying numbers, as being in court and all having been in our little flat.

She recalled a shotgun being put on the shelf above the bed. Reggie had held it on occasion. She talked about going shopping, always with a minder, and how towards the end of it all, a uniformed policeman had come to the door.

Platts-Mills for the defence did his usual inquisition on what went where, up, down, kitchen, toilet, bedroom, day, night, trying to make her look either stupid or devious.

How did she hear a man called Cornell had been killed?

'A newsflash on radio or television, I'm not sure,' she replied.

He pushed her more, about dancing and drinking in the flat and complaining neighbours (they objected to people using their lavatory) – how could this possibly be gangsters lying low? And he couldn't resist a reference to Zorba the Greek.

Perhaps he was a big fan.

He went on and on about the Steeple Bay caravan where our family seaside parties showed how little she, us or anyone else had to fear from the twins.

'How about the Carpenters Arms [a Kray pub in Cheshire Street], did you go drinking there?'

Ronnie must have told his brief.

'Maybe three times.'

'Wasn't it scores of times?'

'Since my husband has been in prison, I have seen the Krays maybe three times,' Christine said.

He seemed to know a hell of a lot. Where were they getting this stuff? Reggie and Scotch Ian's brief came on next to give her a renewed grilling.

I didn't know if I was doing the right thing, or the wrong thing. We had the police on one side of us, the Krays on the other. There was no way out. We knew we were already on the Krays' death-list, whether or not we gave evidence, whether or not we were on the streets, at home, in Steeple Bay or on the Moon. If I was charged and convicted by the police for aiding and abetting the murder of Cornell, I was looking at twelve to fifteen years in prison, while my wife would get three for harbouring a murderer. In the meantime, on a totally separate charge, our mum would be doing five in the company of Moors murderer Myra Hindley – that's if the Krays didn't get us first.

Bobby was on next, Thursday, 16 January. Mr John Leonard for the prosecution gave his full CRO form to the court. It was the usual list of youthful crimes and misdemeanours. He got to the demanding money with menaces conviction in October 1966, to which was added a concurrent year for stealing a motor vehicle.

Bobby did his stuff about the night of the shooting and the flight to Walthamstow, where showbiz agent Sammy Lederman had been behind the bar at the Chequers serving the drinks. Sammy had said, 'You're a cold-blooded murderer, Ronnie,' and Ronnie 'had laughed, saying, "Go on, fuck off then ... "'

Bobby talked about living in the flats in Green Lanes and then Lea Bridge Road, to where he had 'returned once to get some papers and clothes' (it was his passport, hidden behind a picture frame, I'd find out later). He'd seen Ronnie at the caravan site and Reggie once or twice after that. That's what he said anyway.

Then it was the defence turn. Platts-Mills tried the same on Bobby as he'd done on Alfie. Why was he hiding his identity as 'Mr B'? He wasn't hiding, not anymore. He gave it right at the start, clear as day: 'My name is Robert Frank Teale.'

Was it true that he'd been under constant police surveillance since release from prison?

It was.

And why might that be?

'For my personal security,' Bobby replied.

Ronnie's brief then started luxuriating in the blackmail conviction: 'How can the witness say he's not lying under oath when he pleaded not guilty under oath to a trial at the Old Bailey and got convicted by a jury?'

'It is ridiculously wrong to describe me and my brothers as professional blackmailers,' Bobby said.

There's some trying to trip him up on stuff about the night Cornell got shot and what happened afterwards, the drive from Madge's, what really happened in the Chequers, what Sammy Lederman had said, whether Bobby could tell Nobby Clark from Ronnie Clark (he meant Charlie Clark), whether we'd been to any other pub or flats before going to my place.

Next, Bobby was cross-examined about what he'd said about how Reggie and he had lived together in Green Lanes, the trip to Saffron Walden and Cambridge, with the implication that he was making it all up. He was asked about Charlie Clark's place in Chingford and the flat in Lea Bridge Road. Nobody asked how it came to be raided.

Then came something that the defence brief was not going to sneer quite so much about.

'Do you not agree that if by any chance you had applied your mind to this question three years ago just after it happened, made some statement, written it down, thought about it carefully, then it would have been much easier for you to work out the details?' so Platts-Mills asked Bobby.

This is what Bobby said in reply in open court at the Old Bailey: 'I did do something about it three years ago.'

'What do you suggest you did?'

'I got in touch with Scotland Yard and I assisted them in their inquiries.'

'You got in touch with Scotland Yard?'

'Yes – just after the Cornell murder.'

'Was that in March 1966?'

'Yes.'

'With whom did you get in touch?'

'I think it was Tommy Butler.'

'Tommy Butler was then chief of the CID, was he not, at Scotland Yard? How did you contact him?'

'By phone.'

'You actually met him?'

'I met him on one occasion, yes.'

'This is Mr Tommy Butler, a man of enormous distinction, who has just retired from a leading position at Scotland Yard?'

'This is true, yes.'

'And it is your story that he did not take any statement from you whatsoever?'

'Yes.'

'So far as you know, made no investigations whatsoever?'

The judge intervened at that point: 'How can he possibly answer that? He does not know.'

'I was going to suggest to him that he had not really met Tommy Butler,' the defence replied.

'Did you meet some other distinguished police officers?' the defence continued.

'I met one man who I used to explain one or two things to.'

'What sort of things?'

'Look, a murder had taken place,' said Bobby. 'I found myself in a position where I was in possession of a certain amount of information which I felt could help bring these men to justice. I got in touch with Scotland Yard. I met one or two other people who I was in contact with most of the time.'

'Did you get money for that?'

'Not a penny, I didn't expect any.'

'What were you doing it for?'

'Because it was obvious to me that these people were then running around like animals and because I happen to know that they were going to kill a number of people in the area, someone had to do something.'

'Is it not the fact that you did not make a statement to anyone about the supposed knowledge of yours until July 1968, two years after the event? Why was that?'

'It would have put my family in jeopardy. Yes. Well, isn't it obvious, a man walks into a pub and shoots a man in cold-blooded murder, am I going to make a statement and wind up dead myself, or my family?'

'Why would your family be in jeopardy?'

'I knew a murder had taken place. I knew they had a list of people they were going to do.'

'Going back to the time after the shooting, you have told us that you communicated with Scotland Yard and spoke to Tommy Butler. Did you speak to any other officers?'

'Yes, Joe Pogue.'

'Did you tell him about the Cornell shooting?'

'I explained what position I was in. I explained there were going to be some killings.'

'This was about the Cornell killing which had already taken place?'

'Well, I just briefed him on the details that occurred as far as we were concerned. I said my brothers are terrified, they have wives and children. If I am fool enough to get trapped by these animals, then it is my fault.'

'What did you call yourself, speaking to this police officer?'

'I called myself Phillips.'

There were no reporting restrictions this time. The press picked it up eagerly: 'Robert Teale caused a stir when he revealed himself to have been a police spy. He was asked how many times he had seen the police and what information he had given them,' so one paper reported. It was the *Evening News* as I remember. The story was read out to me.

Well, there was quite a stir.

There it was, unlike the no-press-allowed committal in Bow Street, this time for the whole world to see. 'Police Spy in the Firm' was the headline. Bobby was described as 'a brown-haired youth in a suede jacket'. But what the journalists were *not* asking was why Butler had given up on the Krays and left them free to kill again.

Not that the Yard was going to tell them or anyone else.

\* \* \*

Billy Exley was in the witness box next, the ex-boxer who'd come looking for Bobby at Steeple Bay. He was ill with heart trouble. At least he said out loud that the Firm really had 'gone to the Teales' flat in Stoke Newington' and talked about staying at Moresby Road and how Ronnie had said about Cornell in my living room: 'Fuck him! I'm glad he's dead.'

He'd been ordered to get 'underclothes and suits', he said, when we were all in my flat and then take the twins' washing backwards and forwards to their mum in Vallance Road. He'd stayed at Fort Vallance for two or three nights with Scotch Pat Connolly, both cradling shotguns in case the Richardsons came around, he said. In fact, their only visitor had been Olive, Cornell's widow, shouting outside early in the morning – you can imagine what she said. They'd gone to the Lea Bridge Road gaff. Ian Barrie and Teddy Smith had been there, he added.

Detective Chief Inspector Henry Mooney was on after that. He got it hard from the defence. They were doing the old trick of discrediting the police evidence, with Bobby and Butler as the weakest links.

'Have you any knowledge of the communication between Robert Teale and Chief Superintendent Butler?' Platts-Mills asked him.

'I have,' said Mooney. But he had never asked anything of Mr Butler directly about the matter during his own investigation, he admitted. And just why was that? The defence didn't press him further.

What about there being guns in the flat in, where was it, Moresby Road? 'Wouldn't this have provided vital forensic evidence if the police had acted – if indeed there was any truth in the story?' so Platt-Mills asked Mooney.

We were all liars and fantasists; we were made to seem. Especially Bobby with his absurd story about meeting the famous Tommy Butler. We were just making it all up. Mooney did not really know what to say. The police looked like fools or liars or both, the way they'd reacted to the information that half the Firm were holed up in a flat in Stoke Newington. And what had they done?

But the police and prosecution could always produce Pogue to prove that Bobby Teale had been telling the truth. So, Detective Sergeant Joseph Pogue was called. It wasn't part of Read's big plan. His appearance in court could aid the prosecution in confirming the truth of what Bobby had said. Or it might do the very opposite, by making the whole investigation look like a shambles from the beginning, or at least until Read took over.

On the stand, Pogue gave the briefest confirmation of the exist-ence of 'Bob Phillips', who he met 'probably a week after the actual murder'. Under cross-examination by Ronnie's brief, he confirmed the meeting of 'Phillips' with Tommy Butler at Hackney greyhound stadium. But of the meets with Bobby after that, he said he had only made rough notes without dates.

'Robert Teale had never volunteered a written statement,' he said.

Nobody pressed Pogue further. Maybe it suited both defence and prosecution that the story of Phillips the informer and how he had been betrayed should just go away. It certainly seemed to suit the Yard that way.

To my knowledge, Tommy Butler *was* called as a witness (by which side I don't know) but managed to get out of it. He was 'retired', he had insisted.

Nipper Read himself would be on the stand the following day. He was going to be in trouble. This is what he said in his memoirs:

On day eight of the trial, Platts-Mills questioned me directly about [the informer]. I was at a distinct disadvantage. Now the gaping hole in the Yard's file was exposed. He put to me the names of a number of people who had been seen after Cornell's murder and long before I took over the inquiry. I was obliged to answer that there were no notes [of such meetings] or interviews.

Platts-Mills asked questions about the surveillance of the twins and the story of Violet Kray bringing tea on trays to the police watch-ing outside Vallance Road. It sounded ridiculous. Read couldn't comment – he had not been involved. That was Butler's or the local police's operation, it was all before his time.

More to the point was the matter of somebody actually coming forward to tell the police that there 'were guns in some flat in March 1966', as the defence put it. 'Is it really conceivable that the police did not act? Isn't that because the informer and the information [he allegedly gave] was utterly worthless?' so Platts-Mills asked Read.

Read didn't have an answer. He hadn't 'been involved back then', he kept repeating.

Did Inspector Butler ever go to David Teale's flat?

'Not to my knowledge,' said Read. 'I wasn't concerned with the case.'

And of course, he hadn't been.

He stonewalled in court whenever the Moresby Road episode was mentioned, even though it had been his men in summer 1968 who had taken intimate details from neighbours, hire-purchase agents and telephone engineers about 'Mr Lee' and his little family.

Read clearly wanted as little said about Bobby and Butler as possible. Anything to do with Butler and the informer was more than a bit difficult.

Ronnie's brief reeled off a list of members of the Firm whose names this 'Bobby Teale' might have revealed – Sammy Lederman, Nobby Clark, Billy Exley, Harry Jew Boy Cope, Big Pat Connolly, John Dickson. Was there any record of them?

'No,' said Read.

'Of course, that means, doesn't it,' said Platts-Mills, 'that Mr Bobby Teale did not mention any of their names?'

'He certainly did not speak to me about it in 1966,' said Read.

'The Teales at one time shared lodging with Mr McCowan?' asked Platts-Mills.

'Not to my knowledge,' said Read.

'Mr Hew McCowan [who was] the principal witness in the 1965 case of my client ... ?'

Raking up the Hideaway affair was just as uncomfortable for Read.

* * *

After Cornell, the court got on to the Jack 'the Hat' McVitie murder, in which we Teale brothers had not played any part at all. We'd all been inside, although I knew Bobby had given DCI Mooney an account of how Ronnie kept urging Reggie to kill.

Then it was Ronnie's turn in the spotlight. But was he actually going to say anything in his own defence? It looked for a while as if he would not. On 30 January, Platts-Mills announced he was 'frightened to go into the witness box' because of the allegations against him by a 'hooligan mob' of 'self-confessed liars'. Then, having said he wouldn't give evidence, Ronnie suddenly shouted out from the dock that he would. That meant that he could be cross-examined.

Platts-Mills led him through the case as presented by the devious and deceitful prosecution. He had not killed Cornell, it was mistaken identity. He was only on trial, he said: 'Because newspapers and the police had been hostile to him ever since his name had been coupled with that of a "distinguished national servant".'

'The well-known person [Boothby] got £40,000 and all I got was an apology from a daily newspaper,' Ronnie complained (actually, he got a big chunk of the *Mirror* money, as Alfie and I both knew).

There was no gang, never had been, all that stuff about the 'Firm' was an invention by the prosecution. 'All we have is our drinking friends we go out with in the evening,' Ronnie said. Mr Read had

had it in for him ever since the McCowan case, he added. The police had bought all their evidence. And he had *not* been picked out by witnesses when he'd been put on an identification parade to find the Cornell killer. What about our evidence, what we three brothers had said in court?

'I never went to David's flat,' Ronnie insisted. In his version, they'd gone straight to Charlie Clark's (the Chingford house with all the cats).

What about Mrs Christine Teale's testimony, the question about her bedroom door?

'I went there some other night for a drink, for a party,' said Ron. 'It was all lies by them Teales about any murders.'

'This is all part of a police and Home Office conspiracy, is it?' asked Mr Leonard for the prosecution.

'No, but the Teales' mother was on a £25,000 jewel robbery conviction,' Ronnie said. 'She got a suspended sentence. The tale goes round that they [the Teales] are giving evidence against us so that their mother would get off that charge.'

'Is it your contention that the police have bought [the Teales' evidence]?'

'Yes, it is! Yes, it is!' said Ronnie.

\* \* \*

History knows the rest. The twins got life imprisonment, with a non-parole period of thirty years, for the murders of George Cornell and Jack McVitie, the longest sentences ever passed at the Central Criminal Court for murder. Charlie Kray got ten years, Scotch Ian Barrie got twenty.

The Mitchell trial followed just over a month later. There was a different judge and a different jury. Albert Donoghue gave evidence for the prosecution. And Alfie gave evidence about his day out to Dartmoor.

Trying to destroy his credibility all over again, Platts-Mills began his cross-examination with a toe-curling romp through every juvenile misdemeanour and adult crime on Alfie's CRO form sheet. He could not resist reminding him of the evidence he had given in the previous trial, that he'd told the court in the Cornell case that Ronnie Kray had gone into hiding at my flat on 10 March 1966.

Alfie had told the police in his statement that the Dartmoor episode was in May, but the prison visitors' book showed the visit of a 'Mr Walker' on 21 March.

'Was Alfie Teale Mr Walker?'

Alfie had to admit that he was.

And was it March when he made this visit, or was it May, as he had told the police? Did the witness lie like this about everything? Platts-Mills was triumphant. If Alfie had indeed gone on this mission to Dartmoor on 21 March, did it not make his testimony in the previous trial about Ronnie and half the Firm holing up Moresby Road with (my) terrified family look like an invention?

'Are you now telling the jury that when he [Ronnie] was in deep hiding with you and your brothers because of the killing in the Blind Beggar, he was drinking with his brother and lots of other friends in the Grave Maurice within ten days?' Platts-Mills asked Alfie.

'Yes,' Alfie replied.

'It's just stuff and nonsense, isn't it?'

'No, it is not nonsense,' Alfie told him.

\* \* \*

I suppose it was beyond Alfie, it might be beyond anyone, to explain what had really happened in those ten days. How could you convey the madness of that time, the sense of invincibility the twins had? The playing along by us brothers and Christine just to survive, the outings to pubs and social clubs, the desperation to get out of there?

And then Alfie said it out loud: 'I didn't get Ronnie Kray out of deep hiding, you couldn't tell Ronnie Kray what to do.'

He was right, of course. That is what it was all about. But we had, each one of us, found our courage.

We brothers had all faced the Krays and told the truth.

# 23

## A CONFESSION

The Mitchell trial ended on 16 May 1969, with everyone acquitted except Reggie, who got five years to run concurrently with the McVitie sentence for aiding the Mad Axeman's escape. It was over, but it was certainly not over for us Teales.

The Krays lodged an appeal.

Nothing was over till it was really over.

I asked if Christine and I could go away to Spain on holiday but was told we couldn't. I also asked for my photos to be returned but the police said they might be needed, should the Krays appeal.

After the first trial, Alfie, Christine and I were all given police protection, two men for us and a policewoman to protect my wife. That would go on for another year. Bobby had two police to himself, or so I'd be told, as he was considered to be at higher risk. I knew why after what he'd said in court. He'd been a grass since that day the summer before when Scotch Ian Barrie's brief asked him in Bow Street when he'd 'first considered giving evidence'.

And he'd told them. The sky hadn't fallen in then because there'd been nothing in the news as reporting restrictions were clamped down. Then Read's witness protection operation had whisked us all back inside. But after the 'Spy in the Firm' headline?

What I didn't know was that it was Bobby who'd triggered the raid on Lea Bridge Road. It must have been him in his little calls to whoever it was. They'd all be there on such and such a night – Ronnie, Reggie, Scotch Ian, Smithy, Tommy Cowley. I can only imagine how it went.

And then Norman Lucas, the *Sunday Mirror* reporter who'd been on the twins' case for years, put it in his book, *Britain's Gangland*, that came just in time for Christmas 1969. He said directly:

> The police had been tipped off by Bobby Teale, who was working as police spy within the Firm.

The fact of a 'Spy in the Firm' had been in news headlines when the trial was on but here it was in an original paperback on every station bookstall.

Lucas tells a good story. Lots of detail. He got most of it off the twins' cousin Ronnie Hart – who'd come looking for Bobby at my caravan at Steeple Bay that night when Christine was roughed up. Hart had been a Crown witness at the Old Bailey and gave crucial evidence about what happened to Jack 'the Hat' McVitie. He must have told Lucas about what he'd been up to the summer before when he'd been ordered to come after Bobby.

So, what was Bobby going to do now?

Alfie and I knew that he had been put up in some safe house in Ipswich, Suffolk, before the trial. We met him a couple of times after that in London, but never without two police protection officers being present. Even when we met Bobby in a pub they'd be there, armed with shooters, the lot.

Whenever I had tried to get Bobby to talk, in Maidstone, in those snatched asides at Bow Street, and now in the pub, he'd always give me the same answer: 'I can't talk now, I'll explain everything later.'

Then one day, he vanished.

Christine was drinking more than she'd ever done before. We'd argue a lot. The trial was not long over when, one night after a ruck, she told me she had a confession to make. She said: 'Charlie Kray came around one night when you were away and raped me.'

Out it came, through her sobs. Charlie had started giving her money and she'd been grateful. He'd said he wanted to help in any way he could. This went on for a long time before he started making the odd remark, saying what a nice figure she had and generally starting to come on to her.

He'd come around one day with Scotch Pat and given her a ten-pound note. He said, 'I might pop back later.' He did come back, but this time Pat left and went home. Charlie then started touching her and following her when she went into the kitchen. Eventually he began to force her. Christine screamed and kicked, and Charlie said, 'What do you expect after I came round and gave you money?'

They struggled until Charlie eventually forced himself on her.

Charlie Kray then raped my wife.

I felt so angry, I wanted to go straight out and kill him. I was also so confused by my feelings that I started questioning Christine, asking her repeatedly whether she'd encouraged him. Did she really push him off? Why hadn't she told me before?

But Christine was so distressed that I could see she was telling me the truth. She said she had felt ill and depressed ever since, but she hadn't known how to tell me. She didn't want to go to the police because she was too ashamed. When she said that, I knew exactly how she felt.

I'd been through the same experience, of being raped by Ronnie, Charlie's brother, myself. Could I tell her that?

I could not. Already I felt too humiliated. I felt she'd never think of me as a man ever again. In the end I never told her, although now I wish I had. Things stayed very difficult between us.

My wife was pregnant when the Firm all came to camp out at our flat in Moresby Road. She gave birth to our youngest daughter while I was in prison. And then to be raped by Charlie ... What happened was tough on everyone, but it was tougher on Christine than any of us.

\* \* \*

It was a strange time for Alfie and me. We knew we'd done what no one in the underworld ever does – break the code never to grass up our friends. We'd done so under the utmost pressure but that made no difference. What I did in giving evidence against the Krays had to be done. We knew we had no choice, but I wasn't prepared to live the rest of my life looking over my shoulder.

The big problem for Alfie and me right then was that we couldn't get work so we went back to doing what we'd always done, street trading, often with police at our side trying to look the other way. When the police came with us, we'd give them a fiver and they'd take it alright.

There were new temptations, like selling our story to a newspaper. I got an offer soon after the trials were over. One day, Dick De Lillo, one of the police officers who was looking after me, came up and said, 'Listen, Dave, a chap called George Martin down the *Mirror* wants to see you and have a chat with you. He wants to write a story.'

The police said they'd take me there, so we went down to Holborn to the big building opposite Gamages department store. George Martin, the *Mirror*'s crime reporter, said: 'Listen, David, now that the trial is all over, we'd like to run a feature, a real no-holds barred piece about what it was like being close to them, the sexual stuff, everything. We are willing to pay you a lot of money for it.'

I told them I would have a think about it and let them know. Then I went straight to Alfie to talk it over with him. Bobby had gone missing by now. Alfie and I decided together that it was best not to, for all sorts of good reasons.

I assumed by now that the press knew that I had been raped by Ronnie or why else would they have been asking me? When I told the police that I wasn't going to do the story, they immediately got the hump as they would lose their backhander for arranging it all.

About a week later, the police told me that the *Mirror* wanted to see me again. When I got up to George Martin's office, I was told he couldn't see me as his little daughter had accidentally hurt her eye so instead I was ushered into the office of the Sunday crime reporter, Norman Lucas. He'd been doing stuff about the twins for years and was the one behind the 'Peer and a Gangster' story, although I didn't make the connection at the time.

He asked me to sit down and told me that I would make really good money if I would help them with a feature on Ronnie. Not the story of the trial, that had been done, but all the sexual dirt I had on him (who told them about the rape? Only Read's little lot knew about that). But I said no again. It turned out to be a very wise choice and this is why …

Have you wondered why, having given evidence against the Krays, I didn't have to run for my life and neither did Alfie? Well, I'll tell you: we did a deal with the Krays.

It went like this. About two months after the Cornell trial, Alfie and I were having a drink, along with Dick De Lillo and another policeman, outside a pub called The Queen's Larder in Queen's Square, Holborn, when a geezer pulled up in a car. I thought he was asking for directions and walked over.

I recognised Patsy O'Mara in the passenger seat. He was a book-maker and a very good friend of Freddie Foreman and the south London Firm. A money-getter, he was a lovely man who was liked by everyone. The man driving, I didn't know. Patsy wound down the window and called me over, and while Alfie stayed drinking outside the pub with the two coppers, Patsy said to me: 'I've got a message for you from the Colonel.'

My heart was in my mouth: 'Tell me,' I said.

Patsy answered: 'If you don't say anything, about Ronnie, or his family, about anything personal, anything private, and you know what he means, nothing to the press or in print, he will let sleeping dogs lie and leave you and yours alone too.'

I knew what this was about.

When I was raped by Ronnie in Vallance Road I promised him that one day I'd tell everyone what he'd done. Back then, I was an acute danger to myself. But I'd said nothing. I didn't tell Alfie, I didn't tell Christine. So, all I could think of right then was to tell Patsy O'Mara, 'I've got to talk to Alfie,' who was by this time already walk-ing over to join us.

Still I didn't tell Alfie what had happened to me in Vallance Road. Nor what Charlie Kray had done to Christine. How could I in that moment? Alfie and I told one another most things, but that was just too humiliating for me as a man. Not only that I'd been raped, but that I hadn't been able to look after my own wife.

But Alfie knew there were loads of things that Ronnie wanted kept quiet. As far as he was concerned, the deal was about not giving away any of the other personal stuff we knew, like the rent boys Ronnie had ordered him to get, or using my family, my children, to protect himself when he'd done Cornell – that was hardly the act of an East End hardman.

'Tell my brother what you've just told me,' I said to Patsy.

And so he did. After he'd told Alfie, we looked at one another in desperation. Both frightened, we started to walk away from the car to discuss his offer. But as we did so, Patsy called us back, saying: 'No, Ronnie wants to know now. It's a one-time offer only.'

We stood a short distance away from the car, turning our backs as we talked. Alfie came up with the solution. Walking back to the car, he told him: 'We'll do a deal on one condition only. We are going to lodge a letter with a solicitor setting down everything we know, including this meeting. And if any one of my brothers, or any member of our family, is harmed, that letter will go straight to the police and to the press.' (We did write this all out afterwards, although we never actually lodged it with a solicitor in the end.)

Patsy then put his hand out of the window and said: 'This is the hand of Ronnie Kray ... If you say nothing to the papers, you'll be safe.'

I hesitated for a moment. Alfie and I went to walk away to discuss the offer further, but Patsy called out: 'No, this is a one-time offer ... The Colonel says he must have an answer straightaway.'

'It's a deal.'

Then we went back to the two policemen without saying anything about what had just happened. If they had any suspicions, they weren't showing it. We wanted to tell Bobby about the meeting but he'd been missing for eight weeks by this time and we had no idea where he was. I asked the police if we could see Bobby and they said they'd arrange it. It never happened.

So why was Ronnie being so beneficent all of a sudden? It must have been the police who tipped off the *Mirror* to my story – apart from Ronnie and me, they were the only ones who knew. I know for a fact it was the police. And in the way of these things, that must have reached Ronnie.

Christine and I were still young with three daughters and we wanted to have another go at our lives, to start again without the shadow of all that had happened before. In any case, I was frightened of talking to anyone about it, let alone seeing it in the newspapers. The Old Bill hoped to make some money out of it too. It could get very messy. But as time went on, we started to realise we really were safe after all. And we were still here to tell the tale.

I want to say this: when Ronnie raped me, he did more than damage just me, he divided me from my wife. I wanted to tell her and needed to tell her in many ways but it was so horrible, and so humiliating, especially for a young man to have to admit to the woman he loved – and still love. In the meantime, Christine must have sensed I was holding something back. It became very difficult between us. In the end, she never found out.

Mum was not doing so well. She wasn't that old really, but Bobby's disappearance had really affected her. 'Where's Bobby?' she would ask. So, what could I tell her, what could I do? As far as the police would tell me anything, he was dead.

I took my mother up to Scotland Yard. I spoke to the officer on the desk first and asked to see the inspector. We had to fill out some forms and the police asked me if I had any idea what might have happened to him. I said we didn't, and the officer promised to look into the matter and get back to us. No one ever did. A few months later, I took Mum back and we went through the whole thing again.

We did this four or five times and each time we'd be told, 'We understand your position', or 'We'll get back to you soon'. I don't think anyone had a clue. After about three years, they said: 'Assume he's dead, we've got no trace on him, no nothing.'

One day, I said, 'Mum, I've got beautiful news for you. Bobby's all right, he's coming back.'

'Oh, lovely,' she said.

It was a total fabrication. And the funny thing was she seemed to get a bit better after that.

In 1972–3 I opened a cash and carry called Regisand in Brixton. Alfie and I got the money together and Christine was the company secretary. A friend was the frontman. It lasted for about a year and we made a lot of money out of it. During this time, I served all the chaps, all the villains, from south London.

I used to drive lorries and get the goods from all over the place. The twins' word proved as good as their bond as not one villain objected to doing business with us, even though we'd given evidence at the Krays' trial.

There was always the urge to something a bit different. Christine and I had been on a trip to Paris, just on impulse we'd jumped on a plane for a long weekend. We were looking to move abroad, to make a fresh start after all that had happened. But we didn't really like France – feeling that the French didn't really like us Brits much and that it would be hard to make friends.

Then we decided to visit Amsterdam, which we both really liked straightaway. We were drinking in a bar one evening and we got talking to a Dutch antiques dealer called Wally and his wife. They were very friendly and he told me he had a good business and that there was money to be made there. I was really interested. And as soon as that *Lovejoy* loveable rogue antique dealer series came out on British TV, I was made. But money could not help where we really needed it.

Even though Christine was off the drink now, she remained very depressed. She was always talking about wanting to kill herself, so often that none of us believed she would ever actually do anything.

One day, I went out on the piss by myself. I came back. Her body was on the bed, a plastic bag over her head taped round her neck. A bottle of sleeping pills was beside her on the floor. I knew at once she was dead.

It was the end of everything I had loved.

I found out she'd called up our youngest daughter, Christine, the one who was born when I was in prison, in London and told her: 'Look after your father.'

For years I have felt the guilt of Christine's death. She had never even smoked a cigarette before Ronnie told his doctor to give her 'something to calm her down'. Once she started she never really stopped.

The more I think about it now, the more I realise how much all the women involved had to suffer. It is more than a coincidence that first Frances and then Christine took their own lives. Whether it was Frances locking herself in the Ladies at a nightclub to block out Reggie's violence, or a heavily pregnant Christine being made to get up out of bed in the night to 'make a cup of tea for Ronnie', I will wish until my dying day that I could have done something to make it better.

And that I had never let Ronnie and Reggie Kray into our lives.

# LONDON: FORTY YEARS LATER

I had found Bobby on Facebook. He was in Utah. Now the three of us, the survivors, were going to have to meet for real. Of course we were. Me and Alfie would be calling him or it would be him calling us on the old-fashioned phone. It went on like this for about four weeks:

'Come over here!'

'No, *you* come over here!'

I told him I was going to write a book about what had happened to us. No, honestly, I really was going to.

Bobby told us he was coming over: he would come to London after more than forty years. Me and Alfie waited and waited. He did come. But not to see me and Alfie, not straightaway. First, he went to see our sister and one of our younger brothers.

He went to see his daughter, Tracy. That was lovely. He was over about a week staying with her, before he came to me and Alfie. We'd arranged to meet in the Holiday Inn in Holborn, opposite Alfie and Wendy's flat. It was not far from the Rugby Tavern, where Bobby had persuaded us one summer night to go and meet his friend 'Mr Wallace' in a West End pub somewhere. That had been how long ago?

Bobby was waiting in the restaurant and we were in the coffee shop, so even at the eleventh hour we were still missing each other. And there he was.

Alfie moved towards him, beaming wider than anyone could, kissing and cuddling him like a babe. I was not crying, but still full of emotion. It was just the thought he was alive was so wonderful.

*Was it real?*

But with Alfie going into emotional meltdown, I was hanging back a bit. I just had so many questions, so many riddles to solve, so much to be angry about. There was one person in the world who knew the answers and there he was back in front of me again. If Alfie was good cop, I was going to be bad cop.

When we met him with his armed guards a couple of times after the trial was over, I'd ask what the fuck it had all been about. He'd just say: 'I can't talk now, I'll explain everything later.'

Well, now was the time to do just that.

All of it went back to that night on 8 August 1966 when we'd gone on a pub crawl and ended up in a flat in Dolphin Square.

So, who was Wallace? Who was he really?

'Wallace was working for the government,' Bobby explained. 'I'd been told that I was going to be brought in, but I had no idea that meeting this Wallace guy was the way it was going to be done. Well, maybe that was exactly what was happening.'

I was being bad cop now: 'Bob, we were set up,' I said. 'Why didn't you say something?' He said he couldn't, he was working for the police. He was undercover. The police were getting us safe. He thought Wallace was part of doing that. His Yard contact had told him, 'You'll know when it's happening, just go along with it.'

'So how did you meet him?'

'I first met Wallace in a smart pub in Knightsbridge,' Bobby told us. 'I can only assume he'd been following me. I ordered a gin and tonic and he walked straight up and started making conversation about the weather or something. He told me his name. I said, "Is that your first, or last name?" He said, "Just call me Wallace." That was that. From then on, I called him Wallace. I met him several times more and even borrowed his car a few times [Wallace would accuse him of stealing it, Bobby was prosecuted]. Then one day later, we were having a drink and he said, "Why don't you get hold of your brothers and we will have a party back at my flat?"'

And so, Alfie and I went with him to Dolphin Square ... to be nicked by six plainclothes coppers coming in the door at 7.30 the next morning.

So, being bad cop, I say: 'Bob, why didn't you ask this Wallace geezer where he was going in the middle of the night?'

'I was asleep.'

'Bobby, why didn't you say something to the people you'd been talking to, at the Yard, I mean?'

He said he did.

'OK, Bobby, why didn't you say something at our trial? I mean, make a full disclosure of what you'd been doing?'

He couldn't say.

I told him directly: 'When I was in Maidstone, other prisoners would ask me what I was inside for. I'd tell them, "I don't know." How do you think that felt?'

'I don't know. Bad, I guess. I'm sorry.'

'Bobby, how could you let me associate with real hardmen in prison? I mean, friends of the Firm, that would have killed me if they knew what you had done. We were in more danger there than outside.'

He couldn't answer.

'Bobby, why did you lock yourself away in your cell and not let me know I was in danger?'

'Bobby, why did you run away after the trial and leave me and Alfie to fight the battle?'

Bobby said the police told him not to speak to me and Alfie.

'Bobby, you took three years out of my life away from my wife and kids ... Why, why, why?'

\* \* \*

By now we're trying to get all that 'Bobby, why the fuck did you do that stuff?' out of the way. Perhaps we'll never be able to work out why, but there's still lots of things that only Robert Teale can tell the world.

He stopped the show at the Bow Street committal (but that part was in camera) and then at the trial (that was in the open) by revealing he'd been a spy in the Firm. In fact, we'd all known that for years since we had first heard him say it in open court. But what did he actually do? Wasn't he terrified? Wasn't he scared for us, for our wives and kids?

Alfie and I knew that Ronnie had let him out of Moresby Road without a minder on the second day. He'd told Ronnie he was going to see our mum. He did just that but on the way there, he'd gone to a big red telephone box.

This is what he told us: he dialled the Scotland Yard switchboard and asked to be put through to a detective called Tommy Butler – he'd seen that name when Ronnie had sent him out of my flat to get the papers. 'I have some information regarding the Krays,' Bobby had told whoever it was he'd been put through to.

Bobby told us in that big debrief that on the next occasion he got out on his own or the one after that, he'd got to central London and been sat in the back of a black Rover parked just off Fleet Street when the man in the front passenger seat turned round and said, 'I'm Tommy Butler.'

'Who killed Cornell?' he asked Bobby directly.

'Ronnie Kray.'

He told Butler all about what was going on at Moresby Road. About the guns, about the list Ronnie kept making.

'Are any of my men on it?'

That was all Butler seemed to want to know. How could Bobby know that?

Now, all these years later, he was telling us how he assumed the police would move in there and then. It was like it had just happened. He'd thought that one call, one meet, would be enough. That the cavalry would arrive, arrest the Krays and the rest of the Firm and that my family, all of us, would be safe.

But Butler had told him the police needed more information. They needed to build a case. The newspapers might have been mad back then for 'Yard Swoops' but it didn't actually work like that. Would he go back in and get more?

Bobby had agreed.

God knows why.

What Butler seemed to want more than anything else was a photo of Scotch Ian Barrie, the second gunman in the Beggar who'd fired into the ceiling. The one who'd got the burn marks on his face.

Butler was after an undercover operation over weeks, months maybe. He'd brought Sergeant Joe Pogue, who'd be the contact man, who was in the car beside him. They were introduced. Bobby needed a code name; he decided on 'Phillips'. Butler had told him, 'Be very careful or you will be dead.'

And so it had gone on through that early summer of 1966, Ronnie and the rest of them ducking and diving around Hackney and Chingford, staying with Charlie Clark, moving into Lea Bridge Road.

Making up for lost time perhaps, or more to be the perfect undercover agent, Bobby seemed to be behaving that summer like more of a villain than Alfie and I had ever done. That's what I could remember anyway. He'd left his wife, Pat, on the Isle of Wight and was hanging around the Firm full-time. Moving in with Reggie after the Moresby Road siege while trying to get information to Butler, enough for him to actually do something.

He must have been crazy.

And the police were doing what? I found a statement (long after that first meeting of us brothers in the Holiday Inn) from Joe Pogue in the National Archives about his informant. Pogue had given it to Mooney on 7 October 1968. He had said:

It was arranged that I would meet him daily at a particular place in the Clapton area. If he failed to turn up, the meeting stood for the same time the follow-on day and so on. It was quite obvious that Phillips [Bobby] was terrified of the Kray twins and he admitted this, stating he had difficulty getting away without being missed. This went on for weeks.

I could feel Bobby's terror, it came off the typewritten page. And his bravery too. There were other meetings. Bobby met Pogue in unmarked cars driving around Hackney, Walthamstow, wherever. These times there were always other coppers in the car. What he told Pogue was taped. What Butler really wanted was a snap of Scotch Ian. Bobby, I don't know how, told us he managed to get one.

Pogue went on:

Although Phillips was unwilling at the time to give evidence, he stated he would, if police were able to secure the arrest of the Kray twins and Scotch Ian [Barrie].

Some weeks after meeting Phillips regularly, he failed to show up at the meeting place and I never saw him or heard from him again.

But what Bobby's hearing after a time is that the twins were on to 'Phillips': 'Phillips has been in touch again.' It was coming back to them from someone in the Yard, as he told Alfie and me in the Holiday Inn:

Detective Sergeant Pogue told me that 'they' are trying to stop it from happening – by which he must have meant the high-ups at the Yard – but Pogue must have known how it was happening. That the Krays had an insider. But he told me to be very careful as the Yard felt that one day soon they would be dragging my mutilated body from the Thames.

Always, the police wanted more. Alfie and I had also been in the same danger, Bobby told us in that emotionally charged meeting in the Holborn hotel so many years since it all happened. There was a Yard guy, a detective – Dan or Don something – and Bobby was asking him ever more desperately what he reckoned he, we, should do. He had said: 'We can't put you all into hiding as it will tip off the twins. You do and say absolutely nothing to Alfie or David or they will panic.'

He was right about that.

The detective (he'd been with Pogue on an earlier meet) went on: 'I will handle it. Leave it all to me, and don't worry, it's all under control and it will all be taken care of. Just remember, whatever happens, go along with it and don't say a word to a soul.'

Which is what he did. Bobby had already made up his mind to take a gamble. He would tell Butler just where the twins were, the flat above the hairdresser's in Lea Bridge Road. He explained it to us:

> I got word to Butler where the twins were. I told the Yard when it would be the best time to hit the gaff. I described the internal layout, the exit routes. There was a little alley at the back. I told Pogue's guy in no uncertain terms that they had better get it right. Nick the twins. Nick Scotch Ian. And keep them nicked.

But Butler and the Public Prosecutor screwed it up. DI Michael Hyans and his armed team out of the Yard went in alright (I'd find the record of that in the National Archives after our meet in the Holiday Inn), but after the identity parade fiasco the twins walked. And so did Scotch Ian. Smithy seemed to vanish. So, what could Bobby do? He explained that if he ran then they'd know he was the grass – he had to bluff it out.

So, he went back in as if nothing had happened. Reggie said: 'Let's have a drink at Madge's.' Which is what they did that Saturday night after the photo call with the men from the *Mirror* and the other papers. 'Come round to Vallance Road tomorrow morning,' he told him. 'We'll have a nice breakfast, then take a little drive.'

It was Sunday, 7 August 1966. Violet made Bobby a cup of tea, of course she did. Bobby told us what happened:

Reggie said he wanted me to go with him to Epping Forest. He made it sound as if we had to pick up some bags of cash hidden in the woods. I asked him what it was really for. 'You will see when we get there,' he said. We got to the forest and we got out of the car and Reggie pulled out a gun and started shooting at the trees. Then he said, 'Take this bottle and hold it out.' But I wouldn't, so he threw the bottle in the air and started shooting at it. So, I ran and he's laughing and shooting in my direction. As I run, he's shouting, 'Stand still.' I hid in some trees.

'Come on out, we've got to go!' he shouted. 'I'm not going to hurt you.'

I knew then for certain that he was going to kill me. My friend Reggie Kray had been sent by Ronnie to take me out to the forest and kill me.

Then Reggie couldn't shoot straight. He put a bullet in the air, whining past my head.

I ran for my life.

First, Bobby thought he should go to Steeple Bay in Essex to my caravan. Christine and the kids were already down there. That's the first place they'd come looking. And they did. Ronnie sent Ronnie

Hart and Frosty down there. They got there late that same Sunday night that Reggie came back from the forest.

Bobby told us, forty years later, that we were all on a list, Ronnie's hit list. He was afraid we were all going to get done. He said he was creeping round as a police agent and couldn't tell us because it would have been too dangerous. The police were going to get us off the streets and he was doing what he did because it was the right thing to do. He'd gone through the contact procedure and thought 'Wallace' was the escape route for all of us.

Sorry about the way it turned out.

By now he was too emotional, we all were, to try and explain a plan to get us to safety made long ago by shadowy people he hardly knew and we had no conception of. And Bobby told us this. When Inspector Read had first come to see him in Maidstone (around the time when Alfie and I were giving our statements – they had met clandestinely outside the prison in the back of a car), Nipper had told him: 'He was very sorry about everything that had happened. But there had been a changeover at the Yard back then. When he'd gone to look for my files, he found "they had disappeared"'.

And it would all have to stay secret for a hundred years.

I've had plenty of doubts about Bobby's version of events since we had that first emotional reunion, so many questions that still won't go away. But none of us could have had any idea of the acute danger we were in that summer of 1966 when a bent copper high up in the Yard was relaying the existence of 'Phillips' back to the murderous twins. Well, with the help of some good friends and the work of a veteran true-crime historian, I now know a lot more. I know who he was. That's all coming in a little while.

Bobby meanwhile could say more about what had happened to him since around that last time we'd seen him with his minders in a London pub in spring 1969. He'd gone through the gates of Maidstone Prison and been taken straight to Tintagel House for more debriefing. Then to a safe house in Ipswich, Suffolk, with two armed police guards. He'd been brought from there for his Old Bailey appearance and the 'Spy in the Firm' admission. Then he'd been put back into hiding. He'd been let out with an undercover escort to visit our mum, he told us. He'd slipped his minders and gone to Paris for a few days. Then one day, convinced his life was in danger as much from Scotland Yard as anyone else, he took the boat-train to France and went on the run.

'Someone in the police told me I should stay away for five years. Call it paranoia, whatever, but I thought I had to get out right then,' he told Alfie and me.

He got to Gibraltar, Canada, then in the end, Utah.

And it had all begun when he'd gone out one morning to a call box near our mum's flat, dialled that famous Yard number, WHI[tehall] 1212, and asked to speak to Mr Butler: 'I have some information regarding the Krays …'

# EPILOGUE

I'd been thinking about it for years. It was like those old lawyer shows on TV when the plot twist is explained right at the end. Everything that had happened to us from the time around our arrest in Dolphin Square went back to the Yard.

Bobby's cover ('Bob Phillips') had been blown to the twins by someone high up. It was in the days running up to 7 August 1966. But who was he?

This is the best explanation I've seen. Deputy Assistant Commissioner John Du Rose said in his 1971 memoirs, *Murder Was My Business*, that as the Richardson gang was being taken down,[33] he 'selected an officer to take charge of a major investigation into the Krays'. He doesn't say precisely when, but he does name him as Detective Superintendent Ferguson McGregor Walker of C.1, a 50-year-old career policeman with an 'extensive knowledge of the underworld from Soho to the East End'[34].

---

[33] The Richardson arrests were on 30 July.
[34] Ferguson McGregor Walker, 'born 8 January 1916, joined Metropolitan Police in 1938, retired 1968 as Chief Superintendent with a break for war service 1943–48 [Corps of Military Police]. Multiple commendations 1940–1960.' He became head of security for a major scaffolding company.

I'd never heard of him and I never met him. I've only seen published descriptions of him as having a 'droopy moustache' and a 'whisky galore' Scottish accent.

In fact, this 'major' investigation wasn't much at all. It was Detective Superintendent Walker with two detective sergeants, Leslie Emment and later Alan Wright, under him.

Wright (who would go on to be part of Read's team then become a criminologist) would write almost fifty years later in a US academic magazine (*Trends in Organised Crime*, I found it on the internet): 'The small C.1 unit was put in place for political reasons to prevent Assistant Chief Constable Gerald McArthur [who had led] the Richardson enquiry, from investigating the Krays which the Met top brass regarded as their prerogative'. And McArthur (see footnote p. 215) had been brought in from outside in the first place because of all that corruption in the Met (the files on which are closed until 2060) that had let the Richardsons get away with it for so long. And not just the Richardsons.

It was more Yard spookery. Of corrupt coppers and the twins, Wright would only say: 'In our witness statements, including those of criminal accomplices who gave evidence for the Crown... we had no evidence [against] specific officers who had facilitated the Krays' activities... however corruption was present even at the highest echelons of Scotland Yard including C.1 itself. It would be surprising if there were not some interconnection.'

It certainly would be. Meanwhile, the Boothby-era high-ups had not quite moved on. That old cynic Ranulph Bacon was replaced in March 1966 as Assistant Commissioner, Crime, by Peter Brodie, but 'Rasher' would stay on as Deputy Commissioner until October. Sir Joseph Simpson would die in office in March 1968.

A week after that corrupt copper sting in Hackney, Smithy gave a statement to a 'Detective Sergeant L. Emment' (Leslie Emment, later to be Deputy Chief Constable of the Thames Valley Police). Scotch Ian Barrie did the same, four days after that. Like the twins and Smithy, he'd walked free after the ID parade fiasco and they'd all gone back to Charlie Clark's place.

So at least one of Walker's team were in on that Townsend case in mid-August 1966. It was all about Ronnie, after all. We brothers knew nothing about any of this because we'd been lifted the week before and were banged up in Brixton.

And who ordered the Dolphin Square sting? Nobody seems to know.

So there actually was something new going on with the Yard and the Krays at the time Butler walked away and we got banged up. This so-called 'major investigation' didn't seem to get very far. 'The officers found information terribly hard to come by,' wrote Du Rose in his memoirs. 'Weeks went by ... Walker never gave up trying and after several months did get a line on the Krays. At this critical phase Walker [was promoted] and transferred to another department.'

In fact, he would be replaced by Henry Mooney.

Walker's transfer would seem to have been for a reason. The two detective sergeants under him, Emment and Wright, were straight. Their guvnor, maybe not so.

Many years later, a veteran detective called John Rigbey told the author James Morton for his excellent book *Krays: The Final Word*, that he recalled Walker earwigging him one day in the office when he was talking with 'his informer Charlie Clark on a telephone intercept and Walker wanted to know all about it'.

Charlie was the retired housebreaker with the house in Chingford, Essex, with the wife who had all the cats. On a little visit, looking for stolen goods, Detective Constable Rigbey had noticed a clothing-shop rail laden with expensive suits: they were Ronnie's. Firm member Billy Exley would also much later tell Nipper Read all about the Vallance laundry home-delivery service to the Chingford hideaway – 'suits and shirts' he had taken there in his minivan.

Charlie Clark's gaff was where Ronnie was holed up with Teddy Smith (Smithy) in that crazy summer of 1966. It was where he'd got wired up for their failed amateur police corruption-busting Townsend entrapment on 11 August. And Bobby had been in and out of there all through that summer.

So, in their office encounter, Ferguson Walker suddenly wanted to know all about DC Rigbey's phone chat with Charlie Clark. But he wasn't interested in stolen goods, it was Charlie's smartly dressed house guest that got him excited.

A rail of suits, what a giveaway!

According to Morton:

It would seem, however, that Walker made no use of the information except possibly to pass it on to [the Soho porn king Bernie] Silver for onward transmission.

That could mean he was telling Ronnie that at least one copper had found out where he was hiding. Maybe he should change his arrangements. Ronnie was very sensitive about that. He was going to 'do' Ilford club owner Tony Dove just for having his phone number at Lea Bridge Road, so the Krays' cousin Ronnie Hart would recall.

Ferguson Walker, knowing where he was – well, that didn't matter. He wasn't about to scare up a Yard Swoop for a *Daily Mirror* front page: Walker was on the Firm payroll.

Bobby had already been telling Mr Butler for weeks in his meets with Joe Pogue exactly where Ronnie was. He was ducking around Charlie Clark's little property empire. Bobby told them who would be there and when to hit the place. That's why and how the Flying Squad had made the Lea Bridge Road above Adams Barbers raid on Butler's orders: it all went wrong.

Du Rose does at least credit Bobby with that, saying in his memoirs about the raid: 'The investigating officers received a tip from a police spy working within the Firm.'

So, was Ferguson Walker the Firm spy working within the police?

It looks that way.

The retired detective John Rigbey further told author James Morton: 'One day I'm called in by my boss, who tells me that Fergus Walker of C.l wants to see me. What he wanted to know was if Charlie Clark had said anything to me about the Twins. He hadn't, but I realized that there must have been a bell on him.'

Charlie Clark's phone would have been red-hot in summer 1966. If, that is, Ronnie was foolish enough to drop his guard against snoopers. What was Ferguson Walker hearing? What was he feeding back to the twins from his end? That there was an informer called 'Phillips' for one thing. Then Reggie works out who it is and takes Bobby to Epping Forest to kill him.

Bobby ran and we all got arrested.

That looks like an act of panic by the Yard, by whoever it was running Bobby. The plan to bring us in must have been already in place but it was done in a hurry because of rival plots going wrong, not part of an overarching conspiracy. Or so it would seem. The 'menaces' charge, the coppers' giving evidence, the jury-nobbling allegation, the 'cheque' and the judge's notorious prejudices all made it sure we'd go down.

It's also clear now that Nipper Read, once he took over, knew what Walker had been up to. When he hosted a drink for his team at Tintagel House after the arrests at Braithwaite House, the 'promoted and transferred' Walker decided to put his nose in the door.

Nipper was not best pleased: 'What the fuck are you doing here?' he said. That's what Nipper's co-writer James Morton says happened anyway, although it wasn't like that in Nipper's book – there's no mention of Walker in it at all.

And here's the real scandal: if James Morton is right, the Kray mole was actually *in charge of* the Yard's supposed pursuit of the twins. And he was so in the period when Read said he found 'not a single fact' about a continuing investigation before he took over. And it was when there was nothing on record to say that 'Phillips' had even existed. Read didn't bother to ask Mr Butler, or if he did, he didn't say at the time or afterwards. But then in October 1968, DI Henry Mooney found Sergeant Joe Pogue, who told him that Bobby Teale's fantastic tale was true.

Apart from whatever Joe Pogue might have to say about what Phillips had given up ('a few rough notes, no dates'), the mole had covered his tracks: there was no paper trail leading to him.

So, what had Joe Pogue said to Bobby at one of their last meetings about leaks from the Yard?

'They [the high-ups] are trying to stop it from happening.'

Well, maybe not hard enough, for now.[35]

And what about that other spy in the Firm? What about 'Source'? His information had allowed the government to shut down the Boothby scandal.

---

[35] In December 2020, former DS Alan Wright, now retired after a distinguished academic career, said he regarded 'the allegations against Mr Walker as highly speculative'. He did suggest however that they be referred to The Independent Police Complaints Authority for 'proper investigation'.

'Source' was a 'self-confessed homosexual', apparently already known to the Head of MI5 counterespionage, Malcolm Cumming. An intimate of both Tom Driberg, MP, and Lord Robert Boothby, he'd been around since Esmeralda's Barn days, if not before. 'Unpaid', he was clearly older than Ronnie's usual fancies. He had a 'flatmate' – who had Fleet Street connections and who went to the opera.

A theory I like is that it was cat-burgling skills, all those embassies being broken into, that first brought Smithy and Leslie Holt[36] into contact with MI5, rather than sharing beds with homosexual politicians.

There were others around Ronnie, the bisexual Bobby Buckley and a certain Vincent Hart (a resident of Bristol, aka Paul de Selincourt) noted in a 1971 police file as 'homosexual'. But neither had the big presence of Edward R. Smith. He would have loved the role play, the breathless debriefing by his agent runner, the telephoning, the sheer 'have-you-heard-the-latest?' drama of it all.

As I remembered, whatever was happening, wherever the Krays were, Teddy Smith – Smithy – was there too. Yet when there was an arrest, he would seem to mysteriously melt away. Yes, we used to joke about him being 'mad' but not so crazy that he didn't have an eye to the main chance – he always had money in his pocket.

The word I heard when I was in Ford was that Ronnie had done him after the Mitchell business. For years afterwards, it would be said that he'd been done in April 1967 at Steeple Bay, most likely in a quarrel with Ronnie over some boy. His body was never found. It

---

[36] Leslie Holt never got to tell his story. He died in 1979, after a Harley Street doctor called Gordon Kells administered a lethal overdose of anaesthetic. Charged with unlawful killing, the doctor was cleared by the jury at the Old Bailey in July 1981.

went into the marshes, that is what has long been stated. It's been in books by John Pearson several times over – the Kray 'official' historian always seemed keen to polish him off.

Reggie, not Ronnie, is supposed to have 'confessed' to Smithy's murder in a BBC TV documentary called *The Final Word*, broadcast in March 2001. Recorded speaking from a hospital bed a few days before his death from cancer the previous October, he owned up to Jack the Hat but admitted one further killing (he did not say who). But Nipper Read waded in, saying 'that would be Teddy Smith, he suddenly disappeared'. The press widely reported it. The Yard told the *Daily Mail* 'they would look at any new potential lead for a missing person'. Investigate Smithy's vanishing trick? Well they didn't get very far. But why should any of that, what John Pearson and Nipper had to say, be doubted?

Then in 2017, an online 'gangster' forum claimed that, far from being murdered, Smithy had spent forty years in Sydney, Australia. More and more sightings came out and were posted. In 2004, a Sydney music broadcaster had met him at his home – which was full of 'strange-but-true' books about conspiracy theories apparently. Smithy had even treated his visitor to a wheezy Al Jolson impersonation. He'd returned to Britain to die of lung cancer soon afterwards.

Few further details were given but pictures were posted on Facebook of his passport and a head-and-shoulders shot of a man in his seventies. Several in the forum said it was not proof, that it merely showed someone who might have looked like Teddy Smith. Others thought differently.

I myself was convinced the picture was of Smithy. So was Alfie. Could he have done a Bobby and been spirited to Australia by some agency of the state?

In January 2019, on the fiftieth anniversary of the Krays going down at the Old Bailey, our speculating that Teddy Smith was the 'Source' in the MI5 file featured in the *Mail on Sunday* newspaper. A true Teddy expert was contacted by the reporter, who quoted his somewhat contrary view. It was sixties-born, true-crime historian Ray Rose, who had actually gone to Sydney himself in 2012 on the Teddy trail. He's been kind enough to share some of his discoveries.

Smithy was not somehow magicked off to Australia, that is clear. His parents had emigrated there, so it was a natural destination – but not straightaway. It looks like he pulled out of the Firm as soon as he could after the Mitchell murder in December 1966. Crime author David Seabrook got an account off hardman Albert Donoghue around 2000 sometime and put it in a book called *Jack of Jumps* about a London serial killer of the early sixties. It's quite a story ...

According to Donoghue, Smithy was in the Regency Club in Stoke Newington late one night, extremely drunk and bragging about his part in Frank Mitchell's escape. It was late December 1966. One of the Barry brothers who ran the club phoned Reggie and said: 'Teddy Smith's here, mouthing off about Mitchell.' Reggie phoned Albert Donoghue and said: 'Go and get the cunt out of there.'

So, Albert pulled a couple of the Firm to help out. He went in and Teddy Smith was talking to a couple of girls, which was unusual. Donoghue explained:

> We got him in the car, we got him up the Balls Pond Road, we're going east to Vallance Road. We know what's going to happen. He's either going to get a fucking good spanking or a bullet. Teddy Smith says, 'I want to go for a piss,' so we dropped him for a piss. We never thought about it. Anyway, he's fucking bolted, ain't he?

So, Smithy ran. You can see why. The Mad Axeman affair had begun as a quixotic stunt with humane ends. For a time, those pleas he wrote that appeared in newspapers had captured the nation. It ended in a squalid execution in the back of a van. That had horrified him. Being thought dead himself meanwhile was very convenient.

Edward Smith always wanted to be a playwright and achieved his ambition with the acceptance of a thirty-minute TV drama in July 1967 by the BBC. That was weeks after he was supposed to have been done at Steeple Bay. I like to think he got to see it. *Top Bunk* was broadcast live that October. It was a gritty psychological prison drama with two old lags (prisoners) being told what's what by a wimpy 'public school geezer' who gets dominance ('the top bunk') over them by claiming to be a murderer. It was in colour, a first. He was paid £200. It was not video-taped and only programme notes survive.

Meanwhile, Smithy was hiding in plain sight, it seems. A 2000 Frankie Fraser/James Morton book, *Mad Frank's Diary*, recounts a Holborn newsvendor confiding:

> Teddy's done the sensible thing when everyone's been nicked, and he goes into hiding … then Teddy goes up North or some-where. In 1972 Teddy said he was off to Australia. He wouldn't be the first to have gone that route.

So that's him alive and kicking, getting his name on a TV play while Nipper and Co. still have him in their sights for the Mitchell Dartmoor breakout. In June 1968, Henry Mooney interviewed showbiz agent Samuel Lederman about the whereabouts of Edward

Smith – wanted over the Mitchell case. Old Sammy could not tell them much; his statement is in the National Archives.

And Nipper wanted a word all along. He was on his arrest list for the Mitchell investigation. In the second Old Bailey trial, Mr Read was asked: 'What is the position with regard to the man who has been referred to as Ted or Teddy Smith?'

'I have been actively making enquiries to trace him for some time, but I have been unable to do so,' he answered.

True-crime historian Ray Rose tracked Smithy a few years later to 'Fenwick Chauffeur Service Ltd' in the Charing Cross Road. 'He wore a green jacket and peaked cap', specialising in 'foreign business-men and diplomats' apparently. Man-about-the-Krays Dan Farson recalled meeting him in the street in Soho in the early seventies: there was a tap on the shoulder, look who it isn't!

And Ronnie clearly knew he was alive. Ray Rose acquired the original of a letter written by Ron from prison in 1984 to Dora Hamylton (an amateur author who wanted to pen a biography of Violet Kray) bemoaning Smithy's 'desertion' by not sending a wreath to his mother's funeral – she had died two years earlier.

Ronnie knew how to keep a grudge.

So, making a new life was not about running away from arrest or the threat of violent retribution. Edward Smith did the immigra-tion paperwork at Australia House under his own name. His form sheet (armed robbery) was somehow overlooked. He got to Sydney and spent time with a family to whom he confided some of his past, while drinking too much and bashing out drama outlines on an old typewriter.

What a story he might have told! Someone probably said that was a bad idea.

Teddy Smith was sometimes mad and often bad, but he was not a killer. He was witness to violence, not a participant. In the end, Ronnie's bloody antics utterly repelled him. If he, along the way, had been offered Australian citizenship with no questions asked, plus a 'stay-quiet-and-don't-mention-Boothby' pension, he'd be laughing.

Ray Rose is concerned that some of the MI5 Boothby file is internally contradictory and that Teddy had no immediate reason to flee the Firm as long as the identity of 'Source' stayed secret.

Which it did for fifty years.

Well, it's clear now that Edward Smith took his time in fleeing anywhere. And there's this further clue: About the 'The Picture We Must Not Print' furore in summer 1964, Smithy had spoken to an interviewer shortly before his death. Ronnie had reportedly told him: 'As I couldn't get a picture of myself with Churchill, a snap with Boothby was the next best thing.'[37]

What had Solicitor-General Sir Peter Rawlinson said at the height of the 'sinister rumours' crisis? 'We learned from *a secret source* they [the Krays] were attempting to engineer the same sort of thing with Sir Winston Churchill, specifically a photograph of them together.'

Looks like Smithy provided that little nugget.

How convenient it was all round that 'Source' should take the secrets of Her Majesty's Government's dalliance with the murderous twins to the other side of the world. And never say a word.

---

[37] The Teddy interview was reportedly recorded in May 2004, and a transcript retrieved later by true crime historian Ray Rose. The 'Churchill' line was quoted in David Smith's 2020 book, *The Peer and the Gangster*, in which Mr Rose elsewhere expresses a degree of doubt that 'Source' and Smithy were the same.

# TIMELINE

**24 October 1933**

Twins Reginald 'Reggie' and Ronald 'Ronnie' Kray are born.

**18 November 1939**

Alfred 'Alfie' William Teale is born.

**23 January 1942**

Robert 'Bobby' Frank Teale is born.

**7 March 1943**

David Charles Teale is born.

**1957**

Report of the Wolfenden Committee on Homosexual Offences and Prostitution recommends decriminalising homosexual behaviour between consenting adults in private.

## 1959

'Mad' Teddy Smith takes Alfie Teale to the Double R Club in Stepney and introduces him to Ronnie Kray.

## 1960

**February** Reginald Kray is imprisoned for eighteen months for protection-related threats and while in prison, Polish-born landlord Peter Rachman gives Ronald the Esmeralda's Barn nightclub in Knightsbridge.

**May** Superintendent Tommy Butler makes major investigation of 'The Twins'.

**1 September** The Betting and Gaming Act legalises betting shops, casinos, bingo halls and gaming machines.

**October** Ronnie starts drinking at Ellen Teale's club, the '66', at the Angel, London, N1.

## 1960-3

Operation 'Stockade'. MI5 mounts a widespread bugging operation against London embassies requiring clandestine break-ins.

## 1962

**September–October** Vassall Admiralty spy case spurs 'queer-hunting' panic in the British government.

## 1963

**24 January** 'Mr X' MI5 DG Roger Hollis denies to Radcliffe Committee role of Security Service in homosexual murder investigation (Norman Rickard).

**6 February** 'New source' first goes live for MI5 reporting on homosexual peer Robert Boothby.

**March** David Teale takes money to Ronnie in Jersey to pay off policeman.

**23 March** Conservative War Minister John Profumo tells the House of Commons that there is 'no impropriety whatsoever' in his relationship with 'the model' Christine Keeler.

**5 June** Profumo confesses that he had misled the House and resigns.

**15 June** Neo-Nazi Colin Jordan is brought to Scotland Yard on the PM's instructions to give 'list' of alleged prominent homosexuals (some in government). One of them is Lord Robert Boothby.

**16–19 June** David Teale takes money to Jersey again for Ronnie to give to two Metropolitan Police detectives. 'Mad' Teddy Smith is also there.

**June** Lord Boothby first meets Ronnie Kray at Esmeralda's Barn gambling club.

**18 October** Conservative Prime Minister Harold Macmillan resigns on the grounds of ill health. He is replaced by Sir Alec Douglas-Home. Henry Brooke is Home Secretary.

## 1964

**23 April** Sir Anthony Blunt makes secret confession to MI5 that he has been Soviet spy.

**10 June** The Director of Public Prosecutions (DPP) instructs a meeting of chief constables not to bring criminal charges against homosexuals without consulting him.

**12 July** The *Sunday Mirror* runs the story 'Peer and a Gangster: Yard Probe'.

**13–18 July** The *Daily Mirror* runs more protection racket and cover-up allegations.

**14 July** DPP policy change is leaked to the press and the 'sinister rumours' affair begins, that the British government are shielding high-placed homosexuals.

**15 July** 'Source' at his request gives a big debrief to his MI5 agent runner. He says the *Mirror* story came from the Nashes (three Clerkenwell brothers).

**19 July** 'The Picture We Must Not Print' story appears in the *Sunday Mirror*.

**21 July (afternoon)** Lord Boothby tells the Home Secretary that the *Mirror* is 'frightened to death' and will stop their campaign.

**21 July (early evening)** DI Gerrard interviews Boothby. He tells him that Ronnie Kray had said a man called 'Nash' supplied the picture to the *Sunday Mirror*.

**21 July** MI5 DG Roger Hollis sees the Home Secretary and tells him that Boothby is indeed associated with the Krays and is allegedly homosexual.

**21 July** The Home Secretary puts together a crisis committee to address 'the rumours which were spreading involving members of the Government'.

**24 July** MI5 gives Special Branch a summary of Boothby intelligence: 'we are particularly anxious to protect Source from the threat of savage reprisals if he were blown.'

**31 July** Boothby engages Arnold Goodman as his legal adviser. 'Source' tips off MI5 to the fact.

**4 August** The *Daily Express* publishes Kray-Boothby picture (without chauffeur Leslie Holt in it).

**4 August** MI5's Fleet Street agent says the *Sunday Mirror* is dropping the story. Boothby will not sue as he has too much to hide. The newspaper sacks its editor, Reg Payne, apologises and pays Boothby £40,000.

**August (summer)** Alfie Teale acts as a courier, taking the *Mirror* money from Boothby to Ronnie Kray as his slice.

**September** Esmeralda's Barn is wound up with tax debts. The Krays take over the Glenrae Hotel, Finsbury Park, as a new base.

**Early October** 'Source' reveals to MI5 that Boothby has sacked Leslie Holt as his chauffeur and offered him £2,000 out of the *Mirror* damages (he does not pay). Holt moves to reignite the Boothby scandal.

**15 October** 'Source' tells MI5 that Ronnie Kray has warned off Holt with threats.

**15 October** Labour leader Harold Wilson wins the general election with a narrow majority. Sir Frank Soskice is Home Secretary.

## 1965

**January** The Krays are arrested for demanding money with menaces from wealthy homosexual Hew McCowan, owner of a West End club called the Hideaway. They are remanded in custody in Brixton Prison.

**11 February** Lord Boothby asks a question in the House of Lords as to how long the authorities are going to keep the Krays locked up. They are cleared of all charges and hold a party at the renamed El Morocco club to celebrate.

**19 April** Reggie marries Frances Shea. The marriage lasts eight months, although it is never formally dissolved. She commits suicide two years later.

**23 December** Roy Jenkins is appointed Home Secretary and begins a two-year programme of 'permissive' legislation.

**Christmas** A confrontation between the Krays and the rival Richardson gang at the Astor Club when Richardson associate George Cornell refers to Ronnie as a 'fat poof'.

## 1966

**9 March** Ronnie Kray shoots George Cornell in the Blind Beggar.

**9 March** (6pm) David Teale gets a phone call from Reggie Kray saying, 'Come for a drink' at the Widow's pub in Tapp St. He and his brothers do not leave home straightaway.

(8pm) Ronnie gets a tip off that George Cornell is in nearby Blind Beggar pub. He gets a gun from Vallance Road and shoots him (8.30pm) up at the bar then returns to the Widow's. Very soon afterwards the Teale brothers arrive at Tapp St. With the twins and others, they go to a pub in Walthamstow, a neighbouring flat and then late at night to David's flat, 51 Moresby Road, London, E5, where members of the Firm congregate. They stay there over a week.

**14 March** Bobby Teale phones Scotland Yard and is put in touch with Detective Superintendent Tommy Butler. They meet in central London. Butler asks Bobby to be a long-term informer.

**17 March** Tommy Butler chairs a Yard meeting. They decide a prosecution is not going to work, that the Krays are going to get off, but 'there are other matters in the melting pot which may be successful'.

**31 March** Harold Wilson wins the general election with an increased majority.

**March** Alfie Teale visits Frank Mitchell in Dartmoor Prison at the request of Reggie Kray.

**April–August** Bobby Teale ('Mr Phillips') meets Detective Sergeant Joe Pogue on multiple occasions to pass on information. That there is an informer in the Firm called Phillips becomes known to the Krays. Suspicion falls on Teale.

**Summer** DI Ferguson Walker is appointed by John Du Rose to lead a two-man Kray investigation team.

**June–August** Ronnie Kray holes up in Charlie Clark's house in Chingford, Essex.

**July** Reggie and Ronnie Kray hole up in a flat above a barber's shop at 471 Lea Bridge Road.

**30 July** The Richardsons are arrested.

**2 August** Bobby Teale gets word to Sergeant Joe Pogue that there is to be a big Firm meet at the flat.

**4 August (1.40am)** DI Michael Hyans on DS Tommy Butler's orders leads an armed raid on flat. Reggie and Ronnie Kray and Scotch Ian Barrie are held at separate police stations in east London. 'Mad' Teddy Smith is taken to West End Central, later to be released.

**4 August** Identity parade is a fiasco – witnesses in the Blind Beggar shooting won't go through with it.

**5 August** The Krays entertain newspaper reporters at Lea Bridge Road.

**6 August** Press stories mocking Tommy Butler appear. Reggie Kray orders Bobby Teale to go for a drink that night at Madge's pub.

**7 August (morning)** Bobby Teale goes to Vallance Road, as ordered by Reggie – who drives Bobby to Epping Forest for a bungled execution, which he escapes. Bobby goes through with the request for a meeting procedure on the phone with Scotland Yard detective 'Dan'.

**7 August (evening)** Ronnie Kray sends Ronnie Hart and Frosty to Steeple Bay caravan park, where Christine Teale is staying, to find Bobby. But Bobby is in London.

**7 August (evening)** Bobby meets 'Mr Wallace' in a bar who invites him back to his flat in Dolphin Square, Pimlico, for 'a party'. Wallace is already known to Bobby – he has lent him his Triumph sports car.

**8 August** Bobby contacts Alfie and David at the Rugby pub in Holborn. The three go on a pub crawl, ending up at Wallace's flat that night.

**9 August (early morning)** All three Teale brothers are arrested in a raid on Wallace's flat – and charged with demanding money with menaces from an elderly homosexual. They are held at Rochester Row Police Station.

**9 August** Anonymous letters for Tommy Butler arrive at the Yard, naming Ronnie Kray as the killer of George Cornell.

**10 August** The Teale brothers appear at Bow Street Magistrates' Court and are taken on remand to Brixton Prison.

**11 August** Ronnie Kray claims DS Leonard Townsend demands £50 from him to drink in the Bakers Arms, Hackney.

**14 August** Tape recordings are made of DS Townsend in an attempted sting.

**19–23 August** 'Mad' Teddy and Scotch Ian Barrie give testimony on DS Townsend to one of DI Ferguson Walker's team.
Ronnie Kray refuses to give evidence and goes into hiding.

**23 September** The trial of Robert (Bobby), Alfred and David Teale begins at Number One Court, Old Bailey.

**4 October** The Teales are found guilty of demanding money with menaces and sentenced to three years' imprisonment.

**12 December** The Krays assist Frank Mitchell ('The Mad Axeman') to escape from Dartmoor Prison, but Mitchell becomes increasingly violent and unstable while staying in a flat in Barking Road. He disappears and his body is never recovered.

**Late December** 'Mad' Teddy Smith disappears.

## 1967

**March** DS Alan Wright joins the Walker 'investigation'. DI Harry Mooney replaces DI Ferguson Walker sometime thereafter.

**April** Ronnie Kray emerges from hiding in the Townsend affair.

**7 June** Frances Kray commits suicide.

**27 July** Sexual Offences Act 1967 partially decriminalises homosexual acts in private between two men over the age of 21 in England and Wales – although it excludes members of the Armed Forces and the Merchant Navy.

**18 September** DI Leonard 'Nipper' Read is ordered by Met Assistant Commissioner Peter Brodie to go after the Krays with a team based at Tintagel House remote from the tainted Yard.

**29 October** Jack 'the Hat' McVitie offends the Krays by not carrying out a contract killing. The Krays invite him to a 'party' in Blonde Carole Skinner's flat in Evering Road, Stoke Newington, where Reggie murders him.

**30 October** The BBC broadcast in colour *Top Bunk*, a thirty-minute TV play by Edward Smith.

## 1968

**9 May** Krays arrested. Once they are in police custody, witnesses slowly start to come forward. Read builds the case.

**May** David Teale is transferred from Maidstone to Ford Open Prison.

**July** Committal proceedings begin at Bow Street Magistrates' Court. There is no press reporting. Bobby Teale states on the stand that he was providing police with information through the summer of 1966.

**28 November** Mrs Ellen Teale (mother of Bobby, David and Alfie) receives a suspended sentence for robbery at Number One Court, Old Bailey.

## 1969

**8 January** The trial of Reginald and Ronald Kray for the murders of George Cornell and Jack 'the Hat' McVitie opens at Number One Court, Old Bailey.

**14 January** 'Mr A' (Alfie Teale) gives evidence for the prosecution.

**15 January** 'Mr D' (David Teale) gives evidence for the prosecution.

**15 January** 'Mrs D' (Christine Teale, David's wife) gives evidence for the prosecution.

**16 January** 'Mr B' (Bobby Teale) gives evidence for the prosecution and tells the court about his dealings with Superintendent Tommy Butler and Detective Sergeant Joe Pogue and the fact that he is 'Phillips the informer'.

**8 March** The Krays are both sentenced to life imprisonment.

**April–May** The Krays are back in court and plead not guilty to the murder of Frank 'The Mad Axeman' Mitchell. They are cleared of murder, but Reginald Kray is convicted on 16 May of plotting Mitchell's escape from Dartmoor eleven days before he died.

**Summer** Bobby Teale disappears.

## 1972

**Spring** Sightings of 'Mad' Teddy Smith working as a 'chauffeur' in London are recorded in various memoirs.

## 1979

**13 September** Leslie Holt dies under anaesthetic when operation to remove warts goes wrong.

## 1995

**17 March** Ronnie Kray dies at the age of 61 at Wexham Park Hospital in Slough, Berkshire. He had suffered a heart attack at Broadmoor Special Hospital two days earlier.

## 2000

**1 October** Reggie Kray dies aged 66 at a hotel in Norwich, Norfolk. He'd been freed from prison on 26 August because of his worsening cancer.

## 2004

**August** 'Mad' Teddy Smith dies of cancer in Luton, Bedfordshire, UK.

## 2010

**July** Bobby Teale comes back from the dead.

## 2012

**April** Alfie, Bobby and David Teale's book, *Bringing Down the Krays*, is published.

## 2015

**October** Boothby MI5 file released featuring 'Source'.

## 2017

**June** *Gangsterstuff* website publishes a picture of 'Mad' Teddy Smith in the UK, 2004.

## 2018

**July** Alfie and David Teale identify the Teddy Smith picture.

## 2019

**October** Author James Morton publishes *Krays: The Final Word*, naming DI Ferguson Walker as the Kray spy within the Yard.

## 2020

**7 April** Death is announced of Leonard 'Nipper' Read, aged 95.

**15 December** Robert 'Bobby' Teale, after convincing the US authorities he is not somehow an escaped prisoner on the run (from 1969), becomes a citizen of the United States.

# BIBLIOGRAPHY

Andrew, C., *The Defence of the Realm: The Authorized History of MI5*, Allen Lane, London, 2009

Bloch, M., *Closet Queens*, Little Brown, London, 2015

Du Rose, J., *Murder Was My Business*, W. H. Allen, London, 1972

Lucas, N., *Britain's Gangland*, Pan Books, London, 1969

McConnell, B., *The Evil Firm, the Rise and Fall of the Brothers Kray*, Mayflower, London, 1969

Morton, J., *Gangland Soho*, Piatkus Books, London, 2008

*Krays: The Final Word*, Mirror Books, London, 2019

Payne, L., *The Brotherhood*, Michael Joseph, London, 1973

Pearson, J., *The Profession of Violence* (1st edition), Weidenfeld and Nicolson, London, 1972

*The Cult of Violence*, Orion, London, 2001

Read, L., *Nipper Read: The Man who Nicked the Krays* (with James Morton) Futura Paperbacks, London, 1992

Seabrook, D., *Jack of Jumps*, Granta, London, 2006

Smith, D., *The Peer and the Gangster*, History Press, London, 2020

Teale, R., *Bringing Down the Krays*, Ebury Press, London, 2012

Wright, A., 'Organized Crime and Corruption Control in Britain', *Trends in Organized Crime* (journal), New York, May 2015

Wright, P., *Spycatcher* (with Paul Greengrass), Heinemann (Australia), 1987

### Websites

Gangsterstuff.com gangster memorabilia

iicsa.org.uk Independent Inquiry into Child Sexual Abuse

api.parliament.uk/historic-hansard Hansard

cia.gov/library/readingroom/ US Central Intelligence Agency

### Newspapers and magazines

*The Sunday Pictorial, the Sunday Mirror, the Daily Mirror, the Daily Express, the People, the News of the World, the Times, the Sunday Times, the Observer, the Guardian, the Hackney Gazette, the East London Advertiser, the Tatler, the New Statesman, Spitalfields Life*

### References from the National Archives

p. 7 'Source' KV 2/4097

p. 17 'The Twins' MEPO 2/9974

p. 44 'Kray Wounding and Assaults' MEPO 2/11385 – MEPO 2/11408

p. 45 'dangerous man' HO 391/97

p. 49 'charitable ventures' MEPO 2/11462

p. 75 'Terrible reprisals' KV 2/4097

p. 79 'there are four' PREM 11/4462

p. 85 'shocking picture' PREM 11/4462

p. 89 'the following information' KV 2/4097

p. 94 'Office of the Commissioner, Parliamentary Questions' MEPO 2/9722

p. 102 'concurrently efforts' MEPO 2/9722

p. 111 'opposition was going' PREM 11/4689

p. 114 'name was familiar' LO 2/708

p. 141 'come round several times' LCO 2/8676

p. 143 'inquiries among' MEPO 2/10763

p. 145 'had any trouble' DPP 2/3939

p. 147 'There have been' MEPO 2/10763

p. 150 'white sports car' MEPO 2/10763

p. 152 'Zsa Zsa' MEPO 2/10763

p. 154 'The McCowan family' LCO 2/8676

p. 156 'Irish Johnnie' DPP 2/3939

p. 171 'Another London shooting' MEPO 2/10923

p. 173 'be so stupid' MEPO 2/10923

p. 179 'Mrs Gillian Pellegrini' MEPO 2/10923

p. 180 'undesirable characters' MEPO 2/10923

p. 185 'go down to the caravan' MEPO 2/10923

p. 186 'puffs' MEPO 2/10923

p. 186 'lots of cats' MEPO 2/10923

p. 187 'free of charge' MEPO 2/10923

p. 189 'R. Teale' MEPO 2/10923

p. 195 'to put Ronald Kray' DPP 2/4223

p. 196 'I received information' MEPO 2/10923

p. 199 'This fucking number' MEPO 2/10923

p. 201 'You can drink' MEPO 2/10680

p. 202 'You can use this pub' MEPO 2/10680

p. 207 'National Mercantile Bank' CRIM 4/1974

p. 221 'excessive' MEPO 2/11408

p. 224 'gained the impression' MEPO 2/10923

p. 231 'a very large American' MEPO 2/10923

p. 235 'cold-blooded murderer' MEPO 2/10923

p. 238 'Don't worry' MEPO 2/11386

p. 258 'Ronnie saying' MEPO 2/10923

p. 259 'Dave Tiel' MEPO 2/10923

p. 259 'Craigs' MEPO 2/10923

p. 266 'Mr A' CRIM 1/5130

p. 271 'You know the truth' CRIM 1/5130

p. 274 'a newsflash' MEPO 2/10923

p. 275 'My name is Robert Frank Teale' CRIM 1/5131

p. 284 'Yes, it is' J 82/1328

p. 304 'It was arranged' MEPO 2/10923

# ACKNOWLEDGEMENTS

I'd like to thank all those people who have helped me along the way, especially those concerned directly with making this book possible – my brothers Alfie and Bobby, Jonathan Lloyd, Felicity Blunt and Rosie Pierce at Curtis Brown. A special thank you to Lorna Russell at Penguin Random House for listening to my story and to Amandeep Singh and copy editor Jane Donovan.

Without the help and the understanding of a beautiful lady, my partner Deborah Simpson-Bircham, I could not have even started let alone finished writing this book.

Special thanks to my true friends and gifted writers, Clare and Christy Campbell, for making sense of it.

They and I would like to widen our thanks to the authors, journalists and true-crime historians we've drawn on for help and guidance – including James Morton, Ray Rose, Duncan Campbell and Nick Craven. Thanks to James Morton for permission to quote from *Krays: The Final Word*, and to him and the estate of the late Leonard Read for permission to quote from *Nipper Read: The Man Who Nicked the Krays*. Our gratitude is due to the staff and systems managers of the British Library and the National Archives at Kew, including the Freedom of Information team, who helped us find the statements that I and my family made to the Kray Inquiry headed by D I Leonard Read in 1968, along with much else besides.

They and other Security Service, Home Office, Metropolitan Police and Department of Public Prosecutions documents quoted are Crown Copyright and are reproduced under Open Government Licence v3.0. Special thanks too to Dr Clare Smith, Curator of Records, Metropolitan Police Service Heritage Centre, for providing the career summary (p. 311 footnote) of DS Ferguson Walker.

# PICTURE CREDITS

# INDEX